A PASSION FOR TREES

Also by Maggie Campbell-Culver:

The Origin of Plants: The People and Plants that have shaped Britain's Garden History since the year 1000

A PASSION FOR TREES

The Legacy of John Evelyn

Maggie Campbell-Culver

eden project books

To my grandchildren, Guy and Lorna Elizabeth. May they enjoy
and plant trees as they grow from saplings into maturity.

TRANSWORLD PUBLISHERS
61-63 Uxbridge Road, London W5 5SA
a division of The Random House Group Ltd

RANDOM HOUSE AUSTRALIA (PTY) LTD
20 Alfred Street, Milsons Point, Sydney,
New South Wales 2061, Australia

RANDOM HOUSE NEW ZEALAND LTD
18 Poland Road, Glenfield, Auckland 10, New Zealand

RANDOM HOUSE SOUTH AFRICA (PTY) LTD
Isle of Houghton, Corner of Boundary Road & Carse O'Gowrie,
Houghton 2198, South Africa

Published 2006 by Eden Project Books
a division of Transworld Publishers

A catalogue record for this book is available
from the British Library.
ISBN 9781903919477 (from Jan 07)
ISBN 1903919479

Set in 11/17pt Garamond Classico by
Falcon Oast Graphic Art.

Design by Fiona Andreanelli

Printed in China

1 3 5 7 9 10 8 6 4 2

Papers used by Eden Project Books are made from wood grown
in sustainable forests. The manufacturing processes conform to
the environmental regulations of the country of origin.

Contents

PREFACE *1*
'IN TREE IS SOUL OF LIFE'

CHRONOLOGY *7*

CHAPTER I
'A MOST EXCELLENT HUMOURED MAN,
AND VERY KNOWING' *11*

CHAPTER II
'A DISCOURSE OF FOREST TREES' *45*

CHAPTER III
THE TREES *63*

CHAPTER IV
ARBOREAL HUSBANDRY *211*

CHAPTER V
THE DAWNING OF CONSERVATION *237*

CHAPTER VI
A LASTING LEGACY *253*

TREE INTRODUCTIONS *272*

BIBLIOGRAPHY *274*

ACKNOWLEDGEMENTS *275*

PICTURE CREDITS *276*

INDEX *277*

PREFACE

'In Tree is Soul of Life'

Bartholomaeus Anglicus (fl.c.1220–40)

TREES HOLD A UNIQUE POSITION in the world, combining a spiritual and aesthetic role with practicality. Nothing in the natural world seems able to compete with the aura of benign authority that a tree exudes. Trees trickle slowly into our consciousness, their reassuring presence – a mixture of grandeur and stamina – seemingly unchanging. It is usually in our maturity that we realize that such stalwart giants are vulnerable, and not, as they appear, immortal. For a child, it is often the shape of a tree that is so endearing; and this can sometimes be recalled with that adult inward eye many years later. Trees can be record breakers: they can be one of the oldest living organisms in the world: Californian specimens of *Sequoiadendron giganteum*, the Wellingtonia or Big Tree, are believed to be at least 4,000 years old. They can also be the largest form of life: a Montezuma Cypress which grows in Santa Maria de Tule in Mexico – and which, incidentally, is about 2,000 years old – has a circumference measuring 54 metres (178ft) and is 40 metres (130ft) high. Its weight is estimated to be about 500 tons.

Trees' spiritual influence encompasses the story of Adam and Eve and the 'tree which brings knowledge of good and evil'. Tree worship may be discerned amongst the very first traces of religious development. As early as 4000 BC the Chaldaeans idealized a mystical tree as the abode of the gods. The World Tree of Buddha had attributes of wisdom, perfection and holiness, while the Great Tree of the early Iranians was immortalized with a life-giving juice. In China there was the 'Tree of Immortality', which grew in 'a faraway land'. In North America most native Indian tribes held special sacred trees in awe, as did the Aboriginal people of Australia. Most great cultures reserve a special place for trees in their worship.

The botanical definition of a tree is 'a large perennial plant with a single woody stem and an elevated crown of branches usually at some distance from the

Title page 'Paradisi in Sole Paradisus Terrestris', John Parkinson, 1629, illustrating an idealized landscape with Adam and Eve, a grove of trees, the flowing stream and clearly identified flowers.

ground'. The word 'tree' has a lineage going back to the Sanskrit word of *daru* or *dru*; from that it evolved through Gothic to *tru* and the Old Norse *tré* to the Anglo-Saxon *treo*. The antecedents of the word wood are not as international as the word tree, being associated only with the early northern European languages. Branch, bough and trunk entered the language much later than wood or tree, with definitions not exclusively relating to trees.

Trees can be wonderfully aesthetic in the landscape, and with this ability they make an ideal subject for enhancing man's own surroundings. Their practical use – aided by the discovery of how to chop, cut, saw and carve wood – has been integral to the lives of man and animal alike. They provide shade, shelter and fuel; some are eaten or used in brewing; others are made into cloth and rope, or provide glue, resin or dye. Dead, the wood lasts several thousands of years and when used creatively, in buildings, carving or furniture-making, it again has the ability to give pleasure. Alive, they help clean the atmosphere and allow our planet to grow.

Man has been aware of the tree's diverse nature since the dawn of time, and has long recruited the arboreal world to enhance his own. He recognized that in their natural environment trees rarely show an aggressive or sinister character. In that respect, trees have a distinct advantage over the animal kingdom (including humans): when they are to be used, they do not need to be chased, captured, enclosed or tamed, and rather than roaming for miles in their search for food or a mate they stay growing in the same place. As the thirteenth-century Franciscan Bartholomaeus Anglicus noted in his nineteen-volume *De Proprietatibus Rerum* (On the Properties of Things), 'trees move no wilfully from place to place as beestes do'; they require little or no intervention in the way of nurturing or feeding to survive. This characteristic makes the whole of the arboreal world highly exploitable to man and animals.

There are examples of trees being used both for decoration and for practical purposes from earliest times in the ancient world: palm trees being dug up in Ethiopia and taken to Egypt to decorate the Pharaoh's Palace; cedars being sent from the western Himalayas to China for growing in the Imperial Garden; fruit trees arriving from Asia for cultivation in Egypt. From ancient Iraq there is a poem, *Epic of Gilgamesh*, written possibly during the third millennium BC, which describes Gilgamesh, King of Uruk, travelling to a mysterious cedar forest to fight a terrifying monster and, more prosaically, to collect wood and timber for use in his city. A thousand years earlier in Britain wood was used in the construction of footpaths and trackways across soggy peat-laden land in Somerset; one footway, dated to 4000 BC, was planked in oak and supported by a substructure of posts and stakes. Later, woven hurdles were used, and branches of birch, alder and any other timber that could be found were gathered to facilitate the wooden trackways.

Today Britain is unique in continental Europe, both in its silviculture and in the way it uses trees in the landscape. Whereas European woodland management is first and foremost utilitarian, aesthetic considerations being of secondary importance, in Britain trees are seen as mainly decorating the landscape and utility is almost incidental. The British countryside shows an eclectic mix of trees, with a dominating number of non-native species, whereas Continental silviculture consists mainly of native European material, although these differences also reflect the paucity of British native species and the larger number of European trees.

The beginnings of this fundamentally different approach can be traced to the eighteenth century and the landscape movement. This was inspired by an extraordinarily sophisticated philosophical idea that, in creating landscapes, the designer should consult the 'Genius of the Place', and by doing so, reproduce the sensations and emotional response in an audience that an artist might achieve with a painting. This resulted in a monumental physical change taking place across the British countryside. By contrast, the Europeans have never welcomed the wildness of the natural world within their boundaries – nature is tamed for practical rather than for any emotional gratification. Even today the differences may be seen in the management of the countryside, where trees are often lopped, chopped and shaved more earnestly than they are in Britain. Commercially France has the largest proportion of managed forest and the highest number of managed oaks in Europe, with a thriving cooperage industry playing a significant part in its silviculture (England contains the largest number of aged oaks of any country in the European Union).

One hundred years before the advent of the landscape movement, there is a glimmer of similar ideas in the writing of John Evelyn. Described by Samuel Pepys as 'a man so much above others', Evelyn is well known as a diarist, whose *Hornbeam leaves* writing tells us much about the life and times of the seventeenth century, but it is his interest in nature, gardens, horticulture and trees that concerns us in this book. He was highly knowledgeable about trees' practical value, especially as timber, but also deeply aware of their many nuances and appreciative of their aesthetic qualities. All this he expressed in his book *Sylva: A Discourse of Forest Trees and the Propagation of Timber in His Majesties Dominions*, published in 1664, a pivotal work that inspires us to consider trees and their history, and has arguably been one of the greatest influences on the English feeling for landscape and the place of trees in it.

Enlarged boxwood engraving, executed in 1958 by Reynolds Stone (1909–79).

John Evelyn: Chronology

1620–1706

1620 **September**
The *Mayflower* sails from Plymouth for New England with the Pilgrim Fathers aboard

1620 **31 October**
John Evelyn born at Wotton, Surrey

1622 **15 January**
Birth of Jean Molière, French dramatist (d.1673)

1625 **27 March**
Death of James I; accession of Charles I

1625 Death of Orlando Gibbons, English composer (b.1583)

1629 – 40
King Charles governs without summoning Parliament

1631 **9 August**
Birth of John Dryden, poet (d.1700)

1631 **31 March**
Death of John Donne, Anglican divine and poet (b.1572)

1633 Birth of Samuel Pepys, diarist (d.1703)

1638 Death of John Harvard, founder of Harvard University (b.1607)

1640 Summoning of 'Short' then the 'Long' Parliaments

1641 **12 May**
Execution of Thomas Wentworth, Earl of Strafford, the King's principal advisor (b.1593)

1642 **July**
Outbreak of Civil War between the King and Parliament; Battle of Edgehill

1643 Death of Claudio Montiverdi, Italian composer and creator of opera (b.1567)

1643 Louis XVI (1638-1715) becomes King of France

1644 **January**
Birth of Sir John Vanbrugh, architect and playwright (d.1726)

1645 **14 June**
Battle of Naseby; defeat of Royalist army by the Parliamentarians under Oliver Cromwell

1646 **8 August**
Birth of Sir Godfrey Kneller, portrait painter (d.1723)

1647 **27 June**
John Evelyn marries Mary Browne in Paris

1649 **30 January**
Trial and execution of Charles I

1651 **3 September**
Battle of Worcester; Royalist army defeated by Parliamentarian army

1652 **June**
John and Mary Evelyn take up residence at Sayes Court, Deptford, Kent

1652 **June**
Birth of William Dampier, explorer, hydrographer and pirate (d.1715)

1652 – 54
First Dutch War

1658 **3 September**
Death of Oliver Cromwell (b.1599)

1658 Completion of St Peter's Basilica, Rome

1659 Birth of Henry Purcell, composer (d.1695)

1660 **29 May**
Restoration of King Charles II
(1660-85)

1662 The Royal Society receives its
Charter

1663 *Paradise Lost* completed by John
Milton (1608-74)

1665 **Summer**
Plague in London

1665 Death of Nicholas Poussin,
French painter (b.1594)

1665 – 67
Second Dutch War

1666 **September**
Great Fire of London

1669 Death of Rembrant van Rijn,
Dutch painter (b.1606)

1672 – 74
Third Dutch War

1676 **24 September**
Birth of Sir Robert Walpole,
Britain's first Prime Minister
(d.1745)

1678 Birth of Antonio Vivaldi, Italian
composer (d.1741)

1680 Death of Sir Peter Lely, portrait
painter (b.1618)

1681 Publication of *Absalom and
Achitophel* by John Dryden

1683 **12 September**
Turkish army repulsed from
Vienna

1683 Death of Izaak Walton, author of
The Compleat Angler (b.1593)

1685 **6 February**
Death of Charles II and
accession of James II; birth of
Johann Sebastian Bach, German
composer (d.1750); birth of
George Frederick Handel,
German composer (d.1759)

1687 Publication of *Principia* by Sir
Isaac Newton (1642-1727)

1688 Publication of Part I of *Pilgrim's
Progress* by John Bunyan
(1628–88)

1688 **11 December**
Abdication of James II

1689 **13 February**
Accession of Mary II and
William III

1689 First performance of *Dido and
Aeneas* by Henry Purcell

1694 **4 May**
John and Mary Evelyn move to
Wotton

1694 **28 December**
Death of Queen Mary

1697 Birth of Antonio Canaletto,
Italian painter (d.1768)

1702 **8 March**
Death of William III and
accession of Queen Anne

1702 Outbreak of the War of the
Spanish Succession with France

1704 **2 – 13 August**
Battle of Blenheim; French army
defeated by the Duke of
Marlborough

1706 **27 February**
Death of John Evelyn at Wotton

Ἡ δὲ μετάνοια αὐτὴ φιλο-
σοφίας ἀρχὴ γίνεται.

John Evelyn at the age of twenty-eight, painted by Robert Walker (1607–60) in 1648, the year following Evelyn's marriage to Mary.

CHAPTER I

'A Most Excellent
Humoured Man, and
Very Knowing'

Samuel Pepys (1633–1703)

A VOLATILE MIXTURE OF RELIGION and politics bedevilled the seventeenth century, into which John Evelyn was born. The effects of the English Reformation and establishment of a national Church, combined with the burgeoning power of Parliament as it became determined to control the absolute monarchical ambitions of Charles I (1600–49; reigned from 1625), made for an extraordinarily explosive hundred years. With the Civil War, which began in 1642, the deposing and beheading of the King, the Interregnum, the Restoration of Charles II (1630–85) in 1660, the wars with Holland and France, the Plague followed by the Great Fire of London in 1666 and the Glorious Revolution of 1688, the century seems to have been one of social and political disorder. Most of the population were either random participants or swept up in the momentous events. John Evelyn was no exception. His young adulthood was dominated by the havoc caused by the events that took place and as an ardent Royalist he chose to absent himself from England rather than participate in the upheavals.

Yet in spite of the volatility of the century, or even perhaps because of it, there seems to have been a plethora of great thinkers, philosophers, experimenters, artists and other individuals who pushed forward the boundaries of knowledge. Viewed in an historical perspective, Britain in the seventeenth century shows the rejection of the old order and the early stirrings of the modern age. In particular, scientific discovery began to be disentangled from the medieval

JOANNES EVELYN ARMIG.
REG. SOCIETATIS SOC.

hocus-pocus of fictional facts. It was as if the weight of the Middle Ages had been cast aside like some great crusader cloak, and people were confidently clothing themselves in knowledge instead. Learning, intelligent conversation and experiments became part of civilized society, and suddenly science (from the Latin *scientia*, meaning knowledge) was a word much in vogue. Men – rarely women, I fear – held earnest discussions on subjects as diverse and avant garde as electricity (a word coined in the 1640s), blood transfusions and the usefulness of pollen to plants. In England this 'new age' of enquiry found expression in a group of 'virtuosi' (another new word), who formed a scientific club that by 1662 had evolved into The Royal Society.

John Evelyn, painted at the age of sixty-nine by Sir Godfrey Kneller (1646–1723) in 1689, holding a copy of Sylva.

THE ROYAL SOCIETY

Long before 1662, during the previous century, a tradition had grown up for groups of men to gather together and debate subjects of interest. One such association was centred around William Gilbert (1540–1603), physician to Elizabeth I. Solving navigational problems by applying mathematics was one of the fundamental questions of enquiry, as was the making of accurate instruments to be used for measurements. Gilbert was the first person to use the terms electricity and electric force when carrying out experiments at his laboratory. In 1598 Gresham College was founded when Sir Thomas Gresham (1519–79), the financier and founder of the Royal Exchange, made provision in his will for his house in Bishopsgate Street to become the centre for the new learning of arts and sciences. Seven professors were appointed, and under the terms of the will, each one had to lecture during the three-term year. All lectures were to be given in Latin, and the mathematical and astronomical lectures were to be repeated in English the same day. Gresham College prospered into the seventeenth century, when its members included the brilliant mathematician John Wallis (1616–1703), who had presaged the calculus and the binomial theorem. In about 1648 a number of members migrated – along with the Court of Charles I – to Oxford, and established the Oxford Philosophical Society, carrying on its scientific experiments. Two of its members were the young Christopher Wren (1632–1723), whom Evelyn called 'that prodigious young scholar', and the chemist and physicist Robert Hooke (1635–1703), who would also anticipate the invention of the steam engine, and who theorized on the mathematics of the arch and the balance spring of watches, and made important observations with his own designed microscope. In the summer of 1654, while John Evelyn and his wife Mary were on an extended tour of England, they met the young men in Oxford and Evelyn attended a meeting of the Philosophical Society. Having experienced some of the intellectual activity going on in Europe during his travels, Evelyn was interested in associating with these 'virtuosi'.

Five years later some members had returned to London and resumed their meetings at Gresham College. At about this time several proposals were put forward, including suggestions by Evelyn, for the founding of a 'community of scientists', and on 28 November 1660, following a lecture given by Wren, twelve members remained behind to consider the establishment of a college for the promotion of 'Physico-Mathematicall Experimentall Learning'. As well as Wren and Evelyn, among those present were William Petty (1623–87), who expounded on many ideas, including decimal coinage and a national health service, and later would experiment with designing a double-bottomed ship – Evelyn believed there was 'nothing impenetrable to him'; the Irishman and chemist Robert Boyle (1627–91), who in 1662 propounded the theory that has become known as Boyle's Law; John Wilkins (1614–72), who had written, at the age of fourteen, *Discovery of a World in the Moon*, in which he discussed the possibility of using flying machines to explore the unknown world, and in 1640 when he was twenty-six published *Discourse Concerning a New Planet*, in which he very plausibly argued that the earth was one of the planets; and Lord Brouncker (1620–84), Navy Commissioner, who would later become The Royal Society's first President. Their ideas were based on the Italian model of fostering academic and scientific ideals by forming academic foundations – the Accademia dei Lincei, founded in Rome in 1603; the Accademia del Cimento, founded by the Medici family in Florence in 1657; and the Neapolitan Accademia degli Investignati of 1665. Much earlier, during the 1540s, both Pisa and Padua Universities had formed the first botanic gardens.

Forty people were to be invited to join the new Society, and it was decided to hold weekly meetings. By early December, the King had been acquainted with the proposals, and was a keen advocate of the idea – Charles enjoyed watching experiments taking place and discussing them with the 'virtuosi'. This encouraged the drawing up of a draft constitution, and other details, all of which were recorded in the Society's first journal of 5 December 1660. Four days later,

Evelyn was elected a Fellow of the Society, 'and nominated by his Majestie for one of the Council . . . ' It was known as the Philosophical Society of London, but in the following year the society received its Royal Charter – thus gaining some rights and privileges, one of which was to be allowed to dissect human bodies – and at about the same time John Evelyn first used the name by which it has ever since been known: The Royal Society. Its Charter was sealed on 15 July 1662, with a revision of 22 April 1663, when its name was amplified to The Royal Society of London for the Promotion of Natural Knowledge (*Regalis Societas Londini pro scientia natural promovenda*).

Many discoveries we take for granted today were first explored at this time. For example, the foundations were laid for the study of astronomy in England – mainly by John Flamsteed (1646–1719), whom Charles II appointed the first Astronomer Royal. In medicine there was Thomas Sydenham (1624–89), who has been dubbed the 'Father of English Medicine' for his fundamental work regarding the treatment of smallpox, venereal disease, gout and fevers (he named scarlet fever); his ideas about the recuperative powers of the body were very advanced and not easily accepted by his peers. The engineers Thomas Savery (1650–1715) and Thomas Newcomen (1663–1724) between them invented a series of steam water pumps, for use in mining, and Newcomen was associated with the first fire engines. There was the physician and anatomist Thomas Willis (1621–75), who was renowned for his extensive work on the anatomy of the brain. Born six years later was the great Sir Robert Boyle (1627–91), the father of modern chemistry and a natural philosopher. Five years after that, the architect, mathematician and astronomer Sir Christopher Wren (1632–1723) was born, followed by the inventor and instrument-maker Robert Hooke (1635–1703) and Sir Isaac Newton (1642–1727), the greatest mathematician of the age.

Walnut leaves

This flowering was not unique to Britain but pervasive throughout Europe, despite much of the Continent having been devastated by the Thirty Years War, which ended in 1648 and was followed immediately in France by the Fronde, eleven years of civil war. In northern Europe Johannes Kepler (1571–1630) did pioneering work on optics and general physics. Almost contemporary was the Italian, Galilei (1564–1642), whose astronomical revolution caused a furore and much consternation to the Papacy. There was the Dutch physicist renowned for his invention of the pendulum clock, Christiaan Huggens (1629–93), who was a Fellow of The Royal Society, and in France the chemist Edmé Mariotte (d.1684), immortalized on the Continent for 'Mariotte's Law' – the same law (setting out the relationship between the pressure and volume of a confined gas) that in the US and Great Britain we attributed to Robert Boyle and called Boyle's Law.

The horticultural world too experienced its own revolution. Early in the century the previously allied subjects of horticulture and botany had begun to split into separate fields of study. The divergence was aided by a number of events, one of which was the founding in 1617 of the Worshipful Society of Apothecaries, whose work concentrated on medicinal and useful plants. John Parkinson (1567–1650), himself an apothecary, who helped found the Society, wrote a book celebrating the growing of garden flowers, *Paradisi in Sole Paradisus Terrestris* (1629), the introduction of which was entitled 'Ordering of the Garden of Pleasure'. It was full of sound advice and it shows the beginnings of the two separate disciplines emerging. On its publication Charles I made Parkinson the Botanicus Regius Primarius. Other influential monographs followed, including those of Nehemiah Grew (1641–1712), a cleric who sided with Cromwell in the Civil War and devoted his life to the study of the structure of plants; he published three books, the most influential being *The Anatomy of Plants*. Another botanical work of the time was that of John Ray (1627–1705), who between 1686 and 1704 published *Historia Plantarum Generalis*, which contained scientific knowledge on the classification of plants and their structure.

At the same time hundreds of new and unknown plants arrived in Europe from overseas, either with ships on exploratory and trading voyages or with those engaged in war. Those plants that survived were welcomed with an enthusiasm that we now reserve for football idols. Flora from the North American eastern seaboard, Africa, India, Asia and South America began to establish themselves both on the Continent and in Britain. Given travelling conditions that we would now consider primitive and dangerous for humans, let alone plants, it is surprising how many new introductions retained their viability and were able to become part of the European world of flowers.

A new look was also prevalent in European gardens. This was quite different to the older English style – indeed as different as the modern minimalist look is to an Edwardian garden. In the earlier Elizabethan period much of the inspiration in making gardens had been based both on French and, to a lesser extent, Dutch ideas. The pleasure-garden, which became such a popular feature, was conceived as a grandiose extension of sophisticated living, and demonstrated an ability to subdue nature. It was used for entertaining, and for displaying the rare and unusual plants and trees that had begun to be introduced to Britain. By the time Evelyn was a young man, new ideas from Italy and France were being propounded. Many of the gardens created by previous generations were dug up and discarded in favour of the modern tree-lined ideas of long vistas, green sward and avenues stretching as if into infinity, with terraces and great stretches of water contained in formal shapes. The whole was imposed on the landscape, not fused into it, as in the later eighteenth-century style.

All these developments – political, intellectual, horticultural – were significant in the life of John Evelyn.

*

John Evelyn was born on 31 October 1620 into a family of minor gentry, the younger son of Richard Evelyn, a Surrey squire. He was educated at home and then, because of an outbreak of the plague, sent to his grandmother's home at Lewes, Sussex, to continue his schooling. He said later that he had not received the best education and admitted that he had not applied himself well. At seventeen he enrolled as an undergraduate at Balliol College, Oxford, where he spent his time dancing and socializing, and left without a degree – a fact that belies the intellectual and serious qualities that he was to display later. In 1640, he went to the Middle Temple, London, ostensibly to read for the Bar, although his hedonistic career continued here.

There is no doubt that all his life Evelyn felt the pull of the natural world. From a young age he showed a practical and intellectual interest in estate management and gardens. This interest began, naturally enough, at Wotton, Surrey, the estate owned and lived in by his family from 1579. The family had made its wealth from the manufacture of gunpowder at their mills at Godstone and Long Ditton, and at the time of Evelyn's birth in 1620 was using this wealth to enlarge the family seat of Wotton. It was almost at its zenith by this time, and

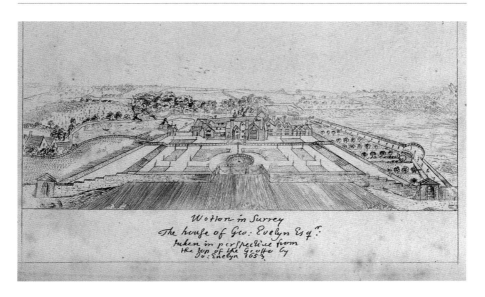

included the manors of Milton, Abinger and Paddington (in Abinger); by 1628
Westcott near Dorking had been purchased, followed eight years later by the
manor of Gosterwood.

The estate had an abundance of mature oak, ash, beech and elm, the timber
from which was used in the production of gunpowder and for iron-making at
Abinger, although by 1676 these stocks were seriously depleted and the woods
comprised little more than beech, birch and holly. Demonstrating an interest in
silviculture and practical detail at an early age, Evelyn records in his diary
watching the husbandmen there sawing down seven-year-old ash trees, noting
how they were stacked and measured, and thus costed, and seeing the skilful
binding of bavins (bundles of twigs), and oak bark being stripped to be sent off
to the tanners at Leatherhead.

It seems extraordinary that the seventeenth century, the most turbulent period in
Britain's history, produced two diarists – John Evelyn and Samuel Pepys. Almost as
amazing is the fact that their two manuscripts survived (both diaries were first
published in the nineteenth century). The two men, who became friends, were
very different characters. While Pepys, the younger by thirteen years, was ebullient,
lusty, hedonistic and streetwise, Evelyn became a restrained, observant and self-
contained diarist. One might hesitate to show a maiden aunt some of Pepys's more
lustful disclosures; Evelyn, on the other hand, was inclined to pomposity and,
unlike Pepys, definitely descendant aware: not a flutter of a scandal or ill behaviour

*Wotton House and
gardens in 1653.
Etching of a drawing
made by John Evelyn.*

touches the pages of his diary, which he 'remodelled' at least once, ironing out all the little indiscretions, until it was pure enough for anyone to peruse.

While the natural world held him most in thrall, Evelyn matured into a polymath, recording in great detail not only all he saw but his subsequent reactions. It is this fusion, also apparent in later work of his, which makes his writings so perspicacious. And it is the juxtaposition of his urbane, cultivated persona with his remarkable knowledge and passion for horticulture, and particularly silviculture, which continues to make him a source of fascination 400 years on.

A Royalist and supporter of the Established Church, Evelyn witnessed both the great trial of Charles I's principal advisor, Thomas Wentworth, Earl of Strafford (1593–1641), and his execution on 12 May 1641, describing in his diary how he watched 'the fatal stroke which severed the wisest head in England'. Such was the distaste Evelyn felt for these events and those that subsequently unfolded in England that he absented himself by travelling abroad, returning during October 1642. Within a month, at the outbreak of the Civil War, he was journeying to join the King's army; he rode to Brentford and was in time to witness the ending of the battle there on 12 November. Three days later, he records, rather priggishly, '[I] was not permitted to stay any longer than the 15ᵗʰ by the reason of the armies marching to Gloucester, which would have left me and my brothers exposed to ruin, without any advantage to His Majesty.' Perhaps this was a tactful way of responding to the 'Hooray Henries' whom the historian C. V. Wedgwood noted were 'young, drunk, victorious and out of control'. Whatever the case, Evelyn decided that being part of such a riotously disorderly equipage was not for him.

In 1643, seeking to escape the turmoil of the war, he spent some time at Wotton, writing: '[I had] resolved to possesse my selfe in some quiet if it might be, in a tyme of greate jealosy.' With the permission of his elder brother George, who by then had inherited the estate, he designed and built a study, and a little triangular fishpond, with some artificial rockwork as well as 'some other solitudes and retirements'. He spent only a few months there, for the chaotic situation grew rapidly worse and later in 1643 Evelyn sought and obtained permission from the King to leave England and 'travel again'. This time he did not return home, except for a period between 1647 and 1649, for nearly ten years. In 1647 he was married in Paris to Mary, the daughter of Sir Richard Browne, the King's Ambassador to the French Court.

While John Evelyn was on the Continent, his brother George asked their cousin, Captain George Evelyn, to help design a temple frontage and a grotto at Wotton. Although Evelyn was travelling, he sent back detailed instructions as to what should be used in the mineral and geological decoration of the grotto. The temple façade and the grotto were so placed that there was an extended view from them northwards back over the garden to the house. Later, on his return to England in February 1652, Evelyn advised his brother that the moat should be filled in with spoil from the mount to make a splendid terrace and a platform to view the garden.

Throughout his extended period of travel through Italy, the Low Countries and France, and then later in England, Evelyn enjoyed visiting other people's gardens, viewing landscapes, visiting new and old gardens, or being shown newly introduced flora. Within a month of his arrival in The Netherlands, in August 1641, he was describing the garden of the Prince of Orange, at The Hague, where the 'adjoining gardens were full of ornament, close-walks, statues, marbles, grotts, fountains, and artificiall musiq'. In almost every entry in his diary that concerns visiting a house, Evelyn makes some pertinent comment. One Parisian garden, belonging to the florist and gardener Pierre Morin, he visited twice. He records his first visit in 1644, when he was twenty-four, remarking what a skilful and remarkable gardener Morin was. 'His garden is of an exact oval figure, planted with cypresse, cutt flat and set as even as a wall: the tulips, anemonies, ranunculus's, crocus's etc are held to be of the rarest.' On his second visit, seven years later, he notes that there were at least 10,000 tulips, and marvels at the 'coralls, minerals, stones and natural curiosities' on display.

He shows a continuing interest in hedges and how they were constructed. When staying in Paris in 1644, he visited the Tuileries and, already having a discerning eye for the layout of a garden, noted 'noble hedges of pomegranates' – not a plant that readily comes to mind in making an ornamental hedge. A few weeks later at the Luxembourg Gardens, also in Paris, he observed high and stately hornbeam hedges and 'hedge-worke'. In the same year, in the town of Richelieu (from which Cardinal Richelieu took his name) he visited the château; he described this as 'a princely pile' and the garden as a 'real paradise'. He also

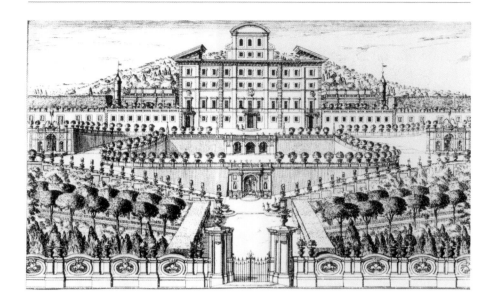

travelled to Chevereuse (south-west of Paris), which he called 'a sweete place'. Situated in the tranquil valley of the River Yvette, it is still 'a sweet place'. The seventeenth-century planting by André Le Nôtre (1613–1700) – the most famous of a dynasty of French royal gardeners – may still be enjoyed today, although John Evelyn was just too early to experience it.

In the autumn of 1644 Evelyn travelled to Italy. Journeying towards Rome, 'After a little riding' he came across 'the Lake of Bolsena, which being above 20 miles in circuit yields from hence a most incomparable prospect'. Then there was the pleasure of viewing the Villa Borghese, which he describes as an 'elysium of delight'. At Padua, he explored one of the first botanic gardens, which included the Garden of Simples. He describes it as 'rarely furnished with plants' and was so enthused by it that he ordered a herbarium collection to be sent to England.

On 29 November he viewed the Aldobrandini Palace for a second time and saw a 'whimsical chayre, which folded into so many varieties as to turn into a bed, a bolster, a table or a couch'. Evelyn took a turn in the garden and then walked uphill to the Pope's Palace of Monte Cavallo, where he 'observed hedges of myrtle above a man's height; others of laurel, oranges, nay of ivy and juniper'.

Villa Aldobrandini at Frascati near Rome. Evelyn visited in 1644 and 1645, calling it 'The most delicious places I ever beheld'.

Evelyn saw many examples of the new gardening style in France and Italy, in which trees were used for adornment in the form of walks, avenues, copses, groves and vistas. He was one of relatively few people in England who saw these developments *in situ*, and was full of enthusiasm for the imposition of such regimental order.

In February 1652, Evelyn returned to England for good. Following Charles II's return from exile and his restoration in 1660, when the turmoil that had plagued Evelyn's early life and made him an exile for so long ended, he began a career of public service. He seems to have got on well with the King, recording in his diary that they enjoyed long discussions; however, he regarded life at Court as frivolous and immoral, and the political intrigue dangerous. Throughout his life Evelyn sought to retain his integrity, and in his service to the Crown was always straightforward. Recognizing that much of the government infrastructure needed reinstating and modernizing, he was public-spirited enough to accept invitations to sit on various commissions. He also produced a number of pamphlets on a wide range of topics, including one in 1661, entitled *Fumifugium*, on London smog, which he described as a 'hellish and dismal cloude of sea-coale'. In 1664 he was asked to join a commission that cared for the wounded of the Dutch Wars, and the following year remained at his post despite a terrible and frightening outbreak of the Plague, particularly in London – he was apparently the only commissioner to do so. In 1672 he was appointed to the Council of Trade and Foreign Plantations. He accepted his last public office in 1695, when aged seventy-five, serving as treasurer to the Hospital for Seamen at Greenwich, an institution which he had been instrumental in founding. He occupied this post for eight years until 1703, when he retired.

THE COUNCIL OF TRADE AND FOREIGN PLANTATIONS

John Evelyn was appointed to this Council as one of eleven salaried Commissioners on 27 September 1672. The Commission had originally been two separate committees, the Council of Trade, and the Council of Foreign Plantations; both existed from 1660 until 1672, when they were amalgamated. Charles II had established these committees under the Great

Seal. In the Council of Foreign Plantations, forty-nine Commissioners had been appointed, none of whom received payment. The nearest analogy today would be the appointment of a Cabinet sub-committee comprising both ministers and civil servants. In the seventeenth century a number of these 'quangos' developed; some were honorary appointments, others were remunerated. Perhaps the most important of them all was the Navy Board, of which Samuel Pepys was the Secretary.

The use of the word 'plantation' needs some explanation: nowadays it is used, almost exclusively, in connection with rural affairs, usually to describe land planted with young trees and from which animals are excluded. The southern states of America use the word for landed property, in a similar sense to the English word 'estate'. However, that usage derives from the original meaning of 'plantation': current in the sixteenth century, it denoted English people being 'planted' or settled in a new or conquered land. The plantation policy was a colonial tool to encourage the political influence and trade of England, and to discourage, subdue and disinherit the 'natives'. This idea – distasteful to us now – was experimented with first in Ulster; it was then taken across the Atlantic to the new lands of Virginia, Barbados, Nova Scotia, and so on. By 1672, when Evelyn was appointed to the reconstituted 'Council of Trade and Foreign Plantations', it was a well-established policy. He only served for a short time, as in 1675 the committee's terms and title were altered yet again, and from then until nearly the end of the century it was one of the committees of the Privy Council for Trade and Plantations. In the early nineteenth century this evolved into the Colonial Office, by which name it was known until 1968, when, under Harold Wilson's premiership, it merged with the Foreign Office, the new hybrid becoming the Foreign and Commonwealth Office.

Evelyn at Sayes Court

From 1652–94 John and Mary Evelyn made their home at Sayes Court, Deptford. Evelyn took up residence first in February 1652 and Mary followed him a few months later in June. Built in the reign of Elizabeth I, the house was three storeys high and triple-gabled. It was part of Crown property and had been Mary Evelyn's ancestral home – the Browne family having long been lessees of the Crown. Since all royal estates had been seized following the execution of Charles I, and the Parliamentary Commissioners administered all Crown property, in 1653 Evelyn purchased a lease for the house from the Commissioners for the sum of £3,500 in order to continue living there.

When Evelyn first arrived at Deptford by water from Gravesend, the old house had been somewhat neglected. He complained that it would have been more cost-effective to have demolished it and built a new house, but he wrote in his diary, 'I was advised to reside in it . . . This I was besides authoriz'd by his Majesty to do.' Earlier, when he had briefly returned to England, Evelyn had sent the exiled King coded information regarding the political situation in London; now a trusted courtier, he had again been charged with gathering secret reports, having been given 'addresses and cyfers to correspond with his Majesty and Ministers abroad'. (The King had promised him that, should he return to England to reign, Sayes Court would be secured for him under a new royal lease. The King was true to his word, and ten years later, in 1663, when all the confiscated estates had been restored to the monarchy, the Crown granted Evelyn a renewal of the lease.)

Sayes Court was well situated for Evelyn to fulfil his secret commission. It was a discreet distance from London, and access to London was easier from here, than, for instance, from Surrey. From Deptford, a small rural village, there was a direct road through to Lambeth (the Colchester road), where he could board a ferry that would take him across the Thames and land him at the Whitehall Steps. He could also travel on the Thames from Deptford, either upstream to London or downstream to Gravesend and, eventually, France. Equally important was the accessibility of Sayes Court to the Kent coast and its Channel ports.

The estate of Sayes Court was about 40.47 hectares (100 acres), and when Evelyn arrived was essentially a self-sufficient farm. It was quite different from Wotton with its voluptuous wooded valleys and hills. The land comprised 'a rude orchard and all the rest one intire field of 100 acres, without any hedge, except the hither holly hedge joining to the bank of the mount walk', all reasonably level, with a stream marking its eastern boundary, and, as an added bonus, direct access via 'the Stayres' to the Thames.

Evelyn immediately began work on the garden. Fortuitously, the 1652 plan of the proposed layout, which he described to his father-in-law as 'the guide of all our designs', has survived. Neither the drawing nor the 126 points of the legend are in his hand, although it seems most likely to have been Evelyn's design. Some ideas were practical, some self-indulgent, others philosophical; all seemed fashionable. His influences were Continental as well as English, in particular gardens he had visited in France, Italy and Holland when residing in Europe, as well as gardens in England. Quite apart from being an enthusiastic diarist, he was also an inveterate note-maker and keen collector of prints and it is likely that he drew on these. Other influences were the many garden books which were then being published, both in English and French.

On 14 January 1653 Evelyn wrote, 'I began to set out the oval Garden at Says Court . . . This was the beginning of all the succeeding gardens, walks, groves, enclosures, and plantations there.' In designing an oval garden, he appeared to be recalling the oval garden of Pierre Morin in Paris, which Evelyn visited in 1644 and again just before his return to England. Like Morin's garden, the Oval Garden at Sayes Court was to be embellished with cypress trees. Evelyn even chose plants from Morin's *Catalogues de quelques plantes à fleurs* of 1651, which presumably he had brought with him from France. A month later, on 19 February, when the wind was from a westerly direction and there was a new moon (which, as Evelyn informs us in *Sylva*, helps to promote growth), he supervised the planting of the area that was to be known as Great Orchard 'with 300 fruit trees of the best sorts mingled, and warranted for 3 yeares upon a bond of 20 pound'. These had been ordered from an East Greenwich nurseryman, Matthew Blissett, who, according to the surviving invoice, supplied 247 trees, made up of 134 cherries of 20 different varieties, 65 apples of 22 different sorts, and 48 pears of 29 varieties. Each tree was charged at 1 s 6 d, and to make the numbers up to 500, Blissett was to supply and plant gooseberries, currants and roses.

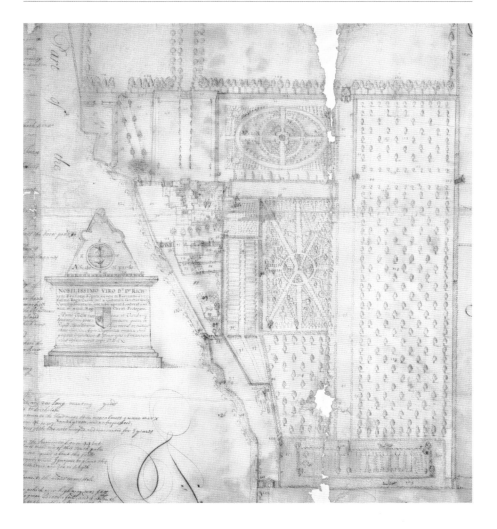

Three years later, in 1656, Evelyn wrote to his father-in-law, Sir Richard Browne, in Paris, where he was serving the King in exile, and asked him to send some citrus trees for the garden. Evelyn had some 'raised of seedes', some of which were 'very faire', but says, 'if I could by any conveyance procure half a dozen bearing trees from Paris, it would exceedingly rejoice me.' One wonders if these were the trees that twenty-six years later supplied the oranges that Evelyn was proud to record serving at a dinner party at Sayes Court. In December of the same year, he was again asking Sir Richard to order fruit trees from France, this time from the catalogue *Le Jardinier François*, out of which Sir Richard would be 'easily able to collect what kind are the best'.

Sayes Court, Deptford – a plan drawn in 1652 of Evelyn's proposed gardens.

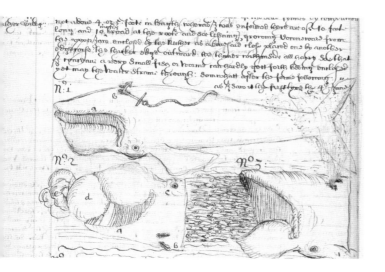

The weather in 1658 proved difficult for such a young garden to cope with. On 2 June Evelyn records 'An extraordinary storm of haile and raine, the season as cold as winter, the wind Northerly neere 6 moneths' (the following day a large whale, 17.68 metres/58 feet long, become stranded between his land 'butting on the Thames' and Greenwich). Then in August, while he was staying with Sir Ambrose Brown at Betchworth Castle, Reigate, Surrey, there occurred a very bad storm with a 'tempestuous wind which threw downe my greatest trees at Sayes Court and did so much mischeife all over England. It continued the whole night and till 3 in the afternoon of the next day.' Evelyn had already written to his father-in-law for 'a pretty quantity of cypresse-seedes [*Cupressus sempervirens*]' saying, 'it would greatly repair the ravage of this winter upon my nursery.'

In designing and planting a grove, 'with the severall walkes, meanders and thickets', Evelyn was again following Pierre Morin's garden. The Grove at Sayes Court included eight main walks, as well as a series of shorter paths which Evelyn called 'spider clawes', each ending in a small glade. The centre of the Grove was, fittingly, bearing in mind its ancient associations, planted with bay, which was itself enclosed with a circular walk of laurel. In each small glade, of which there were fourteen, there were 'Cabinetts of Aliternies' – dens or bowers of *Rhamnus alaternus*. Evelyn was particularly keen on this for hedging and planted a number of long hedges of it at Sayes Court. Also in each of the fourteen bowers he planted 'a great French walnutt' (altogether he planted twenty-four in the Grove), which presumably he had obtained via his long-suffering father-in-law in France. Five hundred large trees were planted: oak, ash, service, elm, beech and sweet chestnut. The thickets were crammed with birch, hazel, thorn and wild fruits (presumably the wild crab and pear trees). Although he does not specifically mention planting holly, of which he was very fond, there were what Evelyn calls 'greenes'. All this planting was seemingly not enough, as in 1654 he stated that he needed to plant a further 800 trees.

Evelyn also made two bowling greens (although there is no evidence of his ever having played), which were walled and divided by gravel walks. The walls supported fruit trees and cypress trees decorated the walks. A double lime avenue led to the entrance to the estate, giving gravitas, one imagines, to one's arrival at Sayes Court.

The development of the estate reflects the eclectic nature of Evelyn's character. There were wide and plentiful long walks, of both gravel and grass. The hedges were much admired, of lilac, buckthorn, laurel, berberis and, notably, holly. In 1683, when he was in his sixties, he wrote: 'I planted all the out limites of the garden and long walks with holly'; they were long indeed – over 122 metres (400ft). There was a miniature banqueting-house for his children to enjoy, and a moat with an island, where asparagus and raspberries grew (a meal in themselves), and there were also a summerhouse and a mulberry tree. He also developed an aviary, where in 1656 the elderly Marquis of Argyll, being shown the grounds by Evelyn, mistook the resident turtle doves for owls.

On a visit to Oxford in 1654, when he visited Wadham College, Evelyn accepted an unusual gift from his 'deare and excellent friend' Dr Wilkins (1614–72). This was a transparent glass apiary, 'built like castles and palaces, and so ordered them one upon another as to take the honey without destroying the bees. These were adorned with a variety of dials, little statues, vanes etc.' He placed it in the working part of the garden, in what he called the private garden, near the house and close also to what he described as 'My Elaboratorie with a Portico of 20 foot long upon Pillars open towards the Private Garden', where he carried out various experiments. When John Wilkins visited Sayes Court in April 1656, Evelyn reciprocated by giving him his 'rare burning-glasse', a concave mirror or lens, by which the sun's rays could be concentrated on an object. The grandest of visitors to the garden were shown the beehive, including Charles II, 'with other persons of quality', on 30 April 1663. Two years later, one May afternoon, Pepys visited the gardens; he records 'among other rarities, a hive of Bees; so as being hived in glass, you may see the Bees making their honey and Combs mighty pleasantly.'

In 1664 Evelyn expanded the planting by encompassing two fields, Homefield (earlier known as Hither or Great Broom Field) and Westfield, with elms. It happened that at the same time elms were being planted at Greenwich Park, and much to Evelyn's chagrin some of his trees were stolen and turned up in

Greenwich, having been 'sold on' and replanted there. How they were identified is not known but Evelyn vowed that if this happened again he would 'complain to His Majesty of it'; he also tried the modern idea of tagging his own trees, but no record remains of the results.

Evelyn obviously loved his garden at Sayes Court, and continued to embellish it until he and his family left to live at Wotton. Over the years he badgered everyone he could to send him seeds or plants and even five months before his move, in December 1693, he was still buying plants, on this occasion from Henry Wise at the Brompton Park Nursery.

Forty years after the original plans for Sayes Court garden had been executed, and as Evelyn was about to retire to Wotton, a survey was made by the famous map-maker Joel Gascoyne (*fl.*1680–1705). It shows that by then the gardened area had grown to include what Evelyn had originally noted as 'An extravagant place mangled by digging Gravell'. However, the Oval Garden was no more and the Grove shown in this new survey seems less elaborate; the whole looks more relaxed, and not quite so fussy.

Evelyn was not selling Sayes Court; he must have hoped it would pass to his son John and family. Initially it was let to Vice-Admiral Benbow (1653–1702) for three years with a condition to keep up the garden. Some time previously Evelyn had written *Directions for the Gardiner at Says-Court*, a document which contains the essentials of the art, simply put, no doubt intended for use by the gardeners when he was away for any length of time. Under Benbow's tenancy, however, he had the 'mortification of seeing every day much of my former labours and expense there impairing for want of a more polite tenant'. By April 1698 he had terminated the agreement with the Admiral, and the house was let to the twenty-five-year-old 'Czar of Muscovy', Peter the Great (1672–1725), who was visiting England for three months, learning about gardens, horticulture and shipbuilding among an eclectic mix of interests. His stay was financed by William III, which was just as well, as this tenancy was even more disastrous for Evelyn. Not only were there were complaints by the servants about the 'house being full of people, and right nasty' but at the end of the Czar's stay, Evelyn was outraged to discover that his beloved holly hedge had been almost destroyed by the exuberant behaviour of his illustrious tenant: the constant pushing and shoving through the hedge of a wheelbarrow carrying the Czar had made huge holes in the smooth sides. As soon as the Czar had departed Evelyn hurried to Sayes Court to inspect the damage, and asked his friends Sir Christopher Wren and the gardener George London (*fl*.1681–1714) to estimate the cost of reinstatement, with the bill to be sent to the King.

Evelyn could not have known that only some twenty-six years following his death in 1706, the house would be demolished, the garden reduced and the building materials recycled to build a workhouse. The Sayes Court Workhouse lasted just over 200 years, until the 1930s, when it was demolished. All that remains of Sayes Court garden (or part of it) today is a small local authority park, within which there is one (vulnerable) mulberry tree; it may be the sole remnant of the glorious garden that was once Evelyn's pride and joy.

Return to Wotton

John Evelyn loved his family home at Wotton all his life, and he kept a benign yet critical eye on the estate, but because he was the younger son, it was his eldest brother, George, and his heirs who inherited it and lived there. The youngest brother, Richard, who was two years younger than John, lived in another of the family houses, at Woodcote, near Epsom, until he died in 1670.

Wotton, Surrey. Watercolour by John Aubrey (1626–97) in The Natural History of Antiquities of the County of Surrey.

At the end of May 1691, George Evelyn's son, also George, died. Under the terms of the family settlement, on George senior's death John and his heirs would therefore inherit the estate. By this time both brothers were elderly (John was seventy-one, George seventy-four) and George invited John and his wife to leave Sayes Court and take up residence with him at Wotton. This was already under discussion at the time of young George's death: only a few days after his son died, George wrote to his brother, ''tis my comfort that you and my nephew are in vivis, to succeed me in the enjoyment of the estate our father left us'.

George – in modern parlance – needed to refinance himself and wished to capitalize on the estate's assets by felling sufficient timber to settle his not inconsiderable debts. This arrangement had to be agreed by the beneficiaries of the family settlement. It is likely that the brothers discussed the situation when Evelyn travelled to Wotton in July 1691, and in November 1691 George wrote to his brother, 'I am now viewing my woods, those that are to be felled for the raising of the £6000 for my own occasions and payment of my debts.' The proposed felling must have utterly depressed Evelyn, who loved the landscape of Wotton. He also realized that nothing had been said about safeguarding the remaining trees, which provided shelter and ornament around the house. It was a while before Evelyn was reassured, and a number of other points were clarified. Significantly he made no comments in his diary about the disagreement, and it was not until the following February 1692, that all was settled and the agreement signed. Even then Evelyn was anxious about how the felling would be conducted; and in the summer he wrote to George, 'I pray brother, spare the aged beech tree, on White Deane as a mark of your clemency: I will ever call it by your name.' No record remains of whether his plea was granted.

Realizing that he would be moving from his home and the garden he had created there over forty years, Evelyn sent to Wotton some 'evergreens', and a promise of a variety of seeds in the spring. He suggested that it would be a good idea to 'add a Conservatory for orange, lemon, and other rare and choice shrubs', but there is no evidence that one was built.

On 4 May 1693 Evelyn and his wife, with four servants, some furniture and two cartloads of books, left Sayes Court to reside at Wotton. It was not the happiest of moves, as Evelyn's forty-four-year-old niece Mary was still living at home. She had recently been married to Sir Cyril Wyche (1632–1707), President of The

Royal Society, and raised a number of difficulties about moving from Wotton. Her husband, who was in Ireland as Lord Justice, does not seem to have been in any hurry to set up the matrimonial home, even though newly married. Six years later, in October 1699, when George Evelyn died, Mary had left Wotton, but despite the settlement (which covered the contents of the house as well as the land), almost everything from the house was sold, leaving it looking desolate and unloved. More family acrimony followed. John Evelyn, apparently still lamenting the felling of the trees, complained bitterly to his Surrey neighbours about the changed view of the woods: 'instead of timber I have nothing but hedgerows!' However, in May of the following year, a 'great Western barge' filled with a hundred bales of furniture, paintings, and thirty cases of books from Sayes Court sailed upriver to Kingston, where all was offloaded and sent to Wotton. Moving house in the seventeenth century was as stressful as it is today. Evelyn wrote to his grandson that his house looked like 'a merchant's store-house'. It was his last move. Evelyn was to live at Wotton until his death in 1706.

John Evelyn: Garden Adviser

As well as being concerned with the gardens and landscape at his homes, Evelyn was asked for help by others in remodelling their grounds, especially during the 1660s and 1670s. His suggestions nearly always involved some degree of formalism and of creating vistas; it was in the detail and structure of his gardens – the orderliness in planting – that Evelyn excelled and which seems to have given him the greatest pleasure. Note, for instance, the precise measurement he gives for the planting of a double avenue of limes 'at 4 yards $^1/_2$ distant' and the endless lengths of crisply kept hedges. Perhaps that was why he developed a particular interest in trees, which have a relatively static structure, rather than quicker-growing plants with all their diversity. He was also admired for his placing of 'evergreens' in the landscape.

In his taste for order, structure and formality, he was, of course, influenced by what he had learned on his Continental travels. Evelyn was just too early to experience the work of André Le Nôtre. He was a near contemporary of Evelyn's, although they do not seem to have met as Le Nôtre began his work at Fontainebleau the year following Evelyn's visit in 1644. However, Evelyn would have been aware of Claude Mollet's book of 1652, *Theâtre des plans et*

Jardinages, which was the main exponent of the classic French designs and garden practices. (Like the Le Nôtre family, the Mollets were a family of great gardeners. Claude's son André Mollet (d.c.1665) spent some time working in England, in 1642 redesigning the gardens of Wimbledon House for Henrietta Maria, wife of Charles I, and then in charge of developing St James's Park.)

One estate John Evelyn was asked to view was Cornbury, at Charlbury, near Oxford, belonging to his friend Edward Hyde (1609–74), Earl of Clarendon, who had been Charles II's principal adviser in exile, becoming his first Chief Minister following the Restoration and subsequently Lord Chancellor. (Cornbury had earlier belonged to Henry Danvers, the benefactor who gave some 2 hectares (5 acres) of land to create the Oxford Botanic Garden.) When Lord Clarendon came into ownership of Cornbury in 1661, he began rebuilding the house and redesigning the grounds. In October 1664 he invited a group of friends and colleagues, including the architect Hugh May (1622–84) and Evelyn, to view the estate; they travelled from London, Evelyn records, in a coach pulled by six horses. Evelyn described Cornbury as 'a sweete park, walled with a dry wall'. He encouraged some tree planting, as it is later recorded that in one year over 2,000 indigenous and foreign trees were planted. Poor Clarendon was not to experience the delights of all this planting, though, as he was forced into exile in 1667 and never returned to England during his lifetime (although he was to be buried in Westminster Abbey). It was at Cornbury during this expansive period that one of the earliest ha-has was built, a feature used to retain uninterrupted views from a residence while preventing animals – cattle, sheep or, in this instance, deer – from grazing too near the house.

In 1667 Henry Howard (d. 1684), later the Duke of Norfolk, invited Evelyn to improve the landscape at Albury Park, near Guildford, the estate which the Howards had purchased in the 1630s. Drawing on Italian ideas, Evelyn created a terrace in the surrounding Surrey hills, added a classical portico and planted the slopes with vineyards. Running parallel with the terrace, he also created a formal canal in the classical French style. He was pleased with the progress of his design when he visited the site in September 1670. A grotto, or 'crypta' as he called it, was in the making, 'through the mountaine in the park, 30 perches in length [150.88 metres (165yd)]. Such a Pausilippe is nowhere in England besides.' This was, in fact, a tunnel, inspired by a visit Evelyn had made to Naples in 1644, when he had 'advanced into this noble and altogether

wonderfull crypt, consisting of a passage spacious enough for two coaches to go on abreast, cut through a rocky mountain neere three quarters of a mile', the drama of it made more marvellous by its proximity to the tomb of Virgil on Mount Posilippo. The Surrey hills do not have quite the ambience of the Bay of Naples or its surrounding mountains, but no doubt Henry Howard enjoyed the novelty of this ambitious and very modern feature.

In autumn 1671 Evelyn was invited to Euston Hall in Suffolk, the home of Sir Henry Bennet (1618–85), later the Earl of Arlington. Sir Henry had earlier been Keeper of the Privy Purse, and at the time of Evelyn's visit he was Secretary of State. He was spending lavishly on both his Suffolk house and his London home, Goring House, later Arlington House and the site of Buckingham Palace. Evelyn stayed in Suffolk for nearly three weeks. The King and the Court were at Newmarket, and Evelyn records, 'the whole house [was] filled from one end to the other with lords, ladys and gallants; there was such a furnished table as I had seldome seene.' Gambling, hunting and hawking took place, as well as 'till almost morning . . . cards, and dice', yet 'without noise, swearing, quarrel, or confusion of any sort'. He continues: '[The] garden [was] handsome, the canal beautifull, but the soile drie, barren and miserably sandy, which flies in drifts as the wind sits. Here my Lord was pleased to advise with me about ordering his plantations of firs, elmes and limes.' Interestingly, bearing in mind Evelyn's association with Cornbury and its use of the ha-ha to improve

Albury Park, Surrey: the design by Evelyn, c.1667, 'for the plat for his Canale and Garden, with a Crypta thro' the hill'.

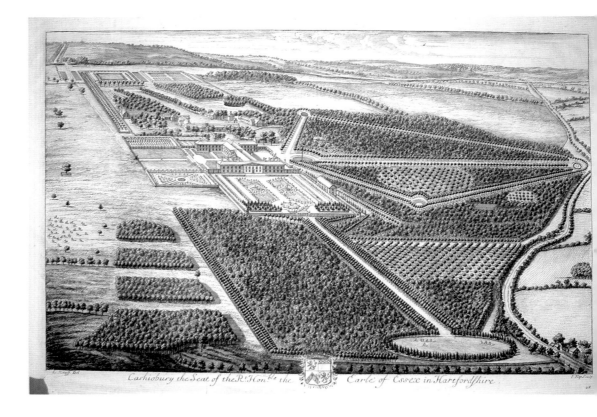

Cashiobury the Seat of the R.t Hon.ble the Earle of Essex in Hartfordshire.

the garden aspect, Evelyn persuaded Sir Henry 'to bring his park so neere as to comprehend his house within it which he resolved upon, it being neere a mile to it'. When Evelyn was invited to stay at Euston Hall six years later in 1677, he 'found things exceedingly improved' and noted that the planting of shelter belts he had recommended to help stabilize the poor soil had been carried out.

As well as advising on improvements, Evelyn visited gardens. He went to see the Botanic Garden at Oxford in 1654 and 1664, and his diary is filled with visits to friends' gardens. One was the garden at Wilton, home of Philip Herbert, 5th Earl of Pembroke (1619–69), which he describes as 'esteemed the noblest in England'. Sion House, belonging to Algernon Percy, 10th Earl of Northumberland (1602–68), he found a little disappointing – 'faire enough, but more celebrated than it deserves'. In 1663 on a visit to Kent, he records a visit to Sir Norton Knatchbull (1601–84), 'who is a worthy person and learned critic' and has 'a noble seat (Mersham Hatch) and a plantation of stately fir-trees', and he saw a grove there that he describes later as a 'delicious plantation

…[which] I beheld with great satisfaction'. Groves of firs and pines always caught Evelyn's eye; there are numerous notes of them in his diary.

In his sixtieth year, in 1680, Evelyn travelled to Hertfordshire 'on the earnest invitation of the Earle of Essex … to his house at Cashioberie'. His host was the scholarly Arthur, Earl of Essex (1631–83), who, with the help of Hugh May, had rebuilt Cassiobury House. The grounds, which were vast, had been remodelled by Moses Cook (*fl.*1660s–1715), who refers to work carried out six years previously in his book *The Manner of Raising, Ordering and Improving Forest Trees*, published in 1675. Moses Cook, like John Evelyn, was eminently practical, and his descriptions of his planting at Cassiobury are detailed: 'having set my Trees straight in their Rows, and trod the Earth close to their Roots, and made my Hills, I then laid round every Tree, upon those Hills, wet Litter taken off from the Dung-hill, a good Barrow-full to every Tree, and covered that with a little Mould, leaving them to take their rest for a time.' Although Evelyn does not appear to have met Cook, he writes: 'The gardens are very rare, and cannot be otherwise having so skilful an artist to govern them … We spent our time in the mornings in walking or riding, and contriving alterations.' Engravings of the time show, and Evelyn confirms, that 'the land about [was] exceedingly addicted to wood', but he complains that the coldness of the site inhibited growth. Nevertheless, there were numerous tree-lined avenues, very much in the French style of Le Nôtre. Evelyn observes that some of the native black cherry prospered 'even to considerable timber' and describes 'a faire walke, set about with treble rows of Spanish chestnut trees'. In 1801, Cassiobury Park was again given a 'makeover' by Humphry Repton (1752–1818). Little evidence remains of all the creative work that took place between the seventeenth and nineteenth centuries, but it is still an open space and some original planting remains in the parkland for the people of Watford to enjoy. The house and its great parterre (the outline of which may be traced in a dry summer) have long since disappeared.

Aged eighty-five, and within a year of his death, Evelyn journeyed to Turnham Green, then a small village on the outskirts of London, and visited the great French traveller Jean Chardin (1643–1713). As a young man Chardin had travelled to India in 1663 to buy diamonds, lived for a time in Persia (Iran) and eventually settled in England, where he wrote a book about his exploits. He became the Royal Jeweller and was knighted by Charles II. The elderly John Evelyn found the gardens 'very fine, and exceeding well planted with fruit'.

John Evelyn: Garden Writer

Throughout his life, John Evelyn wrote prolifically. He was a compulsive educator and, in addition to his diary, composed notes on the history of the navy at the request of Samuel Pepys; in 1661 wrote his pamphlet about London smog, *Fumifugium*; and in 1697 produced *Nusmismata, A Discourse of Medals Ancient and Modern*. His passion for gardens and trees inspired him to develop a singular knowledge and his garden writing was wide-ranging.

He was responsible for a number of publications that were translations from the French. One of his earliest ventures was a gardening book entitled *The French Gardiner: Instructing How to Cultivate All Sorts of Fruit-Trees and Herbs, for the Garden. Together with Directions to Dry and Conserve them in their Natural*, which Evelyn, probably with some assistance from his friend Thomas Henshaw (1618–1700; later Secretary in the French Tongue to the King), translated and published in 1659. The author of the book was Nicolas de Bonnefons (*fl.*1650) and it was first published in Paris in 1651 as *Le Jardinier François*. The original French illustrations were used in the English edition, but it was freely adapted, and Evelyn omitted three of the chapters concerning cooking and preserving. De Bonnefons was 'Le Valet de Chambre du Roi' to Louis XIV, and had a reputation as a culinary expert. Three years later, in 1654, he wrote *Les Delices de campagne* (The Delights of the Countryside), which, in France, is considered to be the first modern cookery book.

Many years later a book written by the garden designer Jean de La Quintinie (1626–88) entitled *Instructions pour les Jardins Fruitiers et Potagers* was translated into English and published under the title *The Compleat Gard'ner* in 1693. For a long time it was assumed that Evelyn was the translator; however, modern research indicates that the translator was George London and that Evelyn merely 'oversaw' the work, and added his by then prestigious name to the publication. London was part of a partnership which had developed the huge Brompton Park Nursery (where the museums of South Kensington now stand). He had been apprenticed to John Rose (*c.*1621–77), who was gardener to the Earl of Essex at his London house. The Earl sent Rose to study with André Le Nôtre in France, and when George London was apprenticed to Rose, he too was sent to France under the tutelage of Le Nôtre. The London–Rose partnership at the Brompton Nursery was of immense significance to many gardens and estates being developed during the latter part of the seventeenth and early eighteenth centuries. Such was the partners' expertise and influence that today it is likely that almost every extant estate still holds somewhere on its land plantings from the Brompton Park Nursery.

Evelyn assisted John Rose in the publication of two books. The first was published in 1666 and called *The English Vineyard Vindicated,* and twenty years later he produced *A Treasure Upon Fruit Trees.* Rose is usually remembered for his connection with the pineapple and the recording of it for posterity in the painting by Danckerts entitled *Rose, the Royal Gardener, Presenting the First Pine-Apple Raised in England to Charles II.* Evelyn records in 1661, 'I first saw the famous Queen Pine brought from Barbados and presented to his Majestie; but the first that were ever seen in England were those sent to Cromwell foure years since.' Seven years later he again writes, after he had seen the magnificent arrival at Court of his friend the French Ambassador Colbert, that 'there was that rare fruit call'd the King-pine, growing in Barbados and the West Indies, the first of them I had ever seene. His Majesty having cut it up, was pleas'd to give me a piece off his owne plate to taste of.' He thought the taste more 'like the quince and melon than of any other fruite'.

Of Evelyn's own projects, the most ambitious was *Elysium Britannicum,* a treatise encompassing everything to do with gardens and gardening. He began writing it in the 1650s (he announced it first in the preface of *The French Gardiner*) and was engaged in expanding and revising it for much of his life. Evelyn wished: 'To comprehend the nature of the Earth and her productions: to be able to discourse of the Elements and to penetrate into the energie and reasons of things with judgement and assurance. In a word, What is our Gardiner to be, but an absolute Philosopher!' Evelyn worked on this mighty thesis for four decades but in the end the manuscript overcame him and it remained unfinished and unpublished. (Evelyn's grandiose vision would eventually be realized in 1822 by the great John Claudius Loudon (1783–1843) with his *Encyclopaedia of Gardening,* an antecedent of the five-volumed *The Royal Horticultural Society Dictionary of Gardening* published in 1951, with a second edition in 1956.) However, sections of *Elysium Britannicum* were finished and published separately. Towards the end of his life, in 1699, Evelyn published *Acetaria: A Discourse of Sallets,* which gave lists of various salad and herb leaves and also detailed why 'the wholesomness of the herby-diet' should be grown and eaten.

Whitebeam blossom

Earlier, in 1664, and also first scheduled as a chapter in *Elysium Britannicum*, was *Kalendarium Hortense or the Gard'ners Alamanac*. This is a calendar of monthly gardening instructions, including a catalogue of 'What Fruits and Flowers are in Prime'. Evelyn divides each month into four sections. The first two describe work that must be achieved 'In the Orchard, and Olitory-Garden' or kitchen garden, and 'In the Parterre, and Flower-Garden'. The third section comprises a list of the fruit either in season or that may be stored and eaten; the fourth and final section concerns flowers 'in Prime or yet lasting'. In providing detailed instructions of what to do, sow and plant, and when, as well as the reassuring catalogue of what can be expected to be in bloom or ready for eating, all laid out so clearly, the *Kalendarium Hortense* was as helpful in its day as, say, BBC *Gardener's World* is today. In fact, it was probably more so, as we have a wide range of detailed information to learn from in an enormous number of horticultural books and web pages – one is almost spoilt for choice – whereas Evelyn's *Kalendarium* was probably the first month-by-month guide of practical advice and catalogue of seasonal fruit and flowers to be published.

Evelyn was writing when England was still using the Julian calendar; under today's Gregorian calendar, which England adopted in 1752, all dates moved forward by eleven days. Taking this into account, a modern reader will find that so much of what Evelyn advised is as pertinent today as it was 350 years ago. If, for instance, the weather is 'over-wet, or hard', Evelyn recommends we should 'cleanse, mend, sharpen and prepare Garden-tools', just as well-organized gardeners do today. In May he says, 'Give now . . . all your house plants (such as you do not think require to take out) fresh Earth at the surface, in place of some of the old earth (a hand depth or so) and loosning the rest with a fork without wounding the Roots.' During June he warns us to keep watering and mulching any late-planted trees.

Evelyn ends his calendar with advice on how to keep through the winter plants that are 'lest patient of Cold'. He divides these into three categories. The first are the most vulnerable and must be 'first into the Conservatory'. He lists about twenty-five exotics, including *Agapanthus,* which is interesting since this mention comes several years earlier than its first known date of arrival in Britain, 1679, and over twenty years before it was grown in the royal greenhouses of Hampton Court Palace. The second group, which must also be

Elm leaves

protected in the conservatory, includes Oleanders, Myrtles and Oranges. The third group, 'not perishing but in excessive Colds', are 'to be last set in or rather protected under Mattrasses, and sleighter coverings, abroad in the Earth, Cases, Boxes or Pots'. The modern equivalent of 'Mattrasses' would be horticultural fleece. This list, the largest, includes *Cineraria, Cneorum, Sisyrinchium* and *Yucca* (this would have been *Yucca gloriosa*, which is said to have arrived from America *c.*1550 and flowered for the first time in Britain about fifty years later in the garden of William Coys in Essex).

A few years before Evelyn's *Kalendarium* was published, Sir Thomas Hanmer (1612–78), a friend and correspondent of Evelyn, had written a similar manual. Hanmer and Evelyn had a lot in common. Both were from Royalist families and had travelled extensively on the Continent (Hanmer for three years from 1638). They both kept a low profile during the Commonwealth, devoting some of their time to cultivating their respective gardens (Hammer having a garden at his home, Bettisfield, in Flintshire); and – to our advantage – they both decided to communicate their horticultural knowledge to a wider audience. Hanmer began writing his manuscript when he was in his thirties – it is dated 1659, five years before Evelyn's was published – but it was not published until 1933. The section devoted to the garden month by month, although similar to Evelyn's, is much shorter, having only two parts. The first is a list of flowers and shrubs in bloom; the second describes 'Remembrances for this Moneth', the equivalent of Evelyn's 'Jobs to be Done'. Hanmer's manuscript is written in a very modern style, with sections including 'How to Preserve Flowers being Planted from Hurtfull Things' and 'Of Watering Flowers'. The largest part is concerned with listing and describing individual plants, organized, just as our horticultural encyclopaedias are today, into different groups. It includes lists 'Of the bulbous Kinds', 'Of Tuberous Plants', 'Of Glandulous Flowers', shrubs, trees, herbs, fruit trees and the Orchard. It is interesting to compare the two manuscripts; there seems little doubt that they knew of each other's desire to publish their gardening manuals and one cannot help wondering how much access Evelyn was granted to Hanmer's work prior to his own being published.

The *Kalendarium* was first published in 1664, encompassed in the first and all subsequent editions of another work that would ensure John Evelyn's lasting reputation as a writer about plants: *Sylva: A Discourse of Forest Trees and the*

Kalendarium Hortense:

OR, THE

GARD'NERS ALMANAC,

DIRECTING

What he is to do *Monethly* through-out the *Year.*

AND

What *Fruits* and *Flowers* are in *Prime.*

The second Edition, *with many useful* Additions.

By *JOHN EVELYN* Esq;
Fellow of the *Royal Society.*

Virg. Geo. 2.
——*Labor actus in orbem.*

LONDON,

Printed by *Jo. Martyn* and *Ja. Allestry,* Printers to
the *Royal Society,* and are to be sold at their
Shops in St. *Paul's* Church-yard.
MDCLXVI.

Propagation of Timber in His Majesties Dominions. No explanation was given for its inclusion, but perhaps Evelyn believed it would receive a wider readership if it was attached to a publication supported by The Royal Society, as *Sylva* was.

The Royal Society was also instrumental in *Pomona*, again included as an appendix to *Sylva*. During the 1660s the Society held a series of lectures on the subject of cider and decided to publish the results of their findings. Evelyn was one of seven contributors, though his paper was the longest. While all the contributors also concern themselves with pears and perry-making, their focus is on the varying taste of cider, and which apple varieties are best used for its production. It seems the most popular apple of the day was one named Red-Strake or Red Streak, which originated in Herefordshire. It also went under the name of Scudamore Crab, a name still in use over 150 years later. *Pomona* is drawn to a conclusion by an anonymous 'Person of Great Experience'. One suspects it is John Evelyn, but whoever it may be, he lists the best apples for cider-making and warns: 'new cider and all diluted and watered Ciders, are great enemies to the teeth, and cause violent pains in them, and rheums in the head'. You have been warned!

CHAPTER II

'A Discourse of Forest Trees'

PUBLISHED IN 1664, *Sylva: A Discourse of Forest Trees and the Propagation of Timber in His Majesties Dominions* was a brilliant *tour de force*. Within the first paragraph of its introduction John Evelyn made it clear that the *raison d'être* for his treatise was concern for the growing shortage of timber. Today, the modern world runs on petroleum, but in the seventeenth century it was timber that powered development; and, just as now there is anxiety about the cost of oil, stability of extraction and a steady supply, so 400 years ago there were similar worries about the amount of timber available for powering exploration, manufacturing, transport, building and fuel.

For thousands of years throughout Europe, shortages of timber, particularly of wood for fuel, were recorded. One, during the Bronze Age, happened on the island of Cyprus, when the metal industry collapsed because of a continuing lack of suitable fuel. During the Middle Ages, in Montpellier, France, bakers could not cook bread for the inhabitants because all the suitable fuel had been used up. In England in the seventeenth century shortage of timber had become a serious problem, against a background of centuries of heavy demand, especially by industry.

Two heavy uses of timber for fuel were glass manufacture and the smelting of iron. The latter had been practised in Britain from the Neolithic period and had probably caused the greatest devastation. The iron industry had been centred in southern England, particularly the Sussex Weald which was heavily wooded, although it petered out here during Evelyn's lifetime to re-emerge in the northern counties during the mid-eighteenth century when coal (in the form of coke) instead of timber took over as the principal source of fuel. Domestic production increased during the later part of the seventeenth century, despite large (and alarming) importations from Sweden. The process of glass-making arrived in England from France some time in the fourteenth century. The two

SYLVA,

Or A DISCOURSE Of
FOREST-TREES,

AND THE
Propagation of Timber

In His MAJESTIES Dominions.

By *J. E.* Esq;

As it was Deliver'd in the *ROYAL SOCIETY* the xvᵗʰ of
October, CIƆIƆCLXII. upon Occasion of certain *Queries*
Propounded to that *Illustrious Assembly,* by the *Honorable* the Principal
Officers, and *Commissioners* of the *Navy.*

To which is annexed
POMONA Or, An *Appendix* concerning *Fruit-Trees* in relation to *CIDER*;
The *Making* and several ways of *Ordering* it.

Published by express Order *of the* ROYAL SOCIETY.

ALSO
KALENDARIUM HORTENSE; Or, *Gard'ners Almanac*;
Directing *what* he is to do *Monethly* throughout the *Year.*

————*Tibi res antiquæ laudis & artis*
Ingredior, tantos ausus recludere fonteis. Virg.

LONDON, Printed by *Jo. Martyn,* and *Ja. Allestry,* Printers to the *Royal*
Society, and are to be sold at their Shop at the *Bell* in S. *Paul's* Church-yard.
MDCLXIV.

*Frontispiece to
the first, 1664,
edition of John
Evelyn's* Sylva.

'A Discourse of Forest Trees' 47

CHARCOAL

In seventeenth-century Britain 'char coal', as it was then written, was taken very seriously. It was the preferred fuel for several manufacturing processes and its production had become a specialized industry in itself. Naturally, wood that was closest to hand, and therefore the cheapest, was used first and so local woodlands became centres of felling operations. Beech wood gave the greatest heat, but birch, oak, Holm oak, hornbeam, ash, hazel, poplar, maple and 'plum' have all been recorded in the making of charcoal. Elm is the notable exception: it very seldom grew in woodland, being a hedgerow inhabitant *par excellence*.

There were at least three different grades of charcoal. The lowest was destined for the iron-making industry (see page 46); the most refined was reserved for use by the King, the Court and London. The middle grade was used as a component in gunpowder (which Evelyn's family had manufactured in Surrey during the sixteenth century). Manufacture of this commodity was strictly licensed and, as recorded by Pepys, who knew it as black powder or 'Kings Powder', trading in it was strictly forbidden. Chinese alchemists in the ninth century were the first to use gunpowder. It was made of sulphur, saltpetre and charcoal, pounded and mixed together in certain proportions, and known as serpentine powder. It must have seemed true wizardry when on contact with a naked flame or hot wire the gunpowder exploded with a bang, dense white smoke and a sulphurous smell. It seems almost superfluous to mention that gunpowder is a component of the explosive and sparky firework.

Today artists use charcoal only occasionally but as a drawing medium it is quick and easy to use and making images from charcoal must have been one of the first ideas to have occurred to 'cave men' thousands of years ago. In the sixteenth century the Venetian artist Tintoretto used charcoal. And in the following

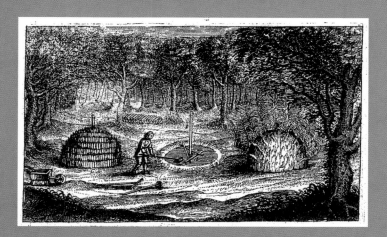

century Dutch draughtsmen experimented with charcoal pencils dipped in linseed oil; this combination increased the blackness of the line and helped the charcoal to adhere to the paper, although over time a thin brown streak developed alongside the darker line.

Along with wood, straw and dried dung charcoal was one of the earliest forms of fuel for fire and heating. By the time the Romans came to Britain in the first century AD, they had perfected the art of underfloor heating, and often used charcoal to fuel the hypocaust. Their iron-making furnaces were also heated by charcoal. Charcoal was also used in the production of saffron: before gas burners were employed, the thousands of stigmas picked from *Crocus sativa* were dried upon a charcoal fire.

There are global records regarding the use or burning of charcoal, and what woods make the best fuel. In southern Somalia the Acacia tree, *Boswellia* spp., of the thorny savannas is used, in Argentina the White Quebracho tree, *Quararibea* spp. Thailand was, before the tsunami of December 2004, an exporter of charcoal, most of it being sent from Phuket as fuel to Malaysia and Singapore, or north to Myanmar. In parts of the Elbruz Mountains of northern Iran, so much felling has taken place that the production of charcoal has had to cease.

Laying out wood ready for making charcoal.

industries were fundamentally different in the way they were fuelled. Iron smelting required great heat and charcoal was required for 'charking' (burning); glass manufacturers used unprocessed wood for fuel. The latter required little capital equipment, but iron-making needed costly water-powered machinery. Both methods of fuelling, though, required wood. The industries reached their peak in timber consumption between 1570 and *c.*1620. Such was the arboreal havoc caused that in 1615 a Proclamation forbade the use of wood as a heat source for the manufacturing of glass. According to Samuel Pepys, in the Forest of Dean slag remaining from the Roman and medieval iron forges or bloomeries was reused.

In the north of England the ancient industry of lead mining and smelting again required a continuous supply of large quantities of wood. By the late fourteenth century on Alston Moor (now part of Cumbria), where lead extraction was prolific, the miners could (unusually) claim the privilege of felling timber 'to roast and smelt ore, and that it was lawful to take the wood for building, burning and hedging, and also to give it to the agents of the mine as wages'. According to the nineteenth-century historian William Wallace, the miners also denied the rights of their overlords to sell or give any timber away and 'claimed that they had such liberty in the woods adjoining the mines from time beyond which there is no memory'. On the other hand, during the fourteenth century in the Forest of Dean in England, there were 'forbid' or Vorbid trees, which by an order from the Mines Law Court (similar to Tree Preservation Orders today), miners were forbidden to fell.

Fuel was needed in the west of England for smelting of tin, which had been extracted there since Phoenician times. Later in Cornwall, during the reign of Charles I, the first experiment was made using coal to fuel the furnace, but it was not a success; even after the 'reverberatory' furnace had been invented, the metal produced was too brittle and so less valuable than that produced by a timber-fired furnace; consequently, timber-fired furnaces remained in use. Timber in the form of pit props was also vital to support the underground passages and shafts of mines.

Fuel played a major part in the manufacture of coloured cloth, for which great vats of liquid dye required heating. Another use for timber was in the brewing industry. First, long poles were needed to support the growing hops – a method

COAL

The output of coal, as a source of fuel, had been steadily increasing from Elizabethan times, and by the end of the seventeenth century, output had reached about 3 million tons yearly (compared with 240 million tons in the early part of the twentieth century). Coal or 'Newcastle coal' was mined in the north-east of England and brought by collier down the eastern seaboard and up the Thames to Tower Wharf, in London. Recognizing that coal could ease the demand for timber, from the 1550s special arrangements were made for churchwardens of each City parish to distribute coal to the London poor from Tower Wharf. Evelyn makes no mention in his diary of his own domestic arrangements but Pepys records deliveries of his coal from 1660 onwards. He describes one delivery on Monday morning, 16 September 1661. Having joined together with other members of the Navy Board, he did not go to the office but was '*busy at home to take in my part of our fraight of Coles, which Sir G. Carteret, Sir R. Slingsby and myself sent for – which is 10 Chalderon…*' (15,240 tonnes, 15 tons). Such was the dependence on coal that six years later, when blockades on the Thames at the height of the Second Dutch War meant coal could not reach the capital, in the panic about invasion, an unfounded rumour spread that the enemy was destroying all the Newcastle colliers.

Windsor Great Park c.1870: collecting wood from the c.1200-year-old 'William the Conqueror's Oak Tree' in the White Deer Enclosure, near Cranbourne Tower.

introduced in 1525 by Leonard Mascall (d. 1589). (He was appropriately the Clerk of the Kitchen to Archbishop Mathew Parker, the second Protestant Archbishop of Canterbury.) Second, after harvesting, the hops had to be dried in an oast house, where a plentiful supply of charcoal was needed for the fire. The discovery of rock salt in Cheshire in 1671 aggravated the shortage of timber in the county with its need for immense quantities of fuel to heat the great pans in which the salt was treated. Most of the valuable woodlands in the area were consumed in a relatively short period.

Apart from the commercial use of timber, wood was used domestically. Tenants and the local poor inhabitants of land belonging to the Lord of the Manor and the Royal Forests benefited from rights protecting the use of wood, established over hundreds of years. Wood could be taken for 'housebote' (house repair), 'hedgebote' (fencing), 'ploughbote' (the making of farm implements) and 'firebote' (fuel). All timber harvestings were overseen by the Wood Mote Court. For whatever purpose the timber was to be used, it had to be gathered from the ground, except that which could be reached and snapped off by hand or by using a crooked pole (by hook or by crook). This was called 'snapwood' or 'snapping wood'. Anyone convicted of woodland offences was sent to prison, fined, or after three convictions, transported for seven years.

There was, of course, a continuing need for timber in the development, construction, repair and enlargement of houses, churches, roads, canals, bridges, carts, carriages, furniture and tools. In the seventeenth century, timber was fundamental to the rebuilding of the country following the Civil War. However, it was shipbuilding and its allied trades that regarded the dwindling timber reserves with the most anxiety.

There was no substitute for wood for the building of a ship – neither stone nor brick could be used, as they could be for land-based items, and only a few sorts of timber were suitable. Requirements for this industry were long term and quite different and more stringent than those for other users, both domestic and industrial. During the seventeenth century new technology in the form of cannons and other equipment required ships to be larger and sturdier, so that they could carry these heavier items. Consequently the navy insisted on higher and higher specifications. It demanded 'designer timber', for which trees needed to have been moulded into the forms desired perhaps many decades before they

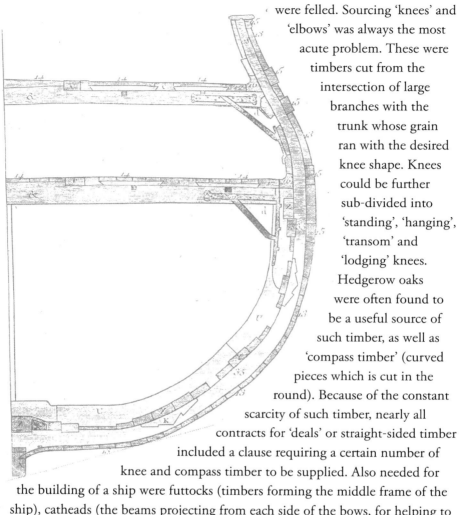

were felled. Sourcing 'knees' and 'elbows' was always the most acute problem. These were timbers cut from the intersection of large branches with the trunk whose grain ran with the desired knee shape. Knees could be further sub-divided into 'standing', 'hanging', 'transom' and 'lodging' knees. Hedgerow oaks were often found to be a useful source of such timber, as well as 'compass timber' (curved pieces which is cut in the round). Because of the constant scarcity of such timber, nearly all contracts for 'deals' or straight-sided timber included a clause requiring a certain number of knee and compass timber to be supplied. Also needed for the building of a ship were futtocks (timbers forming the middle frame of the ship), catheads (the beams projecting from each side of the bows, for helping to raise the anchor), a crutch, a top piece and many others.

The economic world of the seventeenth century was almost exclusively focused on the shipping and maritime trade, the golden objective being trade with 'the East'. In the early part of the century trading conglomerates were the vogue throughout Europe. Merchants had already formed companies in order to trade in various parts of the world. Probably the oldest was the Hanseatic League, first formed during the thirteenth century by the merchants of various north German towns to assist their combined overseas trade. In England there was the Eastland Company, trading with Poland and eastern Europe; the Muscovy

Cut-away section of a ship's hull, showing the complicated use and the different shapes of timber needed.

Company, trading with Russia; and for African trading interests the Royal African (Guinea) Company, which was founded in the sixteenth century and received a new charter in 1662, and again in 1672. But in the seventeenth century, eight European countries, enthralled by the lure of trading with India, Japan, China and Indonesia, set up East India Companies. Of these, five – those of Austria, Scotland, Sweden, Spain and Denmark – made little or no sea-borne impact. The French East India Company began impressively but withered in the late eighteenth century once France had lost its Indian Empire. The most significant were the English and Dutch companies, which both became politically powerful and influential in world trade, all the time the greatest of rivals, continually jostling for superiority.

The English East India Company was incorporated by Royal Charter in 1600, three years before the reign of Elizabeth I ended. By 1609 it had constructed the first of its own dockyards at Deptford and by 1612 its ships were trading with Japan. Politically and physically at the beginning of the 1600s, the Dutch were the dominant maritime nation, and superior to the English navy in both trade and warfare. France too was building a competent navy under Cardinal Richelieu (1585–1642), who, on coming to power, gave himself the title of 'Grande Maître, Chef, et Suprintendant-Général de la Navigation et Commerce de France' and, in 1625, placed an order with the Dutch for five warships. However, the superiority of the English mercantile fleet and navy gradually took hold, and by the end of the century the former had overtaken its European rivals. The Navigation Act of 1651 and its later enlargement of 1660 both had an important impact on trade. The acts decreed that trade imports to Britain were to be carried in British ships – or the ships of the exporting nation – but not those of another country. These impositions implied both a new confidence and an expansion in the naval prowess of Britain. Holland was outraged. Three Dutch Wars followed over a twenty-two-year period from 1652 to 1674; each one lasted only two years but they were painful and destructive to both nations. The necessity of retaining and enlarging a sea-borne fighting force concentrated Parliament's (and to a lesser extent the monarch's) mind on how to obtain and sustain the naval ships: the ready availability of the raw material needed for maintaining such a force, timber, was imperative.

In 1660, at the Restoration of Charles II, the Cromwellian fleet consisted of 156 vessels. By the King's command this fleet was named the Royal Navy, and

although there had been much dockyard activity during the Interregnum,
further shipbuilding began almost immediately. It continued without
interruption, and in one year, 1677, an Act of Parliament commissioned thirty
new ships. This was a triumph for Samuel Pepys, who was by then Secretary of
the Navy Board: he had long been pressing for such a large building
programme. All were to be designed by Sir Anthony Deane (*c.*1638–1721), the
Navy Commissioner and foremost ship designer and shipwright of the day.
There was anxiety about the availability of the major building material, matured
oak. Most materials required by the navy were bought under contract, and often
sourced from overseas; oak was also be available, after protracted negotiations,

from the Royal Forests. Pepys spent much time with various timber merchants negotiating for supplies of oak for the Royal Dockyard; for instance, during 1665 he successfully negotiated a contract with Sir Edward Dering (1625–84) of Pluckley in Kent for the supply of 400 oaks.

There was a lack of first-class timber available not only for building new ships but also for repairing them. Moreover, in his diaries for that period Pepys continually records corruption in the supply of timber. Determined to put a stop to it, he arose particularly early one August morning in 1662 and (after partaking of a dish of eggs at the King's Head at Bow) rode with Sir Anthony

Eighteenth-century view of Blackwell Yard on the north bank of the Thames, east of Greenwich, showing both warships and merchantmen being built. The yard was established in the Middle Ages, and during the seventeenth century was used to build the East India Company fleet.

Deane a friend of John Evelyn, into Waltham Forest. Pepys saw 'many trees of the King's a-hewing' and records, 'he showed me the whole mystery of off-square, wherin the King is abused in the timber that he buys, which I shall with much pleasure be able to correct.' Off-square was a fraudulent method of measuring timber. While they were awaiting dinner, at Ilford, Pepys practised the measuring technique so that he could be sure of understanding it. Later in the day he summoned the Timber Purveyor to the Navy for Epping Forest (and Alice Holt Forest in Hampshire), Samuel Cooper, and quizzed him about the problems he was encountering, as well as Mr Marshall of East Ham, a timber and haulage merchant.

Foreign timber was being purchased from every known continent. Both hardwood and softwood was required but, in particular, timber from the tree then known as 'Fir', *Pinus sylvestris*, was needed for mast wood and spars. The navy's first choice was for trees that had been grown in northern Europe, anywhere between the Baltic shore of Poland and the heartland of Russia, not only because of the straightness, suppleness and durability of the felled trunks but also because of their the retention of resin, which helped ensure the masts' resilience (see also page 162).

Felling and selling oak timber. The owner and his agent discuss prices with the timber merchant. The crooks at the opposite ends of the two felled trunks are probably to be used as ship's timbers.

There had been debate in Britain about the planting of trees and uses of timber for well over a hundred years before the Restoration. An Act of Parliament promulgated in 1544 by Henry VIII laid down regulations for felling in an oak wood in order to conserve fuel. 'Twelve Standils or Storers [young trees], likely to become Timber Trees, shall be left on every acre of Wood or Underwood that shall be felled at or under 24 years Growth; the turning Woodland into Tillage is prohibited; and whenever any Wood is cut, it must be immediately enclosed, and the young Spring of Wood protected for Seven years; and Penalties are appointed for every Transgression against this Law.' Notwithstanding such measures, it was clear that the timber shortage was now acute; and many felt that for years there had been both a profligate use of native wood and a general lack of concern to replenish the species most at risk. Among those who shared this view were Pepys and John Evelyn, who had been acquainted for some years. Both were Fellows of the recently formed Royal Society.

On 10 September 1662, Sir Robert Moray (?1608–73), one of The Royal Society's founders, initiated a discussion about the serious shortage of standing timber and the lack of any forward planning to rectify the situation. By the following week Sir Robert had spoken to the four 'Honourable Principal Officers, and Commissioners of the Navy' and received a paper outlining their concerns. This was referred to a small group of Fellows: Dr Jonathan Goddard (1617–75), a pioneer in experimentation with the telescope; Dr Christopher Merret (1614–95); John Winthrop (1606–76), the Governor of Connecticut; and John Evelyn. Evelyn, aged almost forty-two, was the youngest of the four; they were all mature men who had experienced the upheavals and problems of the Civil War and the subsequent Restoration.

Within a month they had all responded and Evelyn was asked to make a digest of the whole. On 15 October 1662 he wrote in his diary: 'I this day delivered my Discourse concerning Forest-trees to our Society upon the occasion of Certaine Queries sent us by the Commissioners of His Majestties Navy.' The text of the original lecture made such an impression that 'he was desired to print the paper read by him'. Thus was *Sylva: A Discourse of Forest Trees and the Propagation of Timber in His Majesties Dominions* commissioned.

The year 1663 was a busy one for Evelyn. His diary is filled with details of his other work: he sat on numerous committees, including ones for regulating hackney coaches, improving sewers and the commission of the Mint. Attentive to his duties, he also attended Court, and went to various balls, great dinners and plays (none of which he really enjoyed). He was burgled – for the third time. He dined out and entertained when he was in London, and was hospitable when at home in Deptford. It was at the end of April that year that Charles II and his retinue came to Sayes Court, 'to honor my poore villa'. Nevertheless, within this year he did more research and completed the writing of the text of *Sylva*.

In March 1663, the Council of The Royal Society, to which Evelyn had earlier been elected, ordered the printing of the book. Two months later, on 29 May, he wrote a dedication to the King. Six months later, in November, negotiations were successfully completed between The Royal Society and its newly appointed printers. The chosen ones were John Martin (*fl.*1649–80) and James Allestry (d.1670), both well-established booksellers and publishers whose shop was in St Paul's Churchyard in the City. Allestry was already stationer to the King. Pepys patronized both booksellers. Their shop and its contents were to be destroyed during the Great Fire of 1666, as were those of so many other booksellers in the vicinity.

On 16 February 1664, Evelyn wrote, 'I presented my "Sylva" to the Society; and next day to his Majestie, to whom it was dedicated; also to the Lord Treasurer, and the Lord Chancellor.' A few days later he recorded that the King thanked him for his discourse. Later, in March, he presented several of his friends with 'my book', and recorded their congratulations. *Sylva* was the first book to be published by The Royal Society.

Sylva consists of twenty-one chapters on individual trees or groups of trees, and eleven other chapters, mainly about the management of trees, felling and the uses of timber and conservation. In analysing the trees Evelyn chooses to write about, it is interesting to note that under half are native trees, while the majority are introductions, mostly from southern Europe and around the Mediterranean, but a significant number from America. This reflects the relative paucity of British trees, but also the keen interest and open-mindedness of Evelyn, who welcomed any tree into the English landscape provided it could, eventually, contribute timber to the effort to become self-sufficient. He also records the visual impact that individual trees should, or could, make when planted in the countryside. Another of the things that is remarkable about the book is the amount of useful practical detail it imparts, which is as relevant today as it was in 1664. All the practical instruction quoted in the following chapter, apart from a few instances, is still valid: one could do the same thing successfully today. However, being an urbane and cultivated person with an eye for beauty, who loved gardens as well as the trees they contained, Evelyn does much more than just promote trees useful for timber and describe how to provide a ready supply. Drawing on history, literature, his own experience as a gardener and his visits to gardens in England and abroad, the book is rich in detail and observation, inspiring us to look at utility afresh. Most importantly, time and again, he shows – as he did in his own and others' gardens – that he appreciated trees for their aesthetic value too.

This dichotomy begins to emerge on the very first page of the introduction, when, tellingly, Evelyn talks of trees that are 'left standing for ornament and service of their country'. The idea of trees as objects of beauty is repeated throughout the book in phrases such as 'copses of infinite delight', 'gleams of sun adorned with the distant landscape appearing through the glades' and, discussing the elm, 'this noble tree for shade and delight'. The title, *Sylva: A Discourse of Forest Trees*, is in many ways an inaccurate description of what he wrote about, as Evelyn widened the scope beyond the forest and trees suitable for timber and instructed his readers in the nuances of a great number of trees, only a few of which could be classed as 'forest' or timber trees. The oak, beech, sweet chestnut, alder, poplar, the willows, birch and pine can all be included in a woodland setting, but others he writes about, such as the mulberry, walnut, cork oak, cedar, arbutus and many more, have never naturalized in the countryside nor been cultivated for utilitarian qualities; they are all grown for the beauty they bring to gardens and parkland. The core message of the work is, without doubt, how to plant and maintain trees so that they can play a pivotal supporting role in society, both aesthetically and practically.

In trying to reconcile his aesthetic nature with the practicalities of the silvicultural and gardening worlds, Evelyn showed both independence and originality. *Sylva* heralded a new movement, which would gather pace in the next century and change the way people thought of trees. Evelyn would be delighted, both by the subsequent strides in tree-growing to sustain the industrial prowess of the nation, and that his great work came to be acknowledged as such an inspiration for the silvicultural world.

Hornbeam
(Carpinus betulus*)*.

CHAPTER III
THE TREES

In the order in which they
appear in Sylva

Of the Oak

Quercus Fagaceae

PEDUNCULATE OR ENGLISH OAK
(*Quercus robur*):
30–40M (100–130FT) IN HEIGHT;
NATIVE IN LOWLANDS; DECIDUOUS;
YOUNG SHOOTS GREEN-BROWN; ACORNS
2–3 ON 4–8CM STALK

JOHN EVELYN GIVES THE OAK TREE star treatment in his book. Not only does it have pride of place as the first of his descriptions of trees, but the account of the Oak is the longest and most detailed, including how and where to plant, what to do to encourage growth, and, once it has been felled, how the timber should be treated; all its habits are described and no nuance overlooked. No other tree comes in for such loving scrutiny and it is clear that he is convinced there is nothing to compare with the English Oak. Like a mother showing off her child prodigy, so with Evelyn: pride in the tree is obvious. He makes it clear that it is because of the influence of earlier writers, and 'the esteem which these wise and glorious people had of this tree above all others, that I will first begin with the oak'; in particular he refers to Pliny the Elder (AD 23–79),

*King of trees:
a major Oak in
Nottinghamshire.*

who because of the 'weightiness of the matter' devoted a whole chapter to the Oak in his *Historia Naturalis*. 'Nothing could be more ravishing', Evelyn writes, 'in his Majesty's Forests' than 'spreading trees at handsome intervals, by which grazing might be improved for the feeding of deer and cattle under them'.

There are over 900 different species of oak in the genus, including some naturally occurring hybrids. Their range is wide, extending from the northern temperate areas to high-altitude tropical regions. About half the species are evergreen, but without exception they all produce acorns. Two species are native to Britain; both are deciduous. The most widespread and prolific is the Pedunculate Oak, *Quercus robur*; the other is the Sessile or Durmast Oak, *Q. petraea*. The distribution of the Sessile Oak is more usual to the north and west of Britain. Its acorn harvest is not as heavy, and its timber not considered as good, as that of the Pedunculate Oak. The feature that distinguishes the two is the length of the stalk attaching the acorn to the branch: in the Pedunculate species (the word pedunculate was not coined until the eighteenth century) the stalks are long and pendulous; in the Sessile Oak (sessile being a word of 1753 meaning having no foot stalk) the stalk is almost non-existent and the acorn looks as if it is attached to the branch.

The Oak was recognized early as an important tree in England. *Quercus robur* was included in the list of words compiled by the Benedictine Abbot Aelfric (*c.* 955–1020) of Eynsham, Oxford, in AD 995, entitled *The Glossary to Grammatica Latino-Saxonica*. Drawn up to improve the learning of Latin, this list consists of familiar everyday words; it is the first Latin–Anglo-Saxon vocabulary, and scattered throughout the list are the names of some 130 plants and trees, including the Oak. Over 600 years later, in 1634, the oak was listed as *Quercus vulgaris*, first by Charles I's Royal Gardener, John Tradescant senior (*c.*1570–1638), and again in 1648 in *The Catalogue of the Trees and Plants in the Physicke Garden of the University of Oxford*, compiled in both Latin and English by Jacob Bobart (1599–1680), the Oxford Botanic Garden's first curator.

ABOVE, RIGHT:
Sessile Oak
(Quercus petraea*).*

ABOVE, LEFT:
Pedunculate or
English Oak
(Quercus robur*).*

In this chapter Evelyn writes of several different oaks. He dismisses one, the Turkey Oak, *Quercus cerris*, remarking that it is 'goodly to look on but for little else'. In the twentieth century W. J. Bean (1863–1947) of the Royal Botanic Gardens, Kew, confirmed this opinion: he wrote that 'as a timber tree it has very little value'. The timber is very hard, and in south Devon and Cornwall this is acknowledged by its local name of Iron or Wainscot Oak. However, Evelyn acknowledges that it is a noble tree, as indeed it is – it can reach over 36.58 metres (120ft) high. A native of southern Europe and south-west Asia, the tree was supposedly not introduced into Britain until 1735, long after Evelyn's demise, although he could not have failed to notice it while on his Continental travels. On the other hand, its earlier arrival may have gone unrecorded, although this seems unlikely as it was not listed in the Lambeth garden of John Tradescant senior, nor later by his son, also John Tradescant (1608–62), nor by Bobart in the Oxford Botanic Garden. In whatever century it was introduced, the tree soon made an impact, particularly in southern England, where it began behaving like a native, spreading among hedgerows and woodland.

Up to the time of Linnaeus (Carl Linné; 1707–78), in the eighteenth century, the evergreen Holm or Ilex Oak, *Quercus ilex*, the next oak Evelyn discusses, was known as the Holly Oak, or in Latin *Ilex quercus*. Its ovate shaped leaves are indeed very holly-like, in maturity being dark green and shiny. The tree is recorded as having arrived in England some time during the early 1500s, although a century later Evelyn gives the impression that it was rarely grown in England. It thrives in Spain, where it is indigenous, as well as throughout south west Europe and the Mediterranean region. He praises it for the many uses the timber can be put to: it was the choice timber in the making of handles (stocks) for tools, mallet heads, chair axletrees, wedges or anything that required very hard wood. Later he remarks that 'it supplies all Spain almost with the best and most lasting of charcoales, in vast abundance'. He also calls it by its Spanish name 'Enzina' (encina is now the common name for the evergreen *Quercus agrifolia*, introduced from California in 1843).

Holm Oak
*(*Quercus ilex*).*

Holm Oak growing in its native Spain.

Since then the tree has been mainly planted in the south – it likes a warm, rather light soil – and thrives as a coastal tree; with its leather, holly-like leaves it is able to resist salt winds, and it can also act as a superb windbreak. At Mount Edgcumbe House in Cornwall, the eighteenth-century carriage drive which winds its way around the western shore of Plymouth Sound is fringed with the trees, which, with a mighty 3.66-metre (12ft) high hedge also of Holm Oak, help to filter the wind and sea spray from the Formal Gardens. The tree's one drawback is the timing of its leaf drop. This occurs during May and June and as the leaves are leathery they take a long time to rot. However, it is a handsome tree that adds dignity and gravitas to a landscape with its large size and height of 21.5–27.5 metres (70–90ft), as well as a touch of the Mediterranean, particularly when it is producing its grey felty new shoots, when – in a good light, and with a little imagination – it could almost pass for an Olive, *Olea europaea*. The best example of Ilex Trees in Britain is to be seen at Goring in West Sussex, where some 170 years ago David Lyon of Goring Hall planted a mile-long avenue, known as Ilex Way, or Ilex Avenue. The 400 trees create a rather special, quiet atmosphere. Several of the original trees were felled in the Great Storm of 1987 and some replanting had to be done. Today the avenue is open to walkers, cyclists and horse riders.

'Ilex major glandifera or great Scarlet Oak,' Evelyn writes, 'thrives manifestly with us; witness His Majesties Privy Garden at White-Hall where once flourished a goodly tree of more than fourscore years growth, though there be now but a sickly impe [sucker] of it remaining.' This must indeed have been an outstanding specimen, as John Evelyn mentions it twice in *Sylva*. Earlier, in

1597, John Gerard (1545–1612) had also described 'Ilex glandifera; (seu yren scarlet Oake). The euergreene Oake' in *The herball; or general historie of plantes*. The name *Ilex glandifera* is not now in use, and the evergreen oaks – which were originally classed with hollies – were moved into the oak or *Quercus* genus by Linnaeus. Sir Thomas Hanmer, writing in his *Garden Book* of 1659, identifies the Whitehall tree: 'In Latine Ilex coccigera, called Scarlet not from the color of the wood, or leaves which are green at all tymes, but from certaine excrescence growing to some trees, wherein wormes are bred and a graine of which a perfect scarlet color is made', and just to make sure he helpfully continues 'the largest groweth in Whitehall garden'. Nowadays it is often called the Kermes Oak, *Quercus coccifera*. Indigenous to the Mediterranean and Portugal, it is a dense, slow-growing shrub or small tree which usually reaches 1–2 metres (3–6ft), although it has been known to double that height. Both the vernacular names of Scarlet and Kermes reflect the fact that it plays host to the insect *Chermes illicis*, which after treatment produces a beautiful scarlet dye, renowned for its richness and lasting quality; it is known in commerce as 'grain' or 'scarlet grain'. It was of such importance during the Middle Ages that in London the Dyers Company, whose arms were granted during the mid-fifteenth century, used the image of three sprigs of Scarlet Oak on its crest. The tree itself is not believed to have arrived in Britain much before the beginning of the seventeenth century, which is surprising when one considers the importance of the dye in earlier times: Chaucer (*c*.1345–1400) refers to it, as does Shakespeare (1564–1616).

It is strange phenomenon that English oak trees, and the timber they produce, long ago found an almost mythic place in the English mind. The mature tree, standing in a landscape, seems to personify the agelessness of 'Englishness'. Standing true and steady, the tree exudes feelings of solidity and timelessness quite beyond itself; yet at the same time it seems to offer the high comfort value of a familiar friend. No other tree comes close to the affection in which the Oak is held. Throughout history both the tree and its timber have seemed to cast a spell of invulnerability.

The imposition by the Normans of forest law over vast swathes of England, whether pasture, woodland or moor, in order to create royal hunting preserves, caused a nostalgic vision of the greenwood, epitomized by the easily recognizable Oak, to enter the English psyche. In Evelyn's time, when Charles II returned from exile (on his birthday, 29 May 1660) Royalists displayed

branches of oak to commemorate the Battle of Worcester (1651), when Charles hid in an oak tree, along with Colonel William Carlo, to avoid detection. This spontaneous display eventually turned into Oak Apple Day, when sprigs or leaves were worn. Charles II even considered setting up a new order of chivalry and calling it the Knights of the Royal Oak. At the Royal Hospital at Chelsea, London, founded by the King in 1692, encouraged by among others John Evelyn, oak leaves are still worn at the Founders' Day Parade, and the Grinling Gibbons statue of the King is bedecked with fresh oak branches.

The Oak and its acorn are frequently used as symbols in town or county crests, including those of Mansfield (the chief town of the Sherwood Forest area), Cheltenham and Crawley, where acorns are used. Dorking's insignia consists of twelve golden acorns, representing the dozen parishes, with the motto '*E glande quercus*' (from the acorn, the oak).

The significance of the Oak is not confined to Britain: in the ancient world of the gods, Jupiter, the god of thunder, was associated with the Oak Tree. In the Roman world the highest accolade a soldier could receive was to be crowned with a chaplet of oak leaves for saving the life of a comrade. This award was echoed in the twentieth century by the two silver oak leaves on the medal ribbon on the insignia of the Order of the British Empire for Gallantry.

King Charles II depicted in 1651 hiding in an Oak tree at Boscobel, about 30 miles from Worcester; engraving of 1660.

The word oak has its beginnings in the languages of the ancient northern world of Old German, Norse and Frisian. However, pollen grains of the Oak (along with those of the Beech and the Hornbeam), which are at least 26 million years old have been discovered in Britain, dating from long before the last great Ice Age. This event froze out a great number of what had been the established flora, and it was not until the Ice Age slowly waned that plants were again able to establish themselves. First the Pine Tree began to edge itself into, eventually, great swathes of dark forest, and then gradually the deciduous trees were able to move north across the land bridge that existed before Britain became an island. Included in this migration was the Oak, as well as the Ash, Lime, Elm and, last of all, the Beech.

Once felled, oak timber is extraordinarily long-lived, and the hardest of woods, yet supple to use. Used in ship construction, the oak was believed to make ships invincible – oak timber, like a spoilt child, could do no wrong. No wonder there was always much angst and doubt when oak wood had to be sourced from abroad; the use of foreign oak was perceived as if it allowed the enemy (usually the French) to beat at our very shores. Oak trees and their potential use were always a sensitive subject, and one that most of Europe was constantly worried about. It seems extraordinary that the problem of the supply of oak timber (often formed and grown into specific shapes) was never really grasped either in England or elsewhere. One instance that shows the lack of foresight may be seen in the Royal Forest of Sherwood, where two surveys were made. The two documents, both extant, were compiled 175 years apart. The first, undertaken in 1608, records some 23,370 oak trees growing in the Royal Forest. The second survey shows that by 1783 there were only 1,368 remaining – just less than 6 per cent. It clearly indicates that over three or four generations no planned replanting was undertaken. The loss of almost 95 per cent gives an average felling and extraction of 125 oak trees a year – not very many, one would have thought, in replanting terms but replanting was very necessary because of the huge expansion of both naval and commercial shipping that took place. No one, except a few clear-sighted people (John Evelyn included), ever managed to cajole kings, governments or presidents to grasp the nettle, or at least the acorn, and plant for the future.

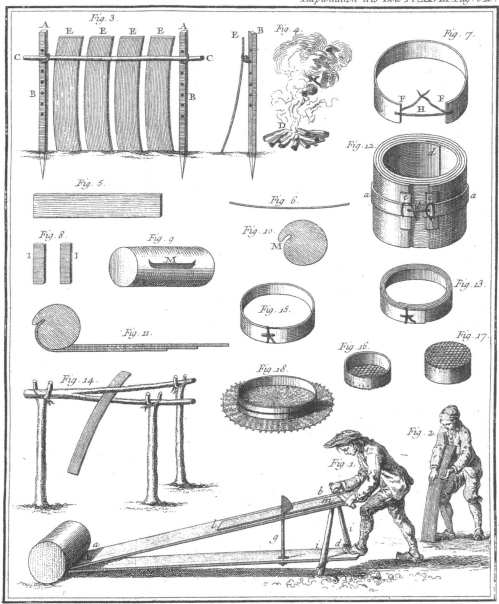

Eighteenth-century
French instructions
showing preparation of
thin strips of wood for
the manufacturing of
cheese moulds.

Barrels, Casks and Tubs

Making a watertight container from planks of wood has always seemed to have a touch of alchemy about it; it seems to defy natural law. Yet from earliest times vessels to hold liquid have been fashioned from plants. The very earliest recorded is from the writings of 'the father of history', Herodotus (*c*.485–425 BC), who refers to palm-wood casks manufactured to carry Armenian wine down the River Tigris to Babylon in Mesopotamia (now Iraq). Wine, milk, honey, ale, oil and much else besides had to be containerized in some way if they were to have any economic value. Trade and transport of goods were prime considerations, as they are today. It was primarily as containers for wine that barrels and casks developed. Amphorae were the usual method of storage until about the third century AD, when wooden containers gradually took over. Over time, timber from a variety of trees has been used in their manufacture – acacia, cypress, chestnut, silver fir, ash, poplar and eucalyptus have all been experimented with – but the supreme material for fashioning barrels is oak wood.

Holding wine in wood encourages natural clarification to take place and an oak flavour to be imparted to the wine. The nuances of the taste of oak can alter considerably, according to age, and it is often the older barrels that the vintner (and the whisky and brandy maker) prefers. The use of different ages of oak and size of casks to achieve particular tastes is a whole science in itself. Suffice it to say that the art of cooperage has so developed that there have been at least 160 different-sized wine casks, each with its own name, ranging from the now extinct Bordeaux Tonneau, one of the largest, which held 900 litres (198 gall), to almost the smallest, the Madeira Baril, capable of holding just 15 litres (3.3 gall). The oak timber for the making of barrels should be at least eighty years old, but as in so much to do with the wood the older it is the better it performs; trees of about a century and a half old are considered the best. Manufactured into staves, these have to be seasoned for at least a

year or two before they can be made into barrels. Today there are two great centres for barrel production: France and the United States. The most fundamental difference between the two lies in the initial way the staves are fashioned: in France the containers must be made from hand-split staves, while elsewhere the staves are machined into shape.

In England, as well as on the Continent, the cooper's trade played an important role in everyday life, and the supply of oak – or any other suitable wood – was crucial. By the end of the ninth century, there were several cooper guilds, who were developing and codifying laws relating to apprenticeships, trading practices and the like. By the seventeenth century cooperage was an important business, and responsible for transporting and storing not only wine but also salted fish and meat, flour, butter, oil, gunpowder and turpentine. Water barrels were always an essential requirement of shipping, and occasionally there was a need for 'barrills' for the packing of plants, both to and from England.

When John Tradescant junior made his three journeys to Virginia between 1637 and 1653, and returned with new horticultural introductions, he would have had wooden containers made in the New World to transport the live material to England. Probably by the time Tradescant arrived in Virginia barrel-making was one of

Cooper at work.

the trades already established, just as it was in the Plymouth Plantation, where the skills of John Alden (*c*.1598–1687), a cooper and earlier *Mayflower* colonist, were flourishing; by 1648 there was a New England Guild of Coopers. Nearly forty years later, Evelyn wrote to Samuel Pepys about some living plant material he was expecting from America, suggesting how it should be transported: 'the nutts in Barills of dry sand: each kind wraped in papers written on. The trees in Barills, their rootes wraped about mosse. The smaller the plants and trees are the better … but the Barill is best'. While wooden casks could be made across the Atlantic, any paper required either for wrapping or for writing the plant details on would have been sent from England, as no paper was manufactured in the New World until the end of the seventeenth century. By the end of that century logs and staves were beginning to be exported to Europe for barrel-making.

Alexander Norman (d.1657), a relation of the Tradescant family, was Cooper to the Ordnance (Artillery) and had a workshop near the Tower of London. He was responsible for, among other things, 'casques, hoopes and cooperage by him made and done and brought into His Majesties stoares and there employed about powder matches and other necessaries'. A wide variety of barrel sizes and shapes were required at that time to contain disparate goods. Among them were double-casked barrels specially designed to hold gunpowder. Smaller were the budge-barrels, which again held powder but had a leather cover with a long neck drawn together like the mouth of a bag. Barrels and casks from the Ordnance were distributed around all the fortifications in Britain and on board naval ships. His was a dangerous occupation, and Norman always supervised the packing of the barrels when they were to be transported.

Of the Elm

Ulmus Ulmaceae

ENGLISH ELM *Ulmus procera* (SYN. *U. campestris*):
NATIVE; CONIC SHAPE; CAN REACH A HEIGHT OF 30M
(100FT) OR MORE; DECIDUOUS; LEAVES ARE OVAL OR
ROUNDED, ROUGH ON THE UPPER SIDE, SHARPLY DOUBLE-
TOOTHED; MATURE SPECIMENS NOW RARE DUE TO THE
IMPACT OF DUTCH ELM DISEASE

TAXONOMICALLY ELMS have always led a troublesome life and, depending on which expert you consult, the number of species ranges from as many as forty-five to fewer than half that number. Botanically elms are cousins of cannabis, nettles and the mulberry, all of which are part of the *Urticaceae* family. Although the European distribution of the genus has not been in doubt, in Britain the English Elm, *Ulmus procera*, syn. *U. campestris*, was usually listed as being introduced by the Romans, who used it for growing and supporting vines. There is a view that the tree's origins lie in the Iberian Peninsula. However, Evelyn took the contrary view, and says that it was Philip II of Spain (1527–98) who was responsible for introducing the Elm to Spain from England after he had spent fourteen months here (during which time he married Mary Tudor). The Spanish king had *U. procera* planted throughout the

walks and vistas of Aranjuez (a shooting lodge in Madrid, where he was creating a summer residence); the trees grew tall and, as was the fashion, they were stripped of all but their uppermost branches. They were also planted in the grounds of the newly built Escorial Monastery, and in other gardens. Unusually, seed was produced from the planting – it hardly ever produced viable seed in Britain – enabling seeds and seedlings to be distributed across Europe. Evelyn received this information from Edward Mountagu, 1st Earl of Sandwich (1625–72), the patron of Samuel Pepys, who was the Ambassador to Spain for

English Elm growing at Powderham Castle, near Exeter, Devon.

three years until 1669. Certainly in the seventeenth and eighteenth centuries in England and France elm avenues were not uncommon. St James's Park was originally planted with elms (later uprooted and replaced by the more fashionable Acacia, *Robinia pseudoacacia*). Blenheim, Stowe, Cassiobury and many other great gardens and parks were all planted with glorious avenues of elm trees.

Without exception Elms are big trees: in maturity all of them reach or exceed 30 metres (100ft). Most are conical shaped, or, as the internationally acclaimed dendrologist Alan Mitchell so expressively remarks, their 'outline billows like a thundercloud'. Evelyn seems to have been an enthusiast for the Elm, for he goes into great detail about its requirements: 'the elm delights in a sound, sweet and fertile land, something more inclined to a loamy moisture ... The elm does not thrive in too sandy or hot ground, no more will it abide the cold and spongy; but loves places that are competently fertile.' Because *Ulmus procera* – the species name means tall – is invariably infertile in England, the suckering shoots are the main means of propagation. Mindful of his aim to encourage planting for timber, Evelyn gives practical advice, explaining a number of different ways of encouraging shoots, including the lopping of a three-year-old tree at the 'latter end of March, when the sap begins to creep up into the boughs, and the buds ready to break to provide material'. Alternatively, having bared the roots near the trunk, using an axe, 'make several chops, putting a small stone into every cleft, to hinder their closure, and give access to the wet; then cover them with three, or four inch thick of earth; and thus they will send forth suckers in abundance'. The suckers from one elm, he assures us, will suffice to stock an 'ulmarium'.

But he goes beyond the practical to show his awareness of its value in the landscape. His description of the Elm as 'a tree of comfort, sociable, and so affecting to grow in company that the very best which I have seen do almost touch one another' gives us the very essence of the tree. It is not a tree for the forest, he says – in a forest there is not enough light and no room for its roots to spread out – but to be planted in avenues and hedgerows. The antiquary John Aubrey (1626–97) confirms Evelyn's observation, saying: 'I never did see an elme that grew spontaneously in a wood.'

Evelyn describes the 'Mountain Elm' and the 'French Elm'. The latter was probably a variety of Dutch Elm, *Ulmus* x *hollandica*. The 'Mountain Elm' may

have been *Ulmus montana*, now known as *Ulmus glabra*, and he may well be referring to the same tree when he writes of the native Wych or Scots Elm, which is *Ulmus glabra*, syn. *U. montana*. This was seen frequently in southern England, but more usually in west and north Wales, and from Yorkshire northwards. Its homelands stretch into northern and central Europe and western Asia. The Wych Elm is a big and spreading tree, with larger and coarser leaves than the English Elm. Evelyn tells us that the bark, which when young is smooth (hence the species name *glabra*), can be used to make bast rope (rope made not from hemp but from the inner layer of a flexible fibrous bark, usually that of the Lime or Linden Tree). The Weeping Elm, *U. glabra* 'Camperdown', which was developed in Angus, Scotland, in 1850, had this elm as its grafted parent.

Evelyn describes the timber of the Elm as 'most singular' and indeed it is. Along with oak, it was one of the major timbers for shipbuilding, being the preferred wood for the keel. It is long lasting when used under water, 'therefore proper for waterworks, mills pipes, pumps aquaducts, ship planks beneath the waterline'. Elm timber can still be found forming part of locks, and in docks and harbours. Elm timber piles were used as support for the old Waterloo Bridge in London, designed by John Rennie and opened by the Prince Regent in 1817. When the bridge was dismantled in 1936 the original elm timbers were found to be still in superb condition. (The present bridge designed by Giles Gilbert Scott does not have timber supports.) The wood of the English Elm is reddish brown and is considered firm, but tough and elastic, to use. It can only be held as seasoned wood for, at the most, about two years before it loses half its weight through drying, when it tends to warp and twist, but it rarely splits – that is its unique quality. It has been the preferred wood where splitting would have been either dangerous or inconvenient, used, for instance, by carpenters to make 'weather boards, chopping blocks, blocks for the hatmaker, trunks and boxes to be covered in leather, for dressers, and shovel board tables of great length', as well as the hubs of wooden wheels, for wheelbarrows, sheep troughs, cheese and dough moulds, as well as good coffin timber (it was usually cheaper than oak) – the list is endless.

Today elm timber is known mostly for its use in furniture-making, especially chair seats, bowls, plates, ball feet on furniture and as a veneer. Craftsmen and turners are able to exploit the grain and colour of the wood. The best English elm timber came from isolated trees or small woods, although the vast majority was extracted from the 620,000 miles of hedgerows.

Caucasian Elm (Ulmus elliptica) bark, smoother and less fissured than the English Elm. A native of the Caucasus, western Asia and western Siberia, introduced to Britain in 1891.

By about 2060 hardly anyone in Europe or North America will be alive who will be able to recall seeing the stolid stateliness of an Elm Tree in the landscape. Indeed the very word Elm, which has been in use for over a thousand years, may well become redundant, and furniture made from elm wood will become rare. The tree's disappearance from the countryside in both Britain and northern Europe in the 1960s and 1970s was startlingly fast, all because of a parasitic fungus, which, like a flu epidemic, was indiscriminate as to what or where it struck. Mycologists know it as *Ceratocystus ulmi*, but it is better known as Dutch Elm disease. It is unfair that the fungus, which is carried by the bark-beetle, is called Dutch, as it was first noted in 1818 in northern France, and a hundred years later the Dutch (who did not at that stage harbour the disease) identified the problem. The fungus was widespread in southern England when in 1927 it was first noticed in London. However, over the following decades it seemed to become less virulent and trees tended to recover from the infestation. Then suddenly in North America during the 1960s a more virulent form of the disease began attacking elms and it has been estimated that thereafter, for over a decade, about 400,000 trees died annually. By the 1970s the invigorated fungal strain had reached Britain, and it was then only a matter of time before the skeletal remains of hedgerow elms, like some macabre reminder of Spartacus's army crucified along the Appian Way, became a familiar sight in the countryside.

The result of Dutch Elm disease: a copse of the dead trees in 1990.

Of the Beech

Fagus Fagaceae

COMMON OR EUROPEAN BEECH *Fagus sylvatica*:
30M (100FT) NATIVE TO SOUTH-EAST AND MIDLAND
ENGLAND, MOST OF EUROPE EXCEPT NORTHERN SCANDINAVIA;
DECIDUOUS; SUPREME TREE ON CHALK SOIL; SHAPE IS HUGELY
DOMED; SILVER-GREY, SMOOTH BARK; THE OVAL OR OBOVATE
LEAVES ARE THE LIGHTEST OF PALE GREEN AS THEY EMERGE,
LATER BECOMING DARK SHINY GREEN

IT SEEMS THAT JOHN EVELYN'S enthusiasm for the Beech was not great, as he fails to give detailed instructions for its propagation or details of its growing habits, and he writes only briefly of its practical merits. Indeed, she tells us that in France walnut wood is infinitely preferred for all domestic utensils, and beech is 'good only for shade and for fire, as being brittle, and exceedingly obnoxious to the worm'. Nevertheless, he shows his awareness of the beech's beauty, writing: 'They make spreading trees, and noble shades with their well furnished and glittering leaves.'

He also mentions that when the wood is burnt, the residual (alkali) ash in a 'proper mixture is excellent to make glass with'. The usefulness of beech wood in firing the furnace for glass-making had been understood since the twelfth

century; the emphasis, though, according to Theophilus, a German monk who wrote in great detail about the glass-making process, was always on 'dry beechwood', which was essential both to reduce the amount of smoke and to encourage a hotter flame for the furnace. Glass-making is an ancient process, known about from the third millennium BC. The blowing of glass developed later, about 100 BC, in Syria, and the making of window glass about AD 100. For the glass-making process to work, the furnace had to reach a temperature of 1,200°C; this normally took at least two days to achieve. Glass manufacturing in England was based in the south-east, mainly in the well-wooded north-west corner of Sussex where beech and other wood was available. By the fifteenth century the enormous quantities of wood required for the process were causing concern. Despite these worries, though, there is evidence that at the beginning of the sixteenth century beech woods were being pollarded – that is, the branches were cut back to the trunk to encourage new young shoots – for fuel; for instance, in the famous Burnham Beeches, and in Epping Forest. This practice lasted long after the end of the use of beech for glass manufacture, and continued into the early part of the nineteenth century, when wood lost its position as the premier fuel to coal.

By 1616 the first glass furnace was in operation in Newcastle-upon-Tyne. In the mid-seventeenth century, in an early case of 'nimbyism', suggestions were being made that all glass manufacture should be transferred from the south-east of England to Ireland, and the newer colonies of America – where there is evidence of a large furnace operating in Jamestown, Virginia, in 1608. By the time Evelyn was writing *Sylva*, it had been discovered that coal gave a superior smokeless heat and was the preferred fuel (see page 51).

The Beech Tree is a native – just. There is some contention as to the date of its arrival, but pollen remains have been found in Hampshire, dated to *c*.6000 BC, about 2,000 years before Britain became entirely surrounded by sea. Small is beautiful in the case of the *Fagus* genus. The two most familiar European species are the Common Beech, *Fagus sylvatica*, which is dominant in the north (except northern Scandinavia), and the tree that Evelyn would have known, while the Oriental Beech, *F. orientalis*, is found further south and east of Bulgaria. The Oriental Beech, which was introduced into Britain only about a hundred years ago, has larger leaves and its autumnal colour is a rich yellow, whereas the Common Beech transforms itself into a golden copper colour, with its leaves

Beech hedge decoratively grown – the Laskett, Herefordshire.

getting a deeper brown as the season progresses. The paper-thin pale green leaves of both are beautifully recognizable in spring.

According to Evelyn, the leaves afford 'the best and easiest mattress in the world to lay under our quilts instead of straw; because, besides their tenderness and loose lying together; they continue sweet for seven or eight years long; before which time straw becomes musty and hard'; he adds: 'they are thus used by divers persons of quality in Dauphine; and in Switzerland I have sometimes lain on them to my great refreshment.' Duvet-makers take note! Until recently (before their emigration to southern France) the elephants of Longleat Safari Park apparently enjoyed nibbling the leaves.

The understorey of a beech wood is quite different from that of most other trees, which, when they are fully in leaf, still allow light to filter through. The beech has a branch system of overlapping flat planes that create a dense canopy of leaves, allowing little chance of any light penetrating through, with the result that most hesitant vegetation beneath the trees is quickly suppressed. Another reason for this is the root system of the beech. A sapling beech quickly develops a taproot, which acts as an anchor and counter balance to the huge weight of the tree above, and then it develops an enormous mat of roots nearer the surface for its nourishment, which also prevent the growth of other plants. As Evelyn says, 'In the valleys (where they stand warm and in comfort) they will grow to a stupendous procerity [loftiness], though the soil be stony and very barren; Also upon the declivity's sides and tops of high hills, and chalky mountains especially; for they will strangely insinuate their roots into the bowels of those seemingly impenetrable places.' For this reason beech trees have often been planted on land where other trees (oak or elm, for instance) could not have survived.

In forestry terms the beech is a slightly difficult tree, as it does not mix particularly well with other native trees, growing – and looking – its best amongst its own kind. In mixed natural woodland it is often missing: whereas you will see single oak, ash or poplar intermixed in woodland you will rarely find a single beech. Although beech is usually associated with the chalk downland of southern England, Reverend William Turner (*c*.1508–68) described the two greatest beeches he had ever seen as growing in his home parish of Morpeth, Northumberland; however, a century after Turner, the agricultural writer John Worlidge (*c*.1630–93) of Petersfield in Hampshire,

Scottish beech wood in autumn.

describing a typical site, said 'the tree is altogether a stranger to most counties in England.' Today there are many fine specimens growing in the Lake District.

In economic terms, beech timber, as Evelyn describes, was of use mainly for domestic purposes: bowls, dishes, stools, boards for dressers, rims for (leather) buckets all were fashioned from the wood, as were bedsteads, hat boxes and 'book covers'. Later in the following century, the Beech found that its real role was to help artistically decorate the landscape. In 1741, the bare terrain of Stourhead, Wiltshire, was planted with beech at the beginning of the creation of that great garden. Lancelot (Capability) Brown (1716–83) certainly helped to spread the use of the Beech Tree (as he did of most other native species): for instance, at Tottenham Park near Marlborough, Wiltshire, then the home of Lord Bruce, the nursery book records his using 14,000 beeches (as well as 21,000 Oaks). Loving order as he did, Evelyn would perhaps have been a little perplexed by the poet and landscape gardener William Shenstone (1714–63), writing in his *Unconnected Thoughts on Gardening*, published posthumously in 1764, that the correct way to plant a beech was 'without any seeming order, or the visible interference of art'. Nevertheless, he would have been delighted to know that a wider audience was finding aesthetic pleasure in the Beech Tree.

Beech
(Fagus sylvatica).

Of the Ash

Fraxinus Oleaceae

COMMON ASH (*Fraxinus excelsior*):
30–42M (100–140FT) IN HEIGHT; NATIVE OF EUROPE
INCLUDING BRITAIN; DECIDUOUS; FOUND WHEREVER THE
SOIL IS BASE-RICH AND DAMP; OPEN TALL-DOMED TREE;
THE 9 – 13 LEAFLETS ARE OPPOSITE TO EACH OTHER
AND ARE PINNATE (FEATHER-LIKE),
20–35CM (8–14IN) LONG

IT IS THE COMMON ASH, *Fraxinus excelsior*, a native of Europe and Asia Minor, that Evelyn describes. Erratically, this does not produce keys (seeds) every year: the tree lives in an eternal perplexity of sexual confusion. Some of its flowers can be all male or all female; however, individual trees may produce both male and female blossoms. The Ash can completely alter its gender from year to year, and indeed even from branch to branch. Not surprisingly, there are a number of beliefs and superstitions connected with the Ash (or esh) Tree. In the seventeenth century it was believed that if no keys were produced, a 'public calamity' would ensue. The year 1648 was 'keyless': none were recorded, and everybody predicted that the wrath of the Ash would descend. Sure enough, early in the following year an awful disaster manifested itself – the execution of Charles I on 30 January.

There are about sixty-five species of *Fraxinus* spread throughout the northern hemisphere, and the Common Ash is native to Europe and the Caucasus. Evelyn probably knew only this one representative, although when travelling on the Continent he might have been familiar with the very ornamental Manna Ash, *Fraxinus ornus*, a native of southern Europe and the eastern Mediterranean. Then called *Ornus europaea*, it was a most important tree, producing the sweet substance of manna sugar, manufactured mainly in Sicily and Calabria in Italy. The tree was reported to have been introduced to Britain in about 1700. It is a handsome tree of medium height, and is one of the flowering ashes, producing whitish flowers during May. Now there are at least another twenty-three or so

Ash buds opening in spring.

species that grow in Britain, nearly all of which arrived during the eighteenth and nineteenth centuries. Being concerned with timber, Evelyn would have been interested in the arrival of the White Ash, *F. americana*, from eastern North America in 1724. Like the native ash, this makes a handsome statement in the landscape, but the wood matures earlier. The timber is of similar quality to that of *F. excelsior* and is still much valued for making oars.

The timber of the native Common Ash was an essential part of the industrial world of the seventeenth century, and, according to Evelyn, used in a wide variety of ways, including the manufacturing of staves for the pike (an infantry weapon), poles for gardening work, arbours and espaliers, and by all the craftsmen: the carpenter, the wheelwright, the cartwright, the cooper, the turner and the thatcher all required the wood of the ash tree. He also reports that cabinet-makers sought the veined timber as they 'prize it equal with ebony, and give it the name of green ebony'. Ash timber bears a similarity to olive wood, the *Fraxinus* genus being in the same family as the Olive Tree, *Olea europaea*.

Because of all these uses, Evelyn obviously believed that one could never grow too many ash trees. There is money, he says, to be made (after forty years), and 'a small and pleasurable industry', from planting the keys (seeds) and growing ash trees. He explains how to do this: '[to] make a considerable wood … dig or plough a parcel of ground as you would prepare for corn, and with the corn (or what other grain you think fittest) sow also a good store of keys …Take off your crop of corn or seed in its season, and the next year following it will be covered with young ash.' However, he warns against planting ash trees adjacent to ploughed land, 'for the roots will be obnoxious to the coulter [the iron blade of the plough]', and the branches drip over the growing corn.

It is interesting that ash wood was used to make pike staves, as in mythological times the tree was dedicated to Mars, the god of war, and the spears of Achilles were fashioned from it; so too were those of the warrior Amazons. Broom handles of ash were *de rigueur* for a witch's broomstick and supposed to protect her from drowning. Perhaps there was a memory of this in the twentieth century, when the designers of the first aircraft used ash timber to make the frames of their flying machines, although more prosaically the reason was the lightness and strength of the timber. In modern use, the tree is the preferred timber of hockey and lacrosse sticks, and tennis racquets.

Of the Chestnut

Castanea Fagaceae

A S EVELYN ACKNOWLEDGES, the Sweet or Spanish Chestnut, *Castanea sativa*, was brought by the Romans from Sardis in Lydia (western Turkey) to Italy, thence into France and eventually to Britain. Modern research shows that the tree is a native not only of western Asia but also of southern Europe and North Africa. Although it is called the Spanish Chestnut, its genus name *Castanea* recalls the name of Castanis in Thessaly, Greece. It has the same name but in different vernacular forms throughout Europe.

The chestnut was, Evelyn tells us, after the oak 'one of the most sought after by the carpenter and joiner', and the timber had no equal in providing the best stakes, poles for palisades (fences) and mill timber such as waterwheels and shafts. The Sweet Chestnut is the supreme coppicing tree, growing fast and straight from the stool, and is a good material for splitting – rather than sawing – poles into long-lasting stakes and staves. As Evelyn points out, it was the timber used for much of the early house building in London; a barn he once owned, 'a very large

one' near the City, was constructed entirely from chestnut timber. Domestically it was used in the manufacturing of chests, tables, chairs, casks and bedsteads. It does indeed have the same qualities as oak timber but with the added bonus of being more resistant to insect attack. Its one fault is its tendency to 'shake': a natural cleft or fissure occurring in the growing wood that renders the timber unusable. Evelyn also declares that chestnut leaves make 'very wholesome mattresses', although he concedes that they make a 'crackling noise', as anyone who has crunched through the dried leaves on an autumn walk will concur. (When he was journeying through Italy he complained in his diary how itchy and uncomfortable a leaf mattress was to sleep on.)

In European terms the Chestnut has always been a significant tree, not just for timber but also for shade and food. It was one of the eighty-nine named plants catalogued by the Emperor Charlemagne (*c*.742–814) in his *Capitulare de Villis* of 800, which were to be grown on imperial land. The first record of *Castanea sativa* growing in England, in the Forest of Dean, is during the twelfth century, although 400 years later William Turner made no mention of the tree in his writings. By the seventeenth century, however, it was listed both in the 1648 *The Catalogue of the Trees and Plants in the Physicke Garden of the University of Oxford*, where it was classified with the Walnut Tree and called *Nux castanea fructu hirsute*, and in 1656 by John Tradescant under the name *Castanea vulgaris*. Its earliest recorded name of Euboean was given to it by Theophrastus

ABOVE: *Trimming the ends of cleft chestnut pales, a traditional woodland craft still practised in the 1950s.*

LEFT: *Silver-grey bark grows in angled spirals.*

(*c.*372–286 BC) and recalls the Aegean island of ancient Euboea (Évvoia). The modern name of *C. sativa* follows Linnaean principles, but Linnaeus placed the Chestnut with the *Fagus* (Beech) genus. Philip Miller (1691–1771), director of the Chelsea Physic Garden, changed its name to *Castanea* in 1754, and it has been known by this name ever since. In landscape terms the Sweet Chestnut was to be one of the major trees employed to enhance the parklands and gardens laid out by 'Capability' Brown during the eighteenth century.

In Evelyn's time one tree in particular, growing beside the parish church of Tortworth in Gloucestershire, had already made its mark with its longevity and extraordinary growth. In 1664 Evelyn called it the 'great chestnut'. Almost fifty years later, in 1712, an illustration in *Ancient and Present State of Gloucestershire* by Sir Robert Atkyns (d.1711) shows the tortuous tree. The London merchant and plant introducer Peter Collinson (1694–1768) remarked in the *Gentleman's Magazine* of 1762 and 1766 that it was the largest tree in England. In 1790 Hayman Rooke, who wrote *Remarkable Oaks in the Park at Welbeck*, considered the tree to be not less than 1,100 years old. The nineteenth century saw the tree engraved and then lithographed. In his *Remarkable Trees*, Thomas Pakenham considers the probability that the Tortworth Sweet Chestnut, still standing today, is over 1,000 years old.

Bark of Horse Chestnut (Aesculus hippocastanum): native to northern Greece and Albania; 30m (100ft) in height; a stately spreading shape, particularly handsome in the late spring when in flower; the leaves are composed of 5–7 leaflets, which are large and obvate, irregularly toothed.

Evelyn believes the nuts of *C. sativa* to be the tree's most important attribute, and goes into great detail about them. In England they were given to the swine to eat, but the chestnut was 'amongst the delicacies of princes in other countries'. He describes how in Italy, having first been roasted in embers, the nuts were eaten with salt, in wine or juice of lemon and sugar. In Piedmont fennel seed was added to the wine to give piquancy, as well as cinnamon and nutmeg; sometimes rose water was used instead of wine. Bread made from the flour of the nuts, he explains, is 'exceedingly nutritive' and 'makes a women well complexioned', although he qualifies this by saying that this was not his own observation but another author's. He also describes the making of fritters with chestnut flour and rose water sprinkled with *parmigiano* and fried in butter; perhaps he enjoyed eating them during his time abroad. In *Aceteria*, Evelyn recommends roasting chestnuts in the embers, or dry frying them until they 'quit their husks', then slitting and eating them in a mixture of orange juice, sugar and claret wine.

In his description about the chestnut Evelyn also comments on the Horse Chestnut, *Aesculus hippocastanum*. While the Sweet Chestnut is in the *Fagaceae* family, this tree is in quite a different family, the *Hippocastanaceae*. When Evelyn was writing, it had not long been established in Britain, having probably arrived only during the early years of the 1600s. A native of Albania and Greece, the Horse Chestnut had been an early introduction into Europe, as Evelyn says spreading via Constantinople (Istanbul) to Vienna, Italy and France.

Interestingly, he also states that its introduction to Britain bypassed Europe and it was brought directly from the Levant. Evelyn may well have noted the tree while he was on his Continental journey – when in flower it makes a very powerful statement – but if so, he makes no comment about it in his diary. He makes no mention of the tree's practical uses – probably because it had only been established a mere fifty years or so. Significantly, the remarks he makes refer only to its decorative nature. He comments that they bear 'most glorious flowers, even in our cold climate' and that it is quite the fashion in France to plant them as an avenue to a château, citing Vaux-le-Vicomte near Melun as an example. Work began on this, André Le Nôtre's first great garden, in 1652, and was, by 1662 when Evelyn was writing, still in the throes of creation. Known in France as *chastagne de cheval*, the tree featured prominently in most of Le Nôtre's gardens.

Noting the tree's foreign antecedents, Evelyn writes, 'we might have ample encouragement to denizen other strangers amongst us' – words that seem prophetic in the light of the many foreign trees that were to find a home on British soil over the following 300 years.

Of the Walnut

Juglans Juglandaceae

COMMON WALNUT (*Juglans regia*):
NATIVE OF EASTERN EUROPE, ASIA
MINOR TO AFGHANISTAN; 18–30M
(60–100FT) IN HEIGHT; LEAVES
20–30CM (8–12IN) OVAL OR OVATE,
COMPOSED USUALLY OF FIVE TO NINE
LEAFLETS, AND ACRID-SCENTED WHEN
RUBBED; FRUIT GREEN AND SMOOTH

LIKE THE CHESTNUT, the Walnut Tree is not a native of Britain. It probably arrived in Britain in the baggage of the Romans, although Evelyn makes no mention of this, or of its origins.

The Common Walnut, *Juglans regia*, has been cultivated for so long that its true home is obscure. Pliny the Elder wrote that by command of the Persian king the nuts were presented to the Greeks, who brought them back to Europe – indeed the tree is often known as the Persian Walnut in America. More prosaically Pliny also said that the oil crushed from the kernels was efficacious as a cure for baldness (as did Nicholas Culpeper (1616–54) later in his *Complete Herbal* of 1653). The tree's regal connection was perpetuated in its old name *Juglans*, associating it with the god Jupiter or Jovis, Emperor of the World (*glans* meaning nuts), and reinforced by Linnaeus when he added the species name *regia*, meaning royal. Its inclusion in the *Capitulare de Villis* compiled by Charlemagne in 800 suggests that it was a very familiar tree and frequently grown during ancient times, and this acknowledgement must have encouraged its wider distribution. *Juglans* is recorded in Aelfric's 995 *Glossary to Grammatica Latino-Saxonica*, though whether the word refers to the nut or the tree is uncertain.

By the middle of the seventeenth century, three species of the fifteen now known were being grown in Britain. The Roman introduction to Britain was the Common Walnut, *Juglans regia*, whose native habitat stretches from south-east Europe to south-west China. The two other species, both of which Evelyn knew, were American natives, brought to Britain during the seventeenth

6

Black Walnut (Juglans nigra): native of eastern and central southern United States; 20–30m (80–100ft) in height; leaflets fragrant when rubbed; male catkins 5–10cm (2–4in) in length.

century. The Butternut, or White Walnut, *Juglans cinerea*, a native of eastern North America, arrived in 1633. It is believed to have first been grown by the Tradescants in their garden at Lambeth, and was listed in their 1634 catalogue as *Nux juglans Canadensis.* In this species the nuts are not the familiar walnut shape but oval, and the leaves are longer than the 45 centimetres (18in) of the Common Walnut, being up to 60 centimetres (2ft) long, thin and bright green; when crushed they give off a scent of warm hay. The second introduction, also grown at Lambeth and listed as *Nux juglans Angliae Novae,* was the New England Walnut, which we now call the Black Walnut, *Juglans nigra*, whose natural habitat stretches from south-east Canada down the eastern seaboard to Texas. It seems they were rare, as despite the fact that Bobart was in receipt of many new introductions and the Tradescants were believed to be generous donors to the Oxford Botanic Garden, Bobart mentions neither tree in *The Catalogue of the Trees and Plants in the Physicke Garden of the University of Oxford* he compiled fourteen years later. The only walnut tree being grown at the Oxford Botanic Garden was the Common Walnut, which was catalogued as 'Nux Juglans'. No doubt Evelyn and his wife Mary noted it when they visited 'the Physick Garden' on 12 July 1654. They would have been familiar with the tree, for as we have seen, Evelyn had obtained walnut trees from France to plant in the Grove at Sayes Court.

Evelyn begins by explaining the difference between the three species. The Black Walnut, he says, 'bears the worst nut' but the timber is 'much to be preferred'. Over the centuries the reputation for the superb quality of its timber has been confirmed. However, all three species were in vogue for furniture-making: a 'wallnot tree tabill' was recorded in 1603 in Scotland, and later in the century a rather grander 'wallnutt tree bed' which graced the palace of Whitehall, decorated in the regal colours of gold and purple. Evelyn states that English cabinet-makers much preferred the burred wood grown from the trees around Grenoble (the burrs, or woody growth, were seldom produced in England).

One of the earliest recorded plantings of *Juglans regia* is in the 1403 Essex manorial presentment, which shows that walnut trees were grown as saplings to be cultivated for harvesting the crop of nuts rather than the timber. There are several surviving records of barrels of 'walnotts' being imported into Kings Lynn in the years between 1503 and 1508, and Nicholas Culpeper later confirms this trade. Samuel Pepys records that as part of a very jolly evening in September 1660, at The Golden Hoop Tavern in Thames Street, he consumed 'above 200 walnuts'. In the twentieth century the pulverized shells were used to clean jet engines and oil wells, and the industrial charcoal made from the shells was employed in the filters of Second World War gas masks. In its native America, the nuts – or nut meal – is used by bakers, and as an ingredient in sweets and ice cream.

Shelling walnuts at Covent Garden Market in London, c.1890.

Evelyn writes that walnuts 'may be prepared by beating them off the tree some days before they quit the branches of themselves'. In this he confirms the old rhyme, or at least part of it:

A woman, a spaniel, a walnut tree
The more you beat them, the better they be.

Controversial the first two may be, but by breaking some of the long sappy branches – which can also be done by pruning – vigorous knocking and hitting encourages shorter and sturdier fruiting twigs. Collecting the nuts in this way also avoids raiding by birds, particularly pigeons and rooks, who are partial to them.

Walnut trees usually make their grand and kingly statement out in the open, as cultivated trees, and are not considered forest trees. Evelyn mentions plantations of them in Surrey, at Leatherhead and Carshalton. Walnut trees obviously did well on Surrey soil, as in 1677 he reported seeing innumerable plantations, 'especially walnuts', on his visit to the Surrey estate of Marden belonging to Sir Robert Clayton (1629–1707), merchant and Lord Mayor of London. (Typically seeing the wider picture, Evelyn also notes all the wild thyme, marjoram and 'other sweete plants' which supported 'neere 40 hives'.) Philip Miller of the Chelsea Physic Garden also knew of the Surrey plantings, and noted that the nuts were harvested 'to the great advantage of their owners'. At the same time Nicholas Culpeper writes – rather exaggeratedly – of walnut trees growing wild 'in many places in Scotland'. That Evelyn appreciated the walnut as a garden tree we know from the fact that he planted them in his Grove.

Two years after Evelyn's death, during the appalling winter of 1708, most of the walnut plantations in the north of Continental Europe were destroyed by severe weather. It was reported that Dutch merchants invested heavily in the fallen woodlands, and made a good profit from the timber. Later, nurseries grew young trees for sale, as for instance in 1730, when Peter Mason of Isleworth, who was reputed to have the best selection of fruit trees anywhere in England, had a collection of 2,000 walnuts. Six years later in Oxford, Mr Thomas Tagg of the Paradise Gardens supplied George Henry Lee, 2nd Earl of Lichfield (1690–1742), with walnut trees for his new estate at Ditchley Park, Oxfordshire. The cost of walnut wood rose steadily, and in the nineteenth century during the Napoleonic Wars the demand for walnut gunstocks sent the

price very much higher. The same thing happened during the Crimean War, and with British timber so depleted, one Birmingham arms factory transferred its operations to the Italian city of Turin, where the supply of the walnut timber could be assured, and where they are said to have converted about 100,000 trees into 3 million blanks to turn into gunstocks.

Harvesting walnuts, which during the seventeenth-century famine in France became an important part of the diet. Even the shells were ground (with acorns) to make a flour.

Of the Mulberry

Morus Moraceae

COMMON OR BLACK MULBERRY (*Morus nigra*):
REACHES TO 9M (30FT); PROBABLY NATIVE OF
WESTERN ASIA; INTRODUCED INTO BRITAIN,
CHIEFLY SOUTHERN ENGLAND ABOUT 1500;
DECIDUOUS; LEAF IS ALWAYS HEART-SHAPED AT THE
BASE AND MAY BE UNEVENLY LOBED OR SIMPLE;
THEY ARE COVERED WITH SHORT ROUGH HAIRS;
FRUIT IS OVOID OR GLOBOSE, AND GROWS TO ABOUT
2.5 CM (1IN) LONG, MATURING IN LATE SUMMER

INCLUDING THE MULBERRY TREE in a book about forest trees seems at first glance to be strange, because it is a tree of the orchard, which John Evelyn acknowledges, but he continues 'we shall soon reconcile our industrious planter when he comes to understand the incomparable benefit of it'. Talking of the Black Mulberry, *Morus nigra*, he describes the usefulness of the timber, for its durability and its wide range of manufacturing uses – the carpenter, wheelwright and joiner were users, and even a ship's carpenter could employ the wood to form the ribs of a small vessel. However, he also wants to encourage the domestic growing of the White Mulberry, *Morus alba*, so that the hesitant silk industry can flourish.

Evelyn gives detailed instructions as to how to collect the fruit, which you 'shake down upon an old sheet, spread under the tree'; today lucky owners of Black Mulberry trees often do the same. For propagation the seeds need to be extracted, and, ever practical, he recommends bruising the fruit through a sieve and swilling the mixture in water 'and the seed will sink to the bottom, whilst the pulp swims'. Sowing the seed should take place during April or May, 'though some forbear even till July and August' (this differs from today's recommendation to sow mulberry seeds in containers out of doors in autumn). Both species of tree of five years' growth, he says, can be transplanted any time between September and November (grown in containers today, they can be planted at almost any time of the year, except the summer months). 'A light, and dry mould [earth] is best, well exposed to the sun and air which above all things this tree affects and hates watery low grounds; In sum, they thrive best where vines prosper most … nor do they less delight to be amongst corn, no way prejudicing it with its shade; The distance for these standards would be twenty or twenty four foot every way, if you would design walks or groves of them if the environs of fields, banks or rivers, highways etc twelve or fourteen foot may suffice but the further distant the better.' It is clear from this passage that John Evelyn had an eye for the wider view of the countryside: as keen in his way to decorate the landscape as 'Capability' Brown would be a century later, he was not only eager to promote the practical aspect of the Mulberry but also its aesthetic side. However, there is no evidence that Evelyn's plea for the decorative placing of the Mulberry was in any way met then or later.

There are in all about ten or twelve species of Mulberry, all natives of the northern hemisphere. The two most commonly grown in England are the White and the Black Mulberry. *Morus nigra* probably derives from western Asia, but as with the Walnut, its true homeland is uncertain. It seems to have been in cultivation in southern Europe and Asia since before recorded history. This species would have been familiar in Europe long before the seventeenth century. In 800 it was one of the plants listed by Charlemagne for planting throughout his empire; in 995 in England Mulberry was recorded by Aelfric as being a word in common use, perhaps known from the dried fruit which the Romans imported. The White Mulberry is indigenous to China, and supposedly introduced into Tuscany from the Middle East in 1434; however, its travels are complicated by the fact that its leaves are the food if not of the gods at least of silkworms, and silk – a fabric which excited all Europe – was being made in Europe long before then.

Silk was first produced in China, where its production can be traced back to the third millennium BC. The silken thread is spun by the Chinese silkworm, *Bombyx mori*, which lives on the leaves of the White Mulberry, in particular. When unwound from the pupae, the thread can be as long as 900 metres (985 yds). It is so light that over 50,000 cocoons are required to produce 1 kg (2.2 lb) of silk. For centuries China jealously guarded its trade secret. However, by about 149 BC sericulture (a word not invented until 1851, meaning silk production and weaving) was taking place in India, and silk caravans were trading with Turkistan and Persia (Iran). From the fourth century AD Uzbekistan was producing its own silk, with mulberry trees being grown along streets and ditches and silk being woven in the Fergana valley (the practice of growing mulberry trees on field boundaries, ditches and beside roads continues today in China, Vietnam and North Korea). Two hundred years later two Persian monks secretly travelled from China, supposedly with silkworms smuggled inside a bamboo cane, to Constantinople (Istanbul); this act of defiance is believed to have led to the beginning of the silk industry in Europe.

Collecting mulberries to feed to silkworms, China, c. nineteenth century. Note how the trees appear to have been pollarded, possibly to keep the lower branches out of reach of browsing animals.

During the tenth century the Arabic invaders of Spain controlled and protected the mulberry trees (along with flax and cotton). In an effort to establish the French manufacture of silk, during the seventeenth century Henri IV

(1553–1610) planted some 20,000 White Mulberry trees in the garden of the Tuileries near Paris. In nineteenth-century Italy, particularly from the 1830s onwards, a silk industry was re-established, notably, in Piedmont and Lombardy, where the parlous state of agriculture was causing concern and the establishment of White Mulberry orchards was begun. All European countries throughout history have vied to produce the gossamer silk, and a mixture of eastern mystery and commercial exploitation led to the spread of the Mulberry Tree.

By the seventeenth century, Britain, like most European countries, had been growing the Black Mulberry for several centuries, but the White Mulberry was rare in northern Europe, and was reportedly not introduced until 1596, the same time as it was being mass planted in Paris. By then mulberry trees, both black and white, were being shipped over in their hundreds from the Continent, encouraged, one imagines, by the publication in 1609 of *Instructions for the Increasing and Planting of Mulberry Trees, Breeding of Silkworms, and Making of Silk*, written by William Stallenge, a 'Searcher of the Port of London' (a customs officer) and a London member of the newly formed Virginia Company. John Tradescant senior had made lavish purchases of the tree for Lord Burghley (1520–98) at Hatfield House – one Mulberry from that first planting still survives – and in the same year, 1609, the King sent instructions encouraging their planting to each English county. The Hertfordshire house of Theobalds, which had been in the ownership of Lord Burghley's father, was also planted with mulberries, which Evelyn noted in 1643, as were 1.62 hectares (4 acres) of ground near St James's Park in London, which gained the name of the Mulberry Garden. The trees were beautifully mature by the time Samuel Pepys strolled through them one May evening in 1664, and even more so ten years later when Evelyn viewed them. By 1703 the garden had become part of what was later to be known as Buckingham Palace. (With a nice sense of history Her Majesty The Queen holds the National Plant Collection of *Morus* in the grounds of Buckingham Palace.)

Queen Anne of Denmark (1574–1619), wife of James I (1566–1625), had been so enthused by the idea of producing silk that in 1616 she had commanded a Silkworm House to be built to a design drawn by Inigo Jones (1573–1652) at the Royal Palace of Oatlands overlooking the Thames near Weybridge, Surrey. Keenness for creating an English silk industry continued all through this period and included the appointment of a succession of Keepers of His Majesty's Gardens, Vines, and Silkworms. Both John Tradescants, father and son, held the title. In 1661 Evelyn viewed a 'wonderful engine for weaving silk stockings, said to have been the invention of an Oxford scholler'. Eight years later, The Royal Society debated William Stallenge's treatise on the culture of mulberry trees and the silkworms. However, for all the royal approval and enthusiasm the English manufacture of silk petered out, because eastern Mediterranean, Italian, Chinese and Indian silk all proved cheaper and easier to make, and because of the waywardness of the worms, who prefer a diet of the leaves of *Morus alba* – which does not thrive in the English climate as well as it does in warmer countries – and spurn the Black Mulberry, *Morus nigra*, which grows with more vigour and is the tree most frequently planted.

The introduction of *Morus alba* and silkworm eggs followed quickly on the discovery of the New World in the fifteenth century, first in Mexico and then later in Virginia, where they were introduced by the English. By the eighteenth century small amounts of raw silk were being sent to England, but at most silk-making remained a cottage industry. However, during the following century 'mulberrymania' swept through America on the back of the arrival from China, via France, of the multi-stemmed *Morus* var. *multicaulis*. Just as with the 'tulpenwoede' or tulipomania which engulfed the Dutch during the 1630s, prices soared, financial speculation was rife, fortunes were made and literally millions of trees were planted, supplies coming particularly from France. It was believed that the tree was a faster and more sturdier grower than the White Mulberry, and that it would therefore be quicker – and easier – to raise silkworms. Within ten years the truth had dawned: *M.* var. *multicaulis* did not cut the mustard as far as silkworms were concerned; nor was there an easy or fast way to manufacture silk. Mulberry orchards were grubbed up, and vast sums of money lost. From then on American belles had to create their gowns from imported silk.

As well as the White Mulberry, the Black Mulberry had been sent to America, where both were recorded as growing in the garden of the Governor of Massachusetts Bay Colony in 1630, and reports were made of a fine native Mulberry Tree. This was duly transported to England, and in 1629, John Parkinson recorded the American Red Mulberry, *Morus rubra*, as growing in his garden at Long Acre in London. A native of the eastern and central United States, the tree was listed by Tradescant in 1634 as *Morus Virginiana*. It was not catalogued as growing in the Oxford Botanic Garden in 1648, but there is another intriguing entry: '*Morus nana Norwegica*', the Norway Mulberry. This is a mystery, as the Norwegian flora does not include a native mulberry. All mulberries find it hard to thrive without great heat and sun, and the American mulberry is no exception; in its native land its leaves are of no interest to the silkworm, and neither are its fruit interesting to humans: they taste quite insipid, and apparently their only use is as food for chickens or pigs.

In the eighteenth century Philip Miller at the Chelsea Physic Garden was growing a relation of the mulberry, named originally *Morus papyrifera* – the Paper Mulberry – and later *Broussonetia papyrifera*. The seed had been collected from Japan, and it throve in the Chelsea garden, growing in the open. It was grown throughout the Far East, being a most important economic plant in the Pacific region for the making of bark cloth.

Despite regal encouragement, and Evelyn's inclusion of it in *Sylva*, the Mulberry is one of our rarer domestic trees. Like the Medlar, *Mespilus germanica*, which Evelyn does not mention, there is ambivalence about its role: is it a tree best grown decoratively in the garden, or is it a tree for the countryside and hedgerow?

The Mulberry Tree, *painted in 1889 by Vincent van Gogh. The tree frequently grows crooked or procumbent with a low broad dome. The bark is dark orange, with fissures and sprouty burrs.*

Of the Service and of the Quickbeam

Sorbus Rosaceae

ROWAN, MOUNTAIN ASH (*Sorbus aucuparia*):
TO 15M (50FT) HEIGHT; NATIVE TO EUROPE
(INCLUDING BRITAIN), NORTH AFRICA AND ASIA
MINOR; DECIDUOUS; THE SHAPE OF THE TREE IS
OBOVOID (EGG-SHAPED); LEAVES ARE PINNATE (FEATHER-
SHAPED) WITH AN AVERAGE OF 15 OPPOSITE LEAFLETS

THERE ARE MORE THAN A HUNDRED species in the *Sorbus* genus, all natives of the northern temperate regions, east to the Himalayas and south to Mexico. The genus includes Service, Rowan and Whitebeam Trees. Evelyn writes about the four that in his time were believed to be native.

The Rowan Tree or Mountain Ash, *Sorbus aucuparia*, was probably domesticated relatively early, as it is included in the list of familiar words drawn up by Aelfric in 995. An adaptable, sturdy yet slight tree, it is certainly the most widely distributed: its native habitat covers the whole of Europe, Siberia (up to the Arctic Circle), Asia and North Africa, and it has become naturalized in America,

having been taken there during the seventeenth century. Evelyn later gives the Rowan a short chapter on its own, and records no fewer than six different names. There was the Quickbeam, the Ornus and the Wild Sorb; then the Pinax – Evelyn could not understand this term, as the word meant a list or an inscribed tablet; and the Quicken Tree, but Evelyn might have got this muddled, as that name is recorded in the Oxford catalogue as the Wild or Common Ash, *Fraxinus bubula*. Lastly, it was sometimes called the Witchen, meaning witch-like – a description used for a number of trees here and in America. Confusingly, for a long time the Rowan Tree was classed with the pear family and called *Pyrus aucuparia*. John Tradescant senior knew it as *Sorbus sylvestris*; however, like all his horticultural contemporaries, he does not seem to have ever used the term Rowan Tree, even though the name was first recorded in 1548. The word rowan comes from *raun*, meaning north, and derives from the old Nordic languages. It is an apt name, as the tree does remarkably well in Scotland, growing at heights of nearly 1,000 metres (3,250ft).

Rowan traditionally had a sinister reputation, similar to that of Elderberry, *Sambucus nigra*, being associated with witches: some believed that once either of the trees was planted, they should never be cut down, as they kept witches at

The Rowan Tree, here growing in Scotland. In May the tree produces creamy-white flowers 1cm across, followed by the fruit in late July. By early August the berries are bright scarlet and are immediately enjoyed by mistle-thrushes, blackbirds and starlings.

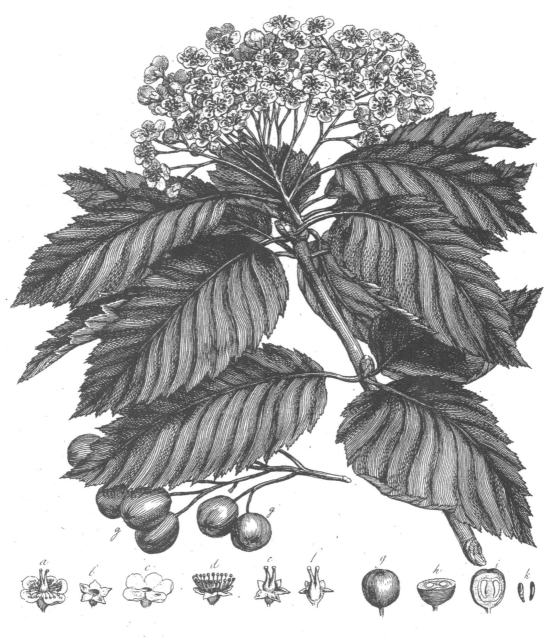

The White Beam Tree

bay. Rowan berries, which colour up voluptuously in early autumn, entice birds to feast off them, as indicated by the species name *aucuparia*, the origin of which means birdcatcher. Evelyn remarks that the thrush was partial to the berries; these days the waxwing, a Scandinavian migrant, has been observed to be keen on them too. Rowan berries are rich in vitamin C and may be eaten; although tart, they make a wonderful jelly to accompany game. Evelyn calls the ale brewed from them 'an incomparable drink', as did Samuel Pepys, who thought it 'the best he had ever tasted'.

The second native *Sorbus* Evelyn describes, saying it is 'the most frequent with us', is the Wild Service Tree, *Sorbus torminalis*. He says that in France it was called the *cormier* (now *Sorbier des oiseaux*). This tree rarely grows north of the border, and its distribution stretches south through Europe to Syria. It is the only *Sorbus* that has a different-style leaf, with a most distinctive shape like a Maple. The shape of the fruit, too, is distinguished: it is obovoid, or the shape of a hen's egg – Evelyn describes it as pear-shaped. He also says how pear-like the timber is. No wonder all the whitebeams were originally included with the *Pyrus* genus. He says it was used by the joiner, by the engraver for woodcuts, and by the carpenter for the manufacture of screws, mill spindles and gunstocks, and 'to counterfeit ebony or almost any Indian wood'. Probably its most useful attribute is implied by its name *torminalis,* meaning effective against colic. Evelyn says the fruit taken with new wine and honey will 'corroborate the stomach' and that the fruit taken alone helps to cure dysentery and diarrhoea. He calls the fruit 'chequers' or 'checker-berries'. This reflects the appearance of the fruit, which is a leathery brown in colour and flecked with lenticels – aeration pores – which give it a patterned or chessboard look.

The Whitebeam, *Sorbus aria*, the third tree John Evelyn describes, is a native and a small tree of great charm. He probably knew it well, as it grows profusely on chalk and limestone soils particularly in southern counties. In Britain it is confined to England, and it is common in southern and central Europe. Perhaps the tree's greatest distinction is in early spring when the leaves are just breaking; these are almost white on the underside (hence its name) and for a few days can give the impression of a mature Magnolia coming into bloom. The clusters of creamy flowers are immensely attractive to insects, so there is always a pleasing hum as one passes by. During the nineteenth century a number of varieties were developed from *S. aria* (then known as *Pyrus aria*), which have been much

The Whitebeam (Sorbus aria) can grow to a height of 25m (80ft). Creamy-white flowers open in May. Fruit ripens from green to red in September and is quickly taken by birds.

planted as street trees, including 'Majestica' in 1858, and 'Lutescens' in 1892. Both are neat and well behaved, the latter having the added advantage of a fleeting pale yellow autumnal show.

Evelyn's fourth *Sorbus* is the True Service Tree, *Sorbus domestica*. In his time this was believed to be a native, but it is now thought to have originated in southern Europe, North Africa and west Asia. It is a handsome but quite slow-growing tree, with ash-like leaves and fruits. The latter are usually shaped like small, hard pears, but occasionally a tree will produce globular-shaped fruit; they are edible only when they have been softened by frost, or when made into an alcoholic fruit beverage. There is evidence that the tree had been introduced into domestic use by the fifteenth century, and there is a record of a young tree being planted in the grounds of Hampton Court Palace in 1530. Later, in 1634, John Tradescant junior recorded *S. domestica* and *S. torminalis* growing in his Lambeth garden.

One imagines that Evelyn, who had written that the shade of the tree was 'beautiful for walks', would have followed with great interest the upward mobility of the *Sorbus* genus from its utilitarian use in the seventeenth century to its decorative and suburban planting today. Although there were signs that the tree (at least the native species) was being grown domestically in the fifteenth century, with the arrival of Chinese species and varieties in the nineteenth and twentieth centuries there was a Rowan revolution. Now there are innumerable varieties, in a wide range of forms and colours to suit many tastes. It is the scale that makes them so ideal for planting in the garden; also their shape and leaf form means the shade they cast is not heavy but dappled. There are the blooms to look forward to in spring and the rainbow-coloured foliage and berries in autumn, ranging from white to pink, yellow and red. Planted in moderately fertile soil in sun or dappled shade, they do well in most gardens. One can admire the many varieties now at our disposal and commiserate with John Evelyn, who had only four *Sorbus* to enjoy.

Of the Maple

Acer Aceraceae

FIELD MAPLE (*Acer campestre*):
4.5–9M (15–30FT); NATIVE THROUGHOUT EUROPE TO
NORTHERN IRAQ AND NORTH AFRICA; ITS DISTRIBUTION IN
ENGLAND IS MAINLY CONFINED IN THE SOUTH THROUGH TO THE
MIDLANDS; RARE IN WALES AND NORTHERN ENGLAND, AND
NOT NATIVE TO IRELAND OR SCOTLAND; OFTEN FOUND IN
HEDGES; THE CROWN IS DOMED; DECIDUOUS; THE FIVE-LOBED
PINKISH LEAVES UNFOLD INTO BRIGHT AND THEN DARK GREEN;
AUTUMN COLOUR CAN BE A RICH GOLD AND LONG LASTING

JOHN EVELYN USES THE NAME then in current use, *Acer minus*, to describe the one indigenous Maple in this large and ornamental family. Aelfric had recorded this name in 995, and some 500 years later John Tradescant senior described it as *Acer minus vulgare*. In 1648, Jacob Bobart of the Oxford Botanic Garden knew it as *Acer minus tenuis* (*tenuis* meaning thin or slender). It was Linnaeus who in the eighteenth century renamed it *Acer campestre*, the species name meaning of the fields; indeed, it is not a woodland tree at all, as its common name, the Field or Hedge Maple, denotes. Both the Latin name *acer*, meaning sharp/acid, pungent/acrid and hard to touch, and the Old English

mapeltrēow were used to describe the tree from earliest times; from the latter comes the shortened word maple, which Geoffrey Chaucer is the first to be recorded as using. The tree originally arrived on British soil thousands of years earlier, after the last great Ice Age and as the landscape that eventually overcame the icy wastes slowly evolved. The Maple, along with the Hornbeam, Ash, Beech and Holly, was among the last of the trees that colonized northwards as temperatures slowly rose and the land gradually began to accommodate plant material from warmer climes.

There are some 200 species in the *Acer* genus, widely distributed throughout the northern temperate zone; many of them are from North America and Europe but with a nucleus indigenous to the Far East. Most of the trees have a handsome but neat habit, and all of them bear samara (winged seeds). But it is the leaves that are the *Acer's* special glory. All grow opposite each other, and the shape, which is palmate and delicate in varying degrees, and their extraordinary autumnal colour make these trees such an ornament in the garden and landscape.

Evelyn writes about maple timber in great detail, extolling its virtues – he considers it far superior to beech in all respects. He quotes Pliny as saying: 'for the elegancey and finess of the wood is next to the very cedar itself'. He describes various different timbers, one the White or French Maple, 'which is wonderfully beautiful'. Perhaps

ABOVE: *Smooth Japanese Maple* (Acer palmatum)*, a native of Japan, China and Korea. The tree was introduced into England in 1820 and is now common in gardens throughout Europe. It grows to a height of 6m (20ft) and the leaves turn red and purple during autumn.*

LEFT: *A maple-wood chair designed by the Canadian Frank Gehry in the late 1980s and created in 1994 by the Knoll Studio in the United States.*

he had in mind the white and close-grained wood of the Norway Maple, *Acer platanoides*, which is native throughout Europe and the Caucasus, and made an early though unspecified arrival in Britain; Evelyn says that 'it grows on that part of Italy, that is on the other side of Po beyond the Alps.'

Evelyn also quotes Pliny's description of a second wood with 'curled grain', the markings of which resemble the swirls of the 'Peacock's Tail', the best apparently being grown in Istria (the borderland of north-eastern Italy). This could have been either the Italian Maple, *Acer opulus*, which is a native of all of southern Europe, or *A. lobelia,* a tree indigenous to southern Italy, closely allied to the Norway Maple and named in honour of the botanist Matthias de l'Obel (1538–1616), whom the Lobelia also commemorates. Perhaps John Evelyn would have noticed and admired both during his travels. The trees arrived in Britain nearly a hundred years apart, the Italian Maple arriving in 1683 and Lobel's Maple nearly a hundred years later in 1752.

In ancient times, Evelyn says of the native *Acer* that the wood was made into tables that resembled the colours of a tiger ('tigrin', he calls it) and of the panther ('pantherine'). When old, the timber is 'admirably figured as it were marbled and therefore much more esteemed by the joiners and cabinet makers'. Evelyn notes: '[by] shredding [pruning] up the boughs to a head I have caused it to shoot to a wonderful height in a little time', an attribute confirmed by evidence of coppicing in our older woodlands, where sometimes the width of a maple stool is twice the height of a man. Quoting Pliny again, Evelyn says that the best polish of all is the hand of a man 'who came warm out of the bath', which conjures up a more pleasing image than that of plain elbow grease as a means of getting a shine on the wood.

Maple wood is tough and hard; the Romans used it as hafts to fit their spears into. The wood has been found made into early Anglo-Saxon harp frames and is still used in the building of violins and pianos. It was part of the ritual Saxon ship burial discovered during excavations in 1939 at Sutton Hoo in Suffolk.

There are at least two further maples that Evelyn might have recognized, both collected from the eastern seaboard of America. The first, which had arrived before he wrote *Sylva*, was the Red, Scarlet or Virginian Maple, *Acer rubrum*. This is said by Philip Miller to have been introduced by John Tradescant junior

CENTRE AND RIGHT: *Sycamore leaves (Acer pseudoplatanus).*

during one of his three trips to the colony, and is listed as *Virgnianum Tradescanti* in Tradescant's 1656 catalogue. Leonard Plukenet (1642–1706), the superintendent of the garden at Hampton Court Palace and the Queen's Botanist, toured the Tradescants' Lambeth garden in 1696 and remarked on both its size and height. In this country it can reach 26 metres (85ft) and have a trunk diameter of 112 centimetres (3ft 8in); in its native habitat it grows larger. Although the leaves explode into fireworks during the fall in America, the tree is not quite so spectacular in Britain. *Acer negundo*, the second of the seventeenth-century American imports, must have arrived about the same time or a little later, as by 1688 the tree was being cultivated by the keen gardener and botanist bishop the Hon. Henry Compton (1632–1713) in his garden at Fulham. Known as the Box Elder or Ash-leaved Maple, it is widespread over North America, growing on swampy or damp soil. This is one of the trees that provided a source of sugar or maple syrup; now it is more ornamentally important, turning a clear yellow during the autumn. Maple traffic was not all one way, for in 1756, John Bartram (1699–1777), an English plant collector who worked in America, sending seeds and plants to England, requested seed be sent of the Norway Maple, *A. platanoides*. Over the years the species has prospered in America, and developed an infinite number of varieties.

A tree which has shuffled around the edge of the *Acer* family, and to which John Evelyn gives a chapter – albeit only two paragraphs – is the Sycamore, *Acer pseudoplatanus*. Some confusion has surrounded the tree. For some time no one was sure whether it was a native or had taken the fancy of some early traveller in Europe, who had brought the winged seed to England. However it arrived, it has subsequently 'gone native'; in fact it is a non-native, from central and southern Europe, but long established and naturalized in Britain. There has been controversy, too, about its antecedents, and of course its name – even Evelyn wrote of the 'sycomor falsely so called'. He records it as *Acer majus*, while Jacob Bobart names it *Acer majus latifolious*, the Great Maple or Bastard Sycamore. The common name Sycamore, used both here and on the Continent, has its roots in the Greek word *sykon*, meaning fig, and *opsis*, referring to its appearance; the leaves do indeed have a fig-like look. The name sycamore developed into the ancient Latin names *Sicimorus*, for the Mulberry Tree, and *Ficus sycomorus*, for the Mulberry Fig Tree, more commonly known as the Sycamore Fig. Although the modern, Linnaean name for the Sycamore places it with the *Acers*, the species name *pseudoplatanus*, meaning False Plane Tree, reflects doubts about its genus; indeed in Scotland the Sycamore is commonly called the Plane Tree.

Evelyn implies that he did not approve of the tree being planted in gardens or avenues, for 'the leaves which fall early turn to mucilage and putrefy … so they contaminate and mar our walks'. Where else, in the twenty-first century, have we heard of the wrong sort of leaves falling?

In England the first mention of the Sycamore occurs in *A Niewe Herball or Historie of Plantes* (1578), an updated translation by Henry Lyte (*c.*1529–1607) of a French version of a book originally written in Flemish in 1554 by the botanist R. Dodoens entitled *Crüÿdeboek*. Here the Sycamore was recorded as a garden tree, as it was again about fifty years later in south-east Cornwall, where 'fourteen sickumers [growing] in the herb garden' were noted. Later in the seventeenth century comes the first indication of the tree being planted in the wider landscape: Norfolk was reported to have sycamores growing in hedgerows then, and again in 1730, while in Cornwall, at the same time, there was a vogue for planting them in churchyards.

It is a pity that sycamores are aggressive colonizers, which often wipe out native and other woodland species, for fully grown sycamores growing in isolation are beautiful. Their timber is much prized; being light but tough, it is often used to make small items, including violins and wooden spoons, and as a veneer in furniture decoration.

Sycamore seen at its best, growing in the Peak District National Park.

Of the Hornbeam

Carpinus Corylaceae

HORNBEAM (*Carpinus betulus*):
CAN REACH A HEIGHT OF 19M (65FT); NATIVE
TO SOUTH-EAST ENGLAND, AS WELL AS EUROPE
FROM THE PYRENEES TO SOUTHERN SWEDEN,
AND EAST TO ASIA MINOR; DECIDUOUS; OFTEN
GROWN AS A HEDGE, PARK OR STREET TREE

LIKE THE FIELD MAPLE, the Hornbeam was a colonizer after the Ice Age. In all there are about forty species in the genus, growing in Europe from Sweden to the Pyrenees and east to Asia Minor. In Britain the tree grows on the fringe of its viability, confined to south-east England. A tree of ancient woodland, *Carpinus betulus*, the only native Hornbeam, is the largest of the genus and makes the most noble of trees: as a solitary specimen in a park its spreading shape is gently pendant. Grown naturally in woodland, the tree lasts about a century or so, but if coppiced its life can be extended by several hundred years.

The Hornbeam's earliest recorded name was Hardbeam, called thus because of its hard, tough and close-grained timber. Its original Latin name was *Betulus* (the name used by Tradescant senior), meaning birch-like, but it had a second name, *Carpinus*, the Latin name for the Hornbeam. In Evelyn's day both words were in use, but confusingly he calls the Hornbeam *Ostrya vulgaris* after the Greek name for the European Hop Hornbeam (now *O. carpinifolia*). The Oxford Botanic Garden list compiled some twenty or so years later uses *Carpinus* with, as its vernacular name, Hedge Beech.

Whatever the tree's name, the Hornbeam is one of those trees that are welcomed both in the planted landscape and when felled as timber. John Evelyn comments that it serves well for mill cogs, heads of beetles (tools for wedge-driving), as well as stocks and handles for tools. However, the timber is not enjoyed by the joiner and carpenter, as the wood is so tough that it is very hard to work and blunts tools; the arboriculturist Henry Elwes (1846–1922) described it in the twentieth century as 'the hardest, heaviest, and toughest' of our native trees. Nevertheless, the timber (like that of the Maple) was valued in the construction of the piano, being the preferred wood for conveying the movement from the key to the hammer, which then strikes the strings. Evelyn also notes that it is good for the fire, 'where it burns like a candle'. It is an excellent hedgerow tree and a component of woodland, where in Evelyn's time it was often coppiced or pollarded; Epping, Hatfield and Hainault Forests all have evidence of its use in this way.

Perhaps its most important feature, and the reason for its association with beech, is its leaves, which it retains throughout the winter, as beech does. Decoratively it makes a superb hedge – as Evelyn tells us, emphasizing its other good points: it is 'so sturdy as not to be wronged by the winds'; 'it leaves no ugly gap between the earth and its commencement of growth';

'it flourishes with a glossy and polished verdure'. Illustrating its decorative appeal, he mentions the 'admirable espalier hedge in the long middle walk of Luxembourg Garden at Paris (than which there is nothing more graceful)'. He visited both the palace and the garden during his time abroad, in 1644.

The two different genus of Hornbeam, *Carpinus* and *Ostrya*, are both deciduous and woodland trees. The genera were disentangled during the eighteenth century, the former by Linnaeus and the latter by Giovanni Scopoli (1723–88), an almost exact contemporary and colleague who was the Professor of Botany and Chemistry at the University of Pavia in Italy. It was Scopoli who named the Hop Hornbeam, *Ostrya carpinifolia*, which nicely encapsulates its similarity to the Hornbeam. The Hornbeam genus *Carpinus* is distributed over a wide area of Europe, Asia and North America, but the smaller group of Hop Hornbeams (*Ostrya*), so named as the involucre (the husk) growing around the flower makes the clusters look very hop-like, are curiously isolated. There are approximately ten species of *Ostrya*, including one in the warmer areas of Europe and Asia, one or two in eastern Asia and one known as Ironwood, *O. virginica*, which John Evelyn could have seen, as its entry into Britain is recorded as 1692, and another in Central America.

Thousands of years previously, the Hop Hornbeam was shedding its pollen over the valleys and slopes of southern Europe, and in early summer some 5,300 years ago a Neolithic man ingested some with his meal. He clambered and scrambled from a valley up above the snowline, where on the Alpine pass of the Hauslabjoch, between Switzerland and Italy (about 3,048m/10,500ft high), he froze to death. The frozen corpse was discovered in 1991, and, nicknamed the Iceman, has been the subject of endless analysis ever since. Dr Klaus Oeggl, a botanist from the University of Innsbruck, made an amazing discovery: in the Iceman's stomach was the intact pollen of the Hop Hornbeam. This enabled Oeggl to deduce not only that he walked up from the south side of the pass, some five or six hours' walk away, but that his death must have occurred sometime between March and June, which is when *O. carpinifolia* flowers and sheds its pollen. He could not have climbed from the north side of the pass, as this area was too cold to sustain the warm-loving tree. Despite the tree's long sojourn in southern Europe (and Asia Minor), it is rare to find it growing in England. Evelyn must surely have met it during his Continental journey, particularly in Italy, but it did not arrive in England until the early eighteenth century.

Of the Lime Tree

Tilia Tiliaceae

COMMON LIME (*Tilia x Europaea*):
IN HEIGHT ABOUT 39M (130FT);
NATIVE; DECIDUOUS; LEAVES ARE
CORDATE OR HEART-SHAPED AT BASE
WITH A SHORT TAPERED APEX, SHARPLY
TOOTHED. DARK GREEN AND SMOOTH
ABOVE, PALE GREEN BENEATH WITH
TUFTS OF HAIRS IN THE MAIN AXILS

THERE ARE THREE COMMONLY planted or indigenous limes. The largest is the Large-leaved Lime, *Tilia platyphyllos*. Its native habitat spreads from northern Spain to Sweden, and from the Crimea, the Caucasus and Asia Minor; there is considerable doubt as to whether it is an English native or a very early introduction. The second is definitely a native. This is the Small-leaved Lime, *T. cordata,* which, like the Large-leaved Lime, is a native across Europe, from northern Spain across the Mediterranean lands to the Caucasus,

The Lime Walk at Knebworth, Hertfordshire, designed by Sir Edwin Lutyens and planted in 1911. The pollarded trees are cut back each winter.

as well as across northern Europe to Siberia. The third is the Common Lime, *T.* x *europaea*, known in the seventeenth century as *T. vulgaris*. This is a hybrid between *Tilia platyphyllos* and *T. cordata*; the cross probably occurred naturally, at some indeterminate early time. During the twentieth century it was the species most favoured for street or avenue planting, despite the fact that its propensity to drop its leaves at any hint of a dry summer and almost certain attack by aphids every year seem to make it an unsuitable candidate for public service. *Tilia*'s erratic habit of interbreeding, not so much in England but certainly in warmer climates, means that a great number of varietal differences occur and nomenclature can be difficult. There are in all about thirty-five species, all found in the temperate northern hemisphere, apart from north-west America. Limes, *Tilia* species, are in no way related to the fruiting Lime Tree, *Citrus aurantifolia*.

Tilia was not one of the familiar Anglo-Saxon words drawn up by Aelfric, but it is on the Tradescant the younger list of 1656 twice, as '*T. mas*. Male Lime Tree, and *T. foemina* Female Lime Tree'. Evelyn, too, refers to two different kinds of lime, male and female, stating that they are 'totally differed as to their form', quoting Theophrastus and his *Enquiry into Plants*, the earliest surviving European horticultural treatise.

Evelyn acknowledges the two vernacular names by which the *Tilia* was known in the seventeenth century, the Lime and the Linden Tree. In Britain the tree was known as Pry up until the sixteenth century, and then more familiarly called the Linden Tree. The word linden derives from *lind*, an Old Saxon word, which itself derives from older northern European languages, such as Old High German and Old Norse, and the Old Prussian *lipe* and the Latvian and Lithuanian *liepa*. The name Linden is used throughout northern Europe, famously in the Berlin street Unter den Linden. In the early part of the seventeenth century, and only in Britain, it started to be called the Lime Tree, and since then it has answered to both names.

The name of the Swedish naturalist Carl Linnaeus is linked to the tree. His surname was coined by his grandfather to commemorate the family's ownership of the Linnegård estate, which itself is derived from the dialect word for the Linden Tree, and to commemorate a great Linden Tree which grew near the house.

Grinling Gibbons (1648–1721)

Grinling Gibbons was English, but born in Rotterdam, and it is interesting that he spent his early years in Holland, where the Lime Tree played an important part in the development of horticulture and lime timber was widely available. For a wood carver, as he was to become, there cannot be a better medium than lime wood. As well as being strong, it is durable, and can be carved against the grain, although curves and swirls, which make Gibbons' style so distinguished, are supreme with the grain. It is a stable timber, which means that it does not warp. English carvers did not originally like lime wood, as it was such a creamy colour, and they were more used to the sturdier and more unforgiving texture of oak timber.

In 1667, as a young man of nineteen, Gibbons moved to England, first to York, and then to London. Evelyn met him in late 1670, 'by mere accident' as he was walking 'neere a poore solitary thatched house in a field in our parish, neere Sayes Court'. He recognized Gibbons' supreme talent for wood carving immediately, and was so enthusiastic about his protégé that within a very short time he swept him off to London. Not only did the King view some of Gibbons' work, but Gibbons was also introduced to the architect Christopher Wren and various other potential clients. Following the Great Fire, there was plenty of rebuilding and reconstruction work to be had, and by 1672 Gibbons had moved from Deptford, with his wife Elizabeth, to Ludgate Hill.

Gibbons' early work was most often of a religious nature, but later he developed and introduced the decorative carving for which he became so well known. Much of his work, in friezes, cascades and picture surrounds, brings to life the still-life paintings of the Dutch and Flemish artists. One of his earliest commissions was to supply lime-wood work to Evelyn's friend the Earl of Essex, who was developing his great house at Cassiobury. By 1685 Gibbons had developed a Covent Garden workshop, and had a number of people working with

him. He was asked to embellish royal palaces by Charles II, William III (who allowed him to use the term 'Master Carver') and George I, and his work may be seen at Windsor Castle, Hampton Court Palace and Kensington Palace. It became fashionable to ask Gibbons to contribute to the decorative detail within a house.

His work was silkily smooth, and for a while scholars were puzzled as to how Gibbons gained such an effect, as sandpaper was an invention of the nineteenth century. In fact he used what Evelyn recommended in *Sylva*: Dutch reed (*Equisetum hyemale*), a member of the horsetail family, commonly used by cabinet-makers of the time. Today the finest wire wool dipped in wax polish gives the smoothest sheen for all woods.

Gibbons' work in churches includes the decorative carving on the choir stalls and organ case in St Paul's Cathedral. Also in London, the carved oak pulpit and the staircase at St Martin-in-the-Fields are attributed to him. In Canterbury Cathedral, Kent, he embellished the Archbishop's throne. Further afield in Worcestershire at the church of St Mary Magdalene in Croome D'Abitot is one of Gibbons' largest carvings, commemorating Lord Coventry and completed in 1690.

Perhaps his most poignant work of all is that in the Deptford Church of St Nicholas, near where Evelyn lived. After all, if Evelyn had not gone for a stroll across the fields of Deptford that day in December 1670, the extraordinary talent of Grinling Gibbons might have gone completely unrecorded. So when Gibbons was asked to carve the reredos in the church he must have done so with a thought or two for

'The cravat' carved from limewood in the style of Venetian needlepoint and worn at least once. Horace Walpole remarked '…he gave wood the loose and airy lightness of flowers'.

his patron. It is a work distinguished for its delicate yet humane rendering of Ezekiel, the Old Testament prophet. He also carved a depiction of the Valley of the Bones, which was originally placed above the entrance to the (separate) charnel house.

Evelyn valued limes for their aesthetic appeal, describing them as 'most proper and beautiful for walks' and recommending that they should be planted in avenues and walks 'at a distance of eighteen or twenty foot'. During the seventeenth century limes became a key feature in big gardens and landscapes, used mostly to delineate avenues and walks. Prior to the Civil War, Wimbledon House, built originally in 1588 as a royal palace, was redesigned to a plan of John Smythson (d.1634). In 1609, there is the first reference to a lime avenue when 131 lime trees were planted within the Great Garden to the south of the house. The great Lime Walk of Buxted in Sussex is believed to have been planted sometime during the 1630s, as was New Hall in Essex, which Evelyn particularly liked, describing in 1656 'the Sweete & faire avenue planted with stately Lime-trees in 4 rowes for neere a mile in length'.

Following the Restoration, royal palaces took the lead in modernizing their landscapes in the Continental style, using limes extensively to create walks and avenues, most notably at Hampton Court Palace: in 1662 Christian van Vranen was granted a pass to travel to Holland to collect 4,000 lime trees, which were planted as avenues. St James's Park was similarly developed with limes.

From the aged evidence remaining of these features, almost without exception it was the Common Lime, *T.* x *europaea*, that was used. That this seemed to be the most popular choice is likely to have been because of its fragrant flowers and because the trees are fast growing, could be bought in bulk and were available in a uniform size – like the equal-sized tomatoes or apples found in supermarkets today. Most importantly it was easy, and therefore inexpensive, to reproduce from its basal shoots.

For the fashionably minded estate owner wishing to indulge in grandiose ideas, limes were readily available. Evelyn complains that, although it is easy to gather the seed and raise the tree here, young limes were commonly imported from Flanders and Holland, at great expense. The trade appears to have been well established: earlier, in 1611, Tradescant senior, on one of his buying trips to Holland for the Earl of Salisbury at Hatfield House, is recorded as buying '200 lim trees', which cost 1s 3d each. Nearly sixty years later £6 was being charged for forty of the 'best Dutch Limes'. Near the end of the century, in a bill sent to Levens Hall in Cumbria from the nurseryman George Rickets (*fl.*1680s–1710s) of Hoxton in London, 'the best and most faithful florist', the cost had fallen to 1s each. Perhaps Evelyn's complaint had been heeded, and these were home-grown trees. Certainly in the following century, there is clear evidence of nurserymen offering locally produced lime trees for sale. In 1753, they were still being sold at the same price per tree. However, in 1766 William Pendar of Woolhampton, Berkshire, was charging only £2 for 200 trees, although they were described as 'small'.

During the eighteenth century the fashion for formally planted avenues waned somewhat as they were incompatible with the free-flowing landscape movement. So we find in a letter written to 'Capability' Brown by John Midgely, the foreman in charge of work Brown had undertaken at Castle Ashby, Northamptonshire, in about 1762: 'I have shorten'd the Spinny and taken down some of the Lims and trim'd some up so as to let your Eye thro' without making a Avenue.' The Lime Tree was criticized for being narrow and erect, rather than what was required, voluptuous and refulgent. Fashion, as ever, was the enforcing discipline, and at Weston Park in Staffordshire, the English poet William Cowper (1731–1800) reported to a friend that the lime trees had been removed 'because, forsooth, they are rectilinear. It is a wonder they do not quarrel with a sunbeam.' However, the planting of lime avenues continued, for instance, at Tatton Park in Cheshire, created during the latter part of the eighteenth century, and in the nineteenth century, at Clumber Park, Nottinghamshire, where a huge 4.85-km (3 mile) double lime avenue was planted.

Lime timber is much prized, as it has been for hundreds of years. The wood is a smooth pale cream colour, light but strong, and excellent for detailed work in carving. On the Continent, in particular, it was the favoured timber for religious statues and often called sacred wood or *lignum sacrum*. Evelyn remarks that 'because of its colour and easy working, architects make with it models for their designed buildings, and small statues and little curious figures have been carved of this wood'. It was also used to carve toys and make apothecaries' boxes; and, Evelyn tells us, the ceremonial white staff 'carried by the Right Honourable the White-stave Officers of His Majesties Imperial Court' was fashioned from lime wood. Most of the carved regalia of the Knights of the Garter in St George's Chapel, Windsor, are made from lime wood.

Lime Tree
*(*Tilia x europaea*).*

Of the Birch

Betula Betulaceae

BIRCH (*Betula pendula*):
12–18M (40–60FT) IN HEIGHT; NATIVE THROUGHOUT THE
WHOLE OF EUROPE (INCLUDING BRITAIN) AND ASIA MINOR;
DECIDUOUS; RELATIVELY SHORT-LIVED TREE (PERHAPS 30–60
YEARS); THE BARK IS AT FIRST SHINY RED-BROWN, THEN DEVELOPS
CHARACTERISTIC SILVERY-WARTY MARKINGS; LEAVES ARE SMALL
AND ROUNDED-TRIANGULAR; AS THE TREE MATURES LONG
SLENDER PENDULOUS BRANCHES DEVELOP

THE BIRCH TREE WITH ITS white bark is easily recognizable and a familiar sight throughout most of Britain. *Betula pendula* and *B. pubescens* are the two species that are indigenous, in a genus of some sixty species spread all across the northern hemisphere. The trees were among the original true colonizers, following the easing of conditions after the last Ice Age. The earliest of all may well have been the Dwarf or Arctic Birch (*Betula nana*). Despite its small size – it is more of a shrub than a tree – and neat habit, this is a tough cookie, occurring, as its common name suggests, in all the most northerly latitudes, including northern Britain. The Silver Birch (*B. pendula*) is probably the most common birch in Britain, and its trunk the most warty – its

earlier name *B. varrucosa* describes its rough-leaved look exactly. The Downy Birch (*B. pubescens*) is also aptly named, having downy twigs and leaves. This species lacks the pendulous graceful habit of the Silver Birch, and is frequently found growing on ill-drained, boggy land. The River or Black Birch (*B. nigra*) was introduced in 1736 from the eastern United States, the seed having been despatched probably by John Bartram and sent to Peter Collinson, a merchant and gardener who distributed material sent to him from various collectors.

The tree's reputation among foresters is not high, as it is short-lived, quick-growing and almost valueless as timber; it is considered something of a weed. Yet viewed in the landscape, birches have a lightness of touch, and their leaves glitter and move to the slightest breeze; some have a happy knack of glowing almost primrose yellow during the autumn. In the seventeenth century the tree caught the eye of the Tavistock-born poet William Browne (1591–c.1643), who referred to it as 'the cold-place-loving birch' in his *Britannia's Pastorals*, a poem he composed about 1613.

The Birch Wood
by Gustav Klimt
(1862–1918).

Evelyn writes a lot about the Birch, making little distinction between the two species, and nearly all of it to do with the tree's sap or, as he calls it, juice. This was drunk as a tonic and general pick-me-up, as well as being recommended for the relief of aching joints. Evelyn gives detailed instructions as to how it can be drawn off the tree and what it may be used for. An incision is made across the trunk when the sap begins to rise, 'About the beginning of March (when the buds begin to be proud and turgid)', he recommends – quoting from Sir Hugh Plat (or Platt; 1552–1608), who wrote *Jewell House of Art and Nature* – tapping about 30 centimetres (12in) off the ground, near the root, on the south-west, warmer side of the tree, where the sap is quicker to rise than it is on the slower, chillier northern side.

Evelyn lists a number of other trees that were also tapped for their sap, including the Sycamore (which was considered especially sweet), the Maple and even the Date – probably the Wild Date Palm (*Phoenix sylvestris*) – describing its 'toddy' as 'a very famous drink in the East Indies'. Few of Evelyn's readers are likely to have tasted the liquor. In fact the 'juice' comes from the flowering spadix of the palm, which is cut before it expands, and a vessel attached to collect the sap. In India in Evelyn's time and up until modern times, the toddy man would climb the tree daily to collect it. When fresh, toddy is a pleasing drink, but it soon ferments and becomes intoxicating. After it is distilled the spirit is known as arrack; if the toddy is boiled the dark brown sugar is called jaggery. Evelyn also recommends 'tree drinks' from 'the coco and palmetto trees', although whether he had tried any of these is doubtful. Birch, he says, makes a 'most brisk and spirituous drink … which is a very powerful opener, and doing wonders for cure of the ptisick [physic]'.

More mundanely but familiarly, he notes the Beech, Alder, Oak, Ash, Poplar and Elder as sources of sap, and goes on to suggest that the 'crabs' (Crab Apple Trees) and 'our very brambles may possibly yield us medical and useful wines'. Wine made from blackberry (*Rubus fruticosus*) is delicious and made today. Evelyn relates how a country neighbour, critically ill with 'a bloody strangury [urinary disease]', drank a draught of oak beer and 'recovered to perfect and almost miraculous health and strength'. Evelyn ends his discourse about saps and their medicinal uses by confessing that 'quacking' was not his trade, apologizing for his discursive writing on the subject and hoping that he has not 'unpardonably transgressed', as he speaks only as a 'simple forester'.

Birch
(Betula pendula).

Of the Hazel

Corylus Corylaceae

HAZEL (*Corylus avellana*):
4–6M (13–20FT) IN HEIGHT; NATIVE TO ASIA, NORTH
AFRICA AND EUROPE, APART FROM THE SHETLANDS; IN
THE WILD IT CAN BE FOUND GROWING TO 615M
(2000FT), WHERE IT FORMS BUSHY THICKETS; PRECURSOR
OF SPRING WITH ITS 5CM (2IN) PALE YELLOW MALE
CATKINS; IN LATE SUMMER THE NUTS ARE FRINGED IN A
GREEN INVOLUCRE OF TWO BRACTS; LEAVES ARE DEEP
GREEN AND HARSHLY HAIRY

LIKE THE BIRCH TREE, the Hazel, *Corylus avellana*, was a very early colonizer as the land slowly warmed up after the Ice Age. It is a widely distributed species, indigenous throughout Europe, western Asia and North Africa. Because of its easy availability, quick growth and edible nuts, it must have been one of the first trees to be used by man. Early in the first millennium, China celebrated the hazelnut as one of five sacred foods of the spirits. In Europe both Charlemagne, in his *Capitulare de Villis* of AD 800, and Aelfric in *The Glossary to Grammatical Latino-Saxonica*, compiled nearly 200 years later, record the Hazel.

There are about fifteen species in the *Corylus* genus, which is very closely allied to the Birch family (Hazels were for a long time ascribed to the *Betulaceae* family). There was (and still is) some confusion about their names. The very earliest name, and the one the Romans used, was *nux pontica*. *Nux* later came to be associated with the walnut; *pontica* indicates origination from Pontus in Turkey (even now the hazelnuts from that area are usually sold under the name Constantinople nuts). Later the tree became *nux avellina*, suggesting that nut production was centred in southern Italy, around the area of Avellino in the Campania region. This name was still in use in the seventeenth century, recorded by Jacob Bobart in his 1648 *Catalogue of the Trees and Plants in the Physicke Garden of the University of Oxford*. However, Evelyn uses two names, *Nux sylvestiris* or *Corylus* to describe the Hazel. A few years earlier Tradescant senior had noted five separate hazels, including *Corylus sylvestris* – all today either *Corylus avellana* or the filbert *C. maxima*, indigenous to the Balkans. Tradescant's hazels included a Red Filbert, *Corylus fructu rubro sativa*, and a Long Filbert, *C. fructu oblongo sativa*, and Evelyn likewise mentions filberts, which suggests that they were widely known and grown then.

Filberts are sometimes confused with cobnuts (which were called cobble nuts). Filberts, from the French *noix de filbert* or St Philibert's Nut, so named as they ripen for his feast day, 22 August – come from *C. maxima*, and have a longer outer husk, which closes over the top of the nut. *C. avellana*, the native species, produces the cob, which has a shorter outer casing, the nut not being enclosed. John Evelyn only mentions nuts to say that trees are best propagated from them, 'which you shall sow … towards the end of February', and advises on how to preserve them against vermin – rats, voles and so on; of course he did not have to contend with the ravenous appetite of the Grey Squirrel (*Sciurus carolinensis*), which was introduced from North America during the nineteenth century. To plant a 'coryletum' or copse of hazel, the nuts should be planted about 'a yard distance' (1 metre), and he recommends letting the plants make at least twelve years' growth before the first felling; after this initial cut, succeeding coppicing can be every seven or eight years.

Hazel wood seems to have been used for a wide range of domestic or industrial purposes, including poles, spars, hoops, forks, fishing rods, springs for catching birds, faggots and cudgels. It was also a good fuel wood for manufacturing gunpowder, until Alder superseded it. Evelyn says there is no wood that clarifies

Filberts.

wine sooner, and riding whips can be made of it, as can rods for divining water or minerals – adding sceptically 'if that tradition be no imposture'. For its usefulness in the making of hurdles and wattles, the hazel is, he says, 'above all the trees of the wood'. Hazel hurdles were good not only for enfolding sheep but for making walkways around Christian oratories; they were also used at Glastonbury for constructing the first buildings. Using them in this way, he tells us, mixed with coarse mortar, loam and straw, to 'enclose divers humble cottages, sheds, and outhouses in the country', was a widespread practice, which commends them as being strong and lasting.

What John Evelyn does not get involved with is the folklore associated with the tree, but it is inevitable that the Hazel, having been so long domesticated, should have beliefs, stories and half-truths attached to it. For instance, there is a superstition that it was a switch of Hazel St Patrick wielded to drive all the snakes out of Ireland, and in Sweden oats had to be stirred with a hazel twig to ensure that the horses eating them were protected from the 'evil eye'. The tree was apparently renowned for its association with Thor, the Teutonic god of thunder, but most sinister of all was the Hazel's connection with witches. The very word witch is derived from the Anglo-Saxon *wie-en*, to bend, which originally referred to the Hazel's natural suppleness and the pliant nature of the wood, and led to the names of wych- or witch-hazel (*wicce* was also an early word for witches). So it is unsurprising that the Hazel was believed to have magical properties.

A Hazel coppice in Dorset.

Of the Poplar, Aspen and Abele

Populus Salicaceae

WHITE POPLAR/ABELE (*Populus alba*):

INTRODUCED AT A VERY EARLY UNKNOWN DATE;
15–20M (50–80FT) IN HEIGHT; CATKINS OUT BEFORE
LEAVES (LATE MARCH) 4–8CM (1.5–3IN) LONG. LEAVES
UNFOLD WHITE FROM DENSE HAIRS, UPPER SURFACE
DEVELOPS SHINY DARK GREY-GREEN, UNDER-SURFACE
REMAINING WHITE

THERE ARE ABOUT THIRTY SPECIES in the genus *Populus*; they are in the same family as the willows and share the willows' liking for having their roots in moisture or growing on the edge of riverbanks. All poplars, John Evelyn writes, are 'hospitable trees, for anything thrives under their shade'. They are native to the northern temperate regions and there are two species indigenous to Britain: the Aspen, *Populus tremula*, and a subspecies of the Black Poplar, *Populus nigra* subsp. *betulifolia*. Growing as if they were natives, but probably introduced and now naturalized, are the White Poplar, *P. alba*, which originated from central and western Europe, and central to west Asia, and the Grey Poplar, *Populus canescens*,

with which the former is often confused. As they are so alike, botanists are unsure about the true origins of the Grey Poplar, which is considered by some to be a hybrid between the Aspen and the White Poplar. Evelyn also knew *P. alba* as the Abele, a word originating in The Netherlands, where the tree was cultivated and grown extensively. He notes that it is a 'finer sort of white poplar', which was imported from the large nurseries in Flanders (like the Lime Tree). The White Poplar is much larger than the Grey. Both sucker freely, which means that they can 'be raised in abundance by every set or slip'.

*LEFT: Lombardy Poplars (*Populus nigra '*Italica'*), introduced from northern Italy in 1758, beside the River Dordogne in France.*

The native Aspen, *P. tremula*, is the smallest of all the poplars, and also the noisiest, because of its very flattened leaf stalk clattering in the wind. The Scots poet Patrick Hannay (d.*c.*1629), a near contemporary of Evelyn, describes the noise in a poem dated 1622 that would have come in for some criticism had he been writing now:

The quaking aspen light and thin,
To the air, light passage gives:
Resembling still
The trembling ill
Of tongues of womankind,
Which never rest
But still are prest
To wave with every wind.

*Aspen (*Populus tremula*) is a native of the whole of Europe, North Africa and Asia. It grows abundantly in northern and western Scotland, and also on damp sites in rocky valley bottoms and on hillsides.*

Bobart's Oxford catalogue of 1648 and Tradescant junior's second list of 1656 record the aspen as *P. Lybica* and *P. tremula sive Lybica* respectively, presumably believing its home was Libya. However, although it is a native of North Africa, it is also indigenous to Europe (including Britain and in particular Scotland) and eastern Asia. Perhaps John Tradescant senior collected a particularly good strain when he joined an expedition sailing from Plymouth in 1620 against the Barbary pirates. He is known to have botanized in Algeria and Spain and returned with a few treasures – including 'a greater or double blossomed wilde pomegranate tree' whose flowers were 'farre more beautifull' (*Punica granatum* f. *pleno*).

No one seems to know why the Black Poplar is so called. The native *P. nigra* subsp. *betulifolia*, which in the male species produces long deep red catkins, is a magisterial tree in the landscape. Evelyn believed it was unusual to see it growing. However, it grows well in East Anglia, and its features can be recognized in the paintings of John Constable (1776–1837) of that region. (Because of its ability to cope with pollution, it later became a familiar sight planted around industrial sites, railway stations and factories, particularly in the north of England, gaining the sobriquet 'Manchester Poplar'.)

Evelyn also writes about 'a poplar in Virginia of a very peculiar shaped leaf, as if the point of it were cut off, which grows very well with the curious amongst us to a considerable stature', continuing, 'I conceive it was first brought over by John Tradescant under the name of the Tulip tree, but is not that I find taken notice of in any our Herbals, I wish we had more of them.' In fact we still know it as the Tulip Tree, *Liriodendron tulipifera*, and it had indeed been introduced only a few years prior to the writing of *Sylva*, so it had had little time to become known or an acceptable tree in the landscape. Tradescant listed it as *Populus alba Virginiana Tradescanti*. Closely related to the Magnolia, Linnaeus gave the tree its own genus of *Liriodendron* and placed it in the *Magnoliaceae* family. A second species was discovered at the beginning of the twentieth century in China and introduced by Ernest Henry Wilson (1876–1930), who was plant-hunting on behalf of the London-based Veitch Nursery. This was called *Liriodendron chinense*, and is a native of China and Vietnam.

As to the poplars' practical application, Evelyn thinks the best use for them is planted as avenues or walks. However, he goes on to say that the timber 'is incomparable for all sorts of white wooden vessels, as trays, bowls, and other turners ware, and of especial use for the bellow-maker'. The lightness of the wood is useful for making carts, and as props for both vines and hops; the prunings and loppings may be stored against a time of expensive fuel, 'but the truth is it burns untowardly and rather moulders away'.

Black Poplar (Populus nigra) bark: grey-brown and very deeply fissured into short broad ridges.

Of the Alder

Alnus Betulaceae

COMMON ALDER (*Alnus glutinosa*):
19M (65FT) IN HEIGHT; DECIDUOUS;
NATIVE OF EUROPE TO SIBERIA
(INCLUDING BRITAIN), AND NORTH
AFRICA

THE WORD ALDER IS an early corruption of the ancient Latin name for the *Alnus* genus, of which there are some thirty-five species in total. In Europe and North Africa, there are five species with numerous sported varieties, but the only one native to Britain is the Common Alder, *A. glutinosa*, 'the most faithful lover of watery and boggy places', as John Evelyn notes.

The tree reaches about 19 metres (65ft) in maturity, and has a rather straggly untidy nature when young, but it later broadens to a conical shape. The male catkins show as dark purple in winter, and shed their yellow pollen over a long period in spring. It grows wild along riverbanks and in boggy land, and can grow at an altitude of up to 488 metres (1,600ft). The Alder has a utilitarian nature, and has never been classed as an ornamental tree. William Bean, the early twentieth-century curator of the Royal Botanic Gardens, Kew, wrote that it had 'not much to recommend it being brought into the garden'.

Evelyn praises the timber as being the most resistant of all timbers to waterlogging: 'it will harden like a very stone [if] it lie continually under water'. He points out that the Rialto Bridge in Venice, 'which bears a vast weight', is supported by alder wood. In Britain, as in Normandy, the wood was prized, rather more mundanely, for the manufacture of clogs and heels for shoes. Evelyn gives a long list of useful items that could be fashioned from the wood, including water pipes, troughs, sluices, pumps, trenchers (flat plates), hop and vine poles; at Windsor Castle in 1253, alder poles were delivered from the surrounding forest, for use in supporting the vines in the King's garden. Not only is the wood useful: the bark is 'precious to dyers', tanners and leather dressers, and ink can be made from a combination of the bark and fruits. Evelyn also advises that fresh leaves 'applied to the naked sole of the foot' will 'refresh the surbated [foot-sore] traveller'.

Like the Birch, the Alder was not highly thought of by the forester, or husbandman, as he was then called. John Evelyn notes that they 'take excessive pains in stubbing up their alders, wherever they meet them in the boggy places of their grounds, with the same indignation as one would extirpate the most pernicious weeds'. As the trees show such resistance to flooding, he is surprised that they are not more planted 'about the Thames, to fortify and prevent the mouldering of the walls, and the violent weather they are exposed to'. Environmental officers take note.

Propagation can be either by seed – 'so they raise them in Flanders, and make wonderful profit' – or by truncheons (stout cuttings), which should be firmly planted some 1.32–1.5 metres (4–5ft) apart during the winter, and 'when they have struck root you may cut them, which will cause them to spring in clumps, and to shoot out into many useful poles'. Evelyn also describes another method, 'after the Jersey manner'. This is to place a bound group of truncheons with their ends in water, and keep them there through the winter, 'till towards spring, by which season they will have contracted a swelling spire or knurr which being set does never fail of growing and striking root'. All three of the methods Evelyn detailed 300 years ago are valid today.

The Alder Tree was recorded twice in early times: first by Aelfric during the tenth century and later in the fourteenth century by Geoffrey Chaucer, himself a forester. The *Alnus* is absent from both of the two seventeenth-century Tradescant lists. However, the Oxford catalogue of 1648 includes *Alnus vulgaris*, the Common Alder, which is obviously *A. glutinosa*, and a second one recorded as the Black Alder, *Alnus nigra baccifera*. This is unknown today. Since *nigra baccifera* means 'black berry bearing', perhaps it was a distinct variety with a darker berry. It could possibly have been the Grey Alder, *A. incana*, which has a wide dispersal over all of Europe, and also in North America; it is recorded as a 1780 introduction into Britain, but as it is the second most common alder after *A. glutinosa* it could have made an earlier entry.

The name alder has also been adopted as the common name of a number of other plants: the indigenous Alder Buckthorn, *Rhamnus frangula*, is one; in America, two plants have 'alder' in their names – a holly, the Winterberry or Black Alder, *Ilex verticillata*, introduced into Britain in the eighteenth century, and a shrub, the White Alder, *Clethra acuminate*, which arrived in Britain a little later in 1806. There are also two trees from South Africa called alder – the Red Alder, *Cunonia capensis,* and the Broad-leaved Alder, *Platylophus trifoliate.*

Of the Withy, Sally Ozier and Willow

Salix Salicaceae

Osier (*Salix viminalis*):
10M (35FT) IN HEIGHT; NATIVE TO
BRITAIN AND CENTRAL AND WESTERN
EUROPE; DECIDUOUS CATKINS OPEN IN
APRIL, MAY BEFORE THE LEAVES; LEAVES
ARE NARROW WITH INROLLED MARGINS
(WAVE-LIKE)

T HE *SALIX* GENUS IS a large one, comprising some 300 species. Botanists had a difficult time identifying them over 200 years ago, when far fewer had been discovered, as Linnaeus remarked; and time has not improved the situation. The reason is that a lot of the species are similar, and there is much blurring of the dividing lines between them. There are at least seventy species indigenous to Europe, of which seventeen or eighteen are native, and all have hybridized freely between themselves.

Evelyn names them as: 'The Common White Willow, the Black, and the Hard-black, the Rose of Cambridge, the Black-withy, the Round-long Sallow, the longest Sallow, the Lesser-broad leaved Willow, Silver Sallow, Upright broad-willow, Repent [creeping] broad-leafed, the Red-Stone, the Lesser Willow, the Strait Dwarf, the Creeper, the Black-low-Willow, the Willow-bay and the Ozier'. Of these eighteen, only six may be identified with any certainty today. The 'Common White Willow' must be *Salix alba*, which retains the same vernacular name. The 'Willow-bay' is *S. pentandra*, and again its name has not altered. This is one of the handsomest of all willows; the leaves are a brilliant green, and when crushed, give off a fragrance. The 'Ozier' is *S. viminalis*; its common name – now spelt osier – is a Gaulish- and Breton-derived word, meaning riverbed. This is a shrub or small tree, frequently coppiced and used for making baskets, fences and hurdles. Evelyn's 'Silver Sallow' may be the Silver Willow, *S. alba* var. *sericea*, its variety name *sericea* meaning silky. The 'Strait Dwarf' may be either the Dwarf Willow, *S. herbacea*, the smallest of all the native species, or *S. reticulata*, which is another prostrate species. Either 'the Creeper' or the 'Repent broad-leafed' could be the modern Creeping Willow, *S. repens*.

When John Evelyn says 'The Withy is a reasonable large tree, and fit to be planted on high banks', he is referring to the Crack Willow, *Salix fragilis*. Native throughout Europe (including Greece) and Russia, with numerous derivatives from the species, the Crack Willow has a string of other vernacular names attached to it, including sally and wully. If left unpollarded, it is a somewhat sprawling tree with wide, spreading heavy branches; the weight of these causes the branches to be easily snapped off, giving it its rather alarming name. Evelyn explains that the Crack Willow root penetrates deeper than other willows, but is the slowest grower; the twigs and the peelings of the branches are of great use as withies for binding together a number of poles, for tying poles in topiary work, in vineyards or when making arbours, for tying espaliered fruit to their frames and so on. He talks of two principal sorts of withies, calling one the 'hoary' and the other the 'red'. According to Evelyn it was Pliny who first recorded the latter as the Greek Willow, 'the toughest and fittest to bind'.

The White Willow, *S. alba*, is the largest of the British species, commonly planted along riverbanks. The leaves, with their silvery grey-green sheen, stand out in a landscape, presumably earning it its name early in its history. A variety,

Creeping Willow (Salix repens): 30–60cm (1–2ft) in height. Native of Europe (including Britain) and northern Asia. Deciduous. Spreads by underground stems.

S. alba var. *caerulea*, is the Cricket Bat Willow. This came to light in Britain some time around 1700, confining its growth to the eastern counties, where it was called the Blue Willow – hence its original name of *S. caerulea* (meaning dark blue). It was only later found to provide the best wood for cricket bats, although other willows, *S. viridis, S. fragilis* and *S. alba*, may also be used.

According to John Evelyn, all willows, including withies and sallys, benefit from being both planted and harvested close to the rising of a new moon, particularly during the early spring. Again Evelyn complains about imports from abroad; most of the osiers for sale in England were from either France (around the Loire) or Flanders. Evelyn says that John Tradescant had earlier returned with a small 'ozier from St. Omers in Flanders, which makes incomparable net works [lattice work]'.

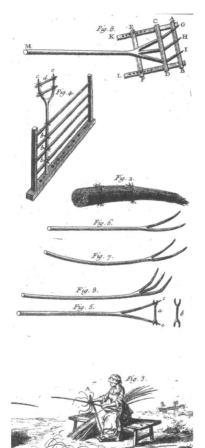

Pole-producing 'sallyes', Evelyn remarks, are held in the greatest esteem. They have a clear close grain, and, as he explains, they are useful once they have made their second year's growth. In the first year the length of the poles will be 2–4 metres (8–12 ft); the third year's growth will produce wood strong enough to make rakes and pike staves; and in the fourth year the hardened timber may be employed by the forester to make utensils, such as trenching ploughs, harrows, rakes (especially the teeth), forks and other heavy tools. Fruit baskets, beehives, pails (using cleft willow), shoemaker's lasts, sieves, backs of chairs (known as dorsers), trenchers and trays are just some of the uses to which he notes the wood can be put.

Stripping bark from osiers ready for basket-making; stages in making tools from a single piece of wood; a bundle of osiers as used by coopers for firing the inside of barrels.

Most of us can recognize a Willow when we see one, but there are two in particular with which we are familiar. One is the Pussy Willow, *S. caprea*, which in the female form has silver catkins. It has two other names, the Great Sallow and, for at least 400 years, the Goat Willow – the latter presumably because goats could nibble the low growth of the shrub. It is a widespread native of Europe and western Asia. Branches are often used to represent the palm on Palm Sunday. The second tree is easily recognizable by its distinctive shape: the

Weeping Willow, *S. babylonica*, which, despite its species name, is indigenous to the western provinces of China, and not to Iraq. John Evelyn probably never saw it growing on the Continent, as it is believed to have arrived in Europe some thirty or more years after his travels; the French traveller and plant collector Joseph Pitton de Tournefort (1656–1708) is credited with the tree's introduction

*The Cricket-Bat Willow (*Salix alba var. caerulea*) is only known as a female clone of a variable hybrid. The tree can reach a height of 30m (100ft). It has strong pyramidal growth and erect branching.*

(probably from the Middle East) some time during the 1680s, but it was supposedly another decade before it was introduced into Britain. However, there was plenty of French influence on gardens in England at that time, and French designers were creating gardens, so it is likely that the tree was already known, having been imported much earlier than its supposed date of about 1699.

The *Salix aquatica* noted on the Oxford Botanic Garden list and the *S. humilis angustifolia* that the Tradescants recorded were both the later single Linnaean-named Purple Willow, *S. purpurea*. This is one of a trio of natives – including the Almond-leaved Willow, *S. triandra*, and the Common Osier, *S. viminalis*. All three are known as osiers and used for basket-making. Between them they seemed to have spawned a great variety of 'different species', as Evelyn says, each with a distinguishing name, including the Gelsters – Horse, Black and Shrivelled, 'in which Suffolk abounds'. There was the Snake Ozier, the Swallow Tail and a collection of Golstones – including the Fine, the Hard and the Soft, which Evelyn singles out as being 'brittle and worst of all the Golstones'. The Red-bud, Dicks, Kecks and Welch were varieties of the Purple Willow. The Common Osier, *S. viminalis*, rejoiced in the names Long Skein, Brown Merrian and Yellow Osier (which Evelyn knew) and was used all over Europe for basketry, while the third species, the Almond-leaved Willow, *S. triandra*, attracted such delights as Jelstiver, Glibskins, Black Mauls, Mottled Spaniards and Pomeranian. Today over sixty named osier species, varieties and cultivars are grown in Britain.

Evelyn writes that the Willow 'yields the most chaste and coolest shade in the hottest season of the day' and that 'physicians prescribe it to feverish persons, permitting them [fresh boughs] to be placed even about their beds, as a safe and comfortable refigerium [consolation]'. Though he makes no mention of it, the Willow had long been known for its efficacy in pain relief – Pedanius Dioscorides in his first-century *De Materia Medica* recommended drinking water in which Willow had been soaked as a relief from all sorts of aches and pains. Nearly 1,800 years later, in 1827, a French chemist succeeded in identifying salicin as the active ingredient in Willow that helped relieve pain, and in 1838 salicylic acid, also present in Willow, was extracted from another damp-loving plant, Meadowsweet, *Filipendula ulmaria*, then known as *Spiraea ulmaria*. In 1899 acetylsalicylic was produced in Germany and given the name aspirin, based on the Meadowsweet's German name, *Spirnsaure*.

Osier (Salix viminalis).

*Willow Trees (*Salix babylonica)*, Hampshire.*

Of Fences,
Quick-Sets, Etc.

COMMON HAWTHORN (*Crataegus monogyna*):
NATIVE TO EUROPE (INCLUDING BRITAIN); DECIDUOUS;
HEIGHT TO 10.5M (35FT); FRAGRANT FLOWERS OPEN
MID-MAY; FRUIT, WHICH CONTAIN ONLY ONE STONE,
RIPEN IN SEPTEMBER

IN THIS CHAPTER JOHN EVELYN departs from his established habit of examining a single tree species and covers the trees and shrubs that he considers are the essential ingredients for creating and maintaining a hedge. This must have been one of the most useful chapters he wrote, and seventeenth-century landowners, farmers and husbandmen could have found in it much helpful advice. He begins with an apt quotation from Thomas Tusser (*c.*1520–80):

If cattle or cony may enter to crop
Young oak is in danger of losing his top.

Evelyn's message is clear: plants must be sufficiently guarded against damage from external causes, as 'Young trees once cropped hardly ever recover. It is the bane of all our most hopeful timber' – a statement that is as true today as it was 300 years ago. The 'wicked hunters' who make gaps in hedges for their dogs and horses, as well as, most disastrously, the 'venomous bitings' and treading of cattle, all compete to cause havoc. John Evelyn makes a plea: if 500 sheep are worth the care of a shepherd, 'are not five thousand oaks worth the fencing and the inspection of a Hayward?' (A hayward was an official employed to ensure that the fencing of enclosed fields was strong enough to withstand cattle grazing on common land.)

The Quickthorn or 'Quick-sets' to which Evelyn refers are hedges or thickets or 'spinetum' (spinneys) that are 'set' with live slips or cuttings of Hawthorn, *Crataegus monogyna*. The word Quickset has been used in the context of hedge-making since at least the middle of the fifteenth century.

Confined to the northern hemisphere, there are over 200 species of *Crataegus*, but Evelyn concentrates on the two native Hawthorns, *C. monogyna* and *C. laevigata*, which are both abundant and variable. These, he says, make the 'very best of common hedges' and should form the backbone of an animal-proof barrier. Although innumerable subspecies and hybrids occur, including the Glastonbury Thorn, *C. monogyna* 'Biflora', the Hawthorn, a shrub or small tree, has never lost its ability to form an impenetrable barrier. It has a long-recorded pedigree in England, despite its small size, scrubby appearance and relatively short life. As Dr Oliver Rackham points out, it is the tree most frequently named in Anglo-Saxon charters, outstripping the oak by a wide margin, which suggests that it was both ubiquitous and recognized by many. Perhaps that is why it is has attracted about sixteen different names, including Agar and Hoppety-haw (for the fruit). In fact single-species hedges of hawthorn did not become a major part of the domestic landscape until the enclosures of the eighteenth and nineteenth centuries, when it has been calculated that some 200,000 miles of Quickset hedges were planted.

Hawthorn blossom.

John Evelyn gives detailed instructions on to how to create a hedge, describing the making of the bank of earth, or fosse, and the planting of the slips – 'two in a foot space is sufficient … adding now and then at equal spaces of twenty or thirty foot, a young oakling or elm sucker, ash or the like, which will come in time to be ornamental standards and good timber'. He mentions that in Hertfordshire the custom is for 'Crab stock' or Crab Apple to be planted in this way as an ornamental tree and warns against leaving 'great trees … that commonly make gaps for cattle'.

In his thorough way, Evelyn goes on to explain how the hedge should be maintained. The young plants should be kept weed free (he emphasizes the need to eradicate the bramble – still sound advice) and after six years' growth, the new hedge will be ready for 'plashing' – that is, weaving or entwining. This is what we know today as layering or hedging, when main growths are partly slashed through (at a slant), bent and woven into the length of the hedge and tied in with sideshoots to thicken the whole. 'This being done very close and thick, makes an impregnable hedge in a few years.' Planting and maintaining good sound hedges to keep animals in or out of cultivated land was recognizably vital work, and one of the fundamental chores of rural communities for generations; today, with the increasing use of mechanical aids and electric fencing in the past hundred years, it has lost much of its significance.

Evelyn discusses the value of a number of different trees and shrubs, mostly native, which he considers might be used for making hedges and thickets. Thickets were small areas of dense underwood and low trees, usually developed on scrub ground where it was difficult either to plough the land or for animals to graze; these were helpful for sheltering stock and later useful for harbouring game birds. One of Evelyn's most seemingly bizarre suggestions for a hedge (in England, anyway) is the 'American Yucca'. However, *Yucca filamentosa*, sometimes known as Adam's Needle, does make a spiky thicket. It is an eastern American plant, found between New Jersey and Florida; Evelyn notes, 'it is a hardier plant then we take it to be, for it will suffer our sharpest winter, as I have seen by experience, without that trouble and care of setting it in cases in our conservatories.' It was probably introduced to England by John Tradescant junior, who records it in his catalogue of 1656 as the 'Virginian Yucca with shorter and narrower leaves, *Jucca Virgininiana angustiore and breviore folio.*' It is just possible that it was pointed out to Evelyn when he travelled to Lambeth to visit John

Tradescant in August of the following year. The Yucca's first recorded flowering in England took place some twenty years later, from plants (probably donated by Tradescant junior) growing in the Oxford Botanic Garden.

Evelyn draws attention to a number of hedging species that can be grown from seed. He recommends propagating Holly this way – refuting a tradition that the seeds 'will not sprout till they be passed through the maw of a thrush', saying 'this is an error as I am able to testify'; likewise Yew, Sloes, Crab Apple, even *Phillyrea angustifolia* – a shrub native to the Mediterranean but recorded in England from the 1590s. Some seeds, he says, 'being invested with a very hard integument [skin, shell or husk] will now and then suffer imprisonment two whole years under the earth, and impatience of this does often frustrate the expectation of the resurrection of divers seeds of this nature'. Again displaying his enquiring mind, Evelyn points out a different way of sowing seeds, first described by the Roman writer on agriculture, Columella in about 60 BC. The method, which can still be used today, involves rubbing seeds (of hips and haws in particular) into the crevices of a bass rope – a rope made from plant fibres – 'and then burying it in a trench'.

Evelyn describes how in Devon 'they build two walls with their stones, setting them edgeways two and one between, and so it rises'. Cornwall secures its land and woods with 'high mounds and on them they plant acorns, whose roots bind in the looser mould [earth] and so form a double and most durable fence, encircling the fields with a coronet of trees.' Another method is to use 'prickly furzes of which they have a taller sort, such as the French employ for the same purpose in Bretaigne [Brittany]'. He calls this plant *Genista spinosa* (as do Tradescant and Bobart), but today its name is *Ulex europaeus*. Commonly now known as Gorse, it was also known as whin or furze. Although it is an aggressive grower, its cheerful yellow flower lightens a journey by road when one is driving past a bank of the golden glory. There always seem to be gorse flowers to admire; as everyone knows, 'kissing's out of fashion when the whin is out of blossom.' Its usefulness for stockproofing

Gorse, Furze, Whin (Ulex europaeus). Dried material was at one time much used for heating both domestic and bakers' ovens.

had been known about for centuries; the Normans are believed to have introduced the shrub into Ireland during the eleventh century for that purpose.

Evelyn is at his most verbose when describing Gorse's qualities. He recommends feeding the young and tender tops to a lean and sickly horse; the wood, he says, is an excellent fuel for the house; the thickets are 'a great refuge for fowl and other game'. The county of Hereford has great 'thickets of furzes' and in Devon – where he believes the best husbandmen come from – gorse seed sown on the worst ground turns the rankest of land into rich wood. In Brittany it 'is sometimes sown no less than twelve yards [11m] thick for a speedy profitable and impenetrable mound'. In Galicia Gorse was called 'tojo' and played an essential part in the rural economy, being the food of the Galician donkeys, as well as their bedding. As usual, all he says is as true today as it was then. John Evelyn makes no mention of the custom, at least in Cornwall, of burning the Gorse off on common land (as a control) or the practice of collecting the remaining burnt wood known as 'smutties' for fuel. The thickets make good refuges for wildlife, including pheasants, and so in the nineteenth and twentieth centuries when Viscount Clifden and the Robarts family of Lanhydrock, near Bodmin, wished to hold a pheasant shoot the timing of the burning was crucial: it had to be delayed so that it did not coincide with the shoot.

The Elder (*Sambucus nigra*), then known as *Sambucus vulgaris*, was another plant that Evelyn considered to be a useful contributor to a hedge. A native shrub, and long in cultivation, it is a tough survivor. Evelyn writes, 'if the medicinal properties of the leaves, bark, berries etc were thoroughly known I cannot tell what our countryman could ail for which he might not fetch a remedy', for instance, an ointment made with butter and the young buds and leaves in May 'is most sovereign for aches, shrunk sinews etc'. However, he makes no mention of the traditional use of the berries in a concoction for soothing sore throats – nor of use of the flowers for making 'champagne'. Evelyn warns, though, that the plant has an insalubrious smell, as does the Box, adding that he would grow neither 'near my habitation'.

A second occasional hedge tree Evelyn recommends is the Spindle Tree, or Prick-timber, *Euonymus europaeus*. He records that it was also known as *Fusanum*, which has an interesting echo in the nineteenth century when a charcoal crayon made from spindle wood – which is very hard – was known as a fusain. Two

*Elder (*Sambucus nigra*).*

other trees he suggests planting intermittently through the length of a hedge are the 'wild cornel' or the Dogwood, *Cornus sanguinea* – whose vernacular name is believed by experts to have nothing to do with the animal but to be a corruption of the old word 'dags', meaning butchers' skewers – and the Wayfaring Tree, *Viburnum opulus*.

Without exception, hedge plants have to be sturdy 'doers', as it is a tough life making one's living in a hedge – sometimes being cut back or layered, putting up with being eaten by sheep or cattle, drought or swamp conditions, and nowadays, depending on the site, continual vibration from passing traffic and pollution. All the trees and shrubs that Evelyn brought to the attention of the seventeenth-century world are still suitable for this purpose today. None is difficult to grow, all are easily propagated by cuttings or growing from seed.

Many hedges and boundaries in Britain were first made by our remote ancestors and have been in use for thousands of years. Adapted over the centuries to different needs and (sometimes) legal requirements, they seemed to reflect the permanent nature of the countryside. However, the invention and use during the last half-century of mechanical diggers and hedge trimmers has enabled the easy removal of boundaries to enlarge fields, widen roads and so on, effecting in many instances a depressing alteration of the landscape. The problem, though, is not new. In 1792 the *House of Commons Journal* reported: 'The grubbing up of Hedge Rows is become general, and the Growth of Timber in them is thereby totally destroyed, owing to the great Price given for Corn since the Bounty took place for exporting of Corn and Beer, which gives every Farmer encouragement to grub Hedge Rows up and convert them into Corn Land' – sentiments that are all too familiar today.

Spindle berries (Euonymus europaeus). Native to Europe (including Britain).

Of the Fir, Pine Pinaster, Pitch Tree

Abies, Picea, Pinus Pinaceae

SCOTS PINE (*Pinus sylvestris*):
TO 36M (120FT) IN HEIGHT; NATIVE TO
WESTERN AND NORTHERN EUROPE (INCLUDING
BRITAIN), AND RUSSIA; CONIFEROUS; BRITAIN'S
ONLY NATIVE PINE

THE WORD FIR HAS BEEN part of the English language since earliest times, but it originated in the heart of fir country – Norway, Finland and the Baltic – and has a pedigree derived from Old Norse and High German, whence it was taken into Middle English. The name has had a muddling life, writers using it indiscriminately to identify two genera, *Abies* (the Silver Fir) and *Picea* (the Spruce Fir), as well as our one native Scots Pine, *Pinus sylvestris*.

John Evelyn is no exception, saying: 'There are of the Fir two principal species, the Male which is the bigger tree most beautiful and tapering, and of a harder wood, the female which is much softer, and whiter … that which knowing

workmen call the Dram.' 'Dram' was short for Drammen, a port in Norway from which the wood was exported. The 'two principal species' Evelyn refers to are *Picea abies*, the Norway Spruce, and *Abies alba*, the European or Common Silver Fir. They are closely related and look very similar. There is a small but simple way of distinguishing a Fir (*Abies*) from a Spruce (*Picea*) and that is by pulling off a living leaf from a shoot: in the Fir the leaf breaks off sharply at the base, leaving it cleanly, but with the Spruce some of the bark is torn away. The timber of both was used, but particular value was placed on the yellow spruce timber for being long and straight. Pepys notes in his diary in June 1662, when as Clerk to the Navy Board he was shown around the Wapping shipbuilding yard, that the wood was 'esteemed much before the white for flooring and wainscot'. There were two other timber types named for the ports of shipment from Norway: Svinesund and Christiania.

Pine, fir and spruce had been exported from Norway and the Baltic into East Anglian ports from early in the thirteenth century; among the first of the records is an order for scaffolding pine poles, for delivery to Ely Cathedral, which was then under construction. Four hundred years later it continued to be imported, for use in shipbuilding. Evelyn writes: 'For masts etc those of Prussia which we call Spruce and Norway (especially from Gottenberg) are the best, unless we had more commerce of them from … New England which are preferable to any of them.' Almost at the same time (1664), Pepys and the Navy

*Norway Spruce (*Picea abies*) seen growing in the great northern forests of the Baltic.*

The Classification or 'Rating' of Warships in the Seventeenth Century

Warships were defined by their rating – that is, the size of the vessel and the number of cannons mounted. There were six rates: first, second and third rates were Ships of the Line. In the twentieth century their equivalents would have been battleships and battlecruisers. First rates mounted one hundred cannons, or more; seconds, ninety or so; and thirds, sixty to eighty cannons. Fourth rates, which mounted fifty to sixty cannon, were the cruisers of the day, while fifth and sixth rates mounted between thirty and fifty cannons; those with thirty or less were classed as frigates. The convention amongst all navies was that fifth- and sixth-rate vessels were not to be fired on by Ships of the Line unless they opened fire first. Usually first and second raters had three gundecks for their cannons, which were mounted broadside; third and fourth had two gundecks and fifth and sixth only one deck. The majority of the armament was fired laterally; there were relatively few bow or stern chasers.

Board were concluding a 'great contract' for the delivery of 3,000 loads of timber. A load was 1.415 cubic metres (50 cu. ft.), so 3,000 loads was 4,245 cubic metres – enough to fill 133 tennis courts. The contractor, Sir William Warren, got supplies where he could, but most undoubtedly came from the Baltic and Norway, including forty-six very large pieces to make into beams for the broadest parts of second raters.

The imported timber was also used for upper works, decks and bulkheads. Spars (undressed timber) of various sizes were used to manufacture bowsprits and booms. Balks were larger pieces of undressed timber, and Norwegian uphroes were extra-long spars of 8.5–9.7 metres (28–32ft) long. All this was pointed out to Pepys on his visit, as well as the fact that timber shipped from Norway was quickly accessible and usually cheaper than that delivered from the Baltic; the cargo did not need to pass through Danish waters, and so did not have to pay dues to Denmark. The everyday name for all this wood was 'Deales', as Pepys calls it – we still use the word deal today.

Imported timber arrived – as it still does – at ports all around the United Kingdom: ports such as Shoreham-by-Sea in Sussex, which handled trade in deal with the Baltic countries, as did Liverpool, where in the eighteenth century the timber trade steadily increased, both with the Old World countries and with the rapidly expanding Empire and America. The various cargoes of timber were consigned to timber merchants; for instance in 1769, wood was imported from Riga in the Baltic by the cargo vessel the *Spring* for sale by the Liverpool firm Beetham and Dowson; six years later in August 1775 the same firm received timber from the *Minerva*, which arrived from Falmouth, Massachusetts. Later it advertised for sale 'all kinds of Mahogany and Oak, either in Logs Planks or Boards; likewise all sorts season'd Boards, Fincan, Walnut, Bark, Sheathing'. John Evelyn would have been interested in all the new and different timbers which were being imported into Britain, and would have been keen to receive the seeds and experiment with growing the trees.

European or Common Silver Fir (Abies alba) can grow at an altitude 800–1800m (2,600–6,000 ft). Its green cones mature to dark brown and measure 12cm x 3cm (4½in x 1½in).

The European Silver Fir, *Abies alba*, is one of about fifty species in this genus of evergreen conifers, whose home stretches across the northern latitudes. The shape of them all is mostly pyramidal and very symmetrical. Philip Miller of the Chelsea Physic Garden, writing nearly seventy years after *Sylva* was published, notes that a Sarjeant Newdigate introduced the tree from central Europe into Britain in 1603. John Evelyn eulogizes it, listing six attributes 'all which highly recommend it as an excellent improvement of husbandry, fit to be enjoyed ... that we may have masts, and those other materials of our own growth'.

The Spruce, *Picea*, is similar in many respects to the *Abies* genus: it is indigenous across the northern hemisphere; it is pyramidal in form; and again it is not a native of Britain. It is no wonder that trees have often been confused with each other over the past 400 or so years – although the Norway or Common Spruce, *P. abies*, has been growing here since the thirteenth century. Bobart's Oxford catalogue, compiled in 1648, seemingly records no Spruces, but does list '*Abies mas*. Male Firretree', and '*Abies foem* Female Firretree' – the same form that Evelyn uses to refer to the Fir and the Spruce. Such was the confusion between the two trees that in the following century Philip Miller was still calling the Norway Spruce *Abies picea*. Later in the eighteenth century Linnaeus named it *Pinus abies*. A hundred years on, botanists changed its name again: it reverted to the *Picea* genus, and the Norway Spruce became *P. excelsa*. Finally in 1881 it received the name *P. abies*, the name by which it is now known.

The tree's popularity has steadily increased, particularly following the Christmas of 1841, when it was singled out by Prince Albert to be brought indoors and decorated, following the custom of his native Germany; thereafter the tree gradually become known and grown as the Christmas tree. As a specimen tree in the landscape it has some merit, but planted in profusion on our upland hills it takes on the demeanour of the dark Arctic winters of its homeland. Even Evelyn noted that 'being planted reasonable close together [the trees] suffer nothing to thrive under them'.

No other spruce trees seem to have been introduced into Britain until the beginning of the eighteenth century, when two arrived. The first was the White Spruce, *Picea glauca,* a tough Canadian that is able to grow at a higher latitude than any other conifer. The leaves, when crushed, are evil smelling. The second was the Black Spruce, *P. mariana*, also a native of the northern USA, including Maryland (hence its name), and reputed to have been introduced first into the gardens of the Bishop of London, Henry Compton, an enthusiastic introducer of new plants to Fulham Palace. His responsibilities included the appointment of missionaries to North America and, being a keen gardener, he always ensured that the appointees were not only of a godly nature but keenly interested in horticulture as well. The Bishop received seeds and plants from the naturalist, botanist and missionary the Reverend John Banister (1650–92) in Virginia, and many others, including the explorer, naturalist and artist Mark Catesby (1682–1749) from North America, as well as Surgeon to the East India

Company Samuel Browne (d.1698) in India. John Evelyn paid a visit to the Bishop's Fulham garden in 1681.

About the planting of 'firretrees' – probably meaning both the Spruce and the Silver Fir – Evelyn says they 'are all of them easily raised of the kernels and nuts which may be gotton out of their cones'. Indeed they are, and unlike some deciduous trees, coniferous trees not only benefit from being grown from seed sown *in situ* as early as possible: they produce a much stronger growth when grown from seed – growing from cuttings is not recommended – and can be planted as soon as the ground is reasonably workable during January or February. On good authority John Evelyn claims that the seeds of pine and fir never fail to sprout if 'rolled on a fine compost made of sheeps-dung and scattered in February'; similarly he records a Spanish acquaintance saying that macerating the seeds 'five days in a childs urine, and three days in water' is 'an expeditious process for great plantations'. He also recommends plunging the whole cone (seeds and all) into an earthenware pot, letting it get frosted, and then applying a little warmth, whereupon the entire 'clod', as Evelyn calls it, will sprout; this is 'the safest course of all'.

There are about ninety species of the genus *Pinus*, which are distributed throughout the world and, like the Spruce and the Fir, originated in the northern temperate regions. The Pine that Evelyn writes about particularly is the Maritime Pine, *Pinus pinaster*, native to south-west Europe and the Mediterranean region. It is a tree long known in England, having been recorded here since the sixteenth century; and, as the name implies, it is the supreme tree for seaside planting, and the best adapted for any sandy soil. In England it became known as the Bournemouth Pine, as it was the most frequently planted pine in the neighbourhood. In the *départements* of Gironde and Landes, in south-west France, over 708,225 hectares (1.75 million acres) of previously arid sand became an economic and stable area after *P. pinaster* was planted there. A mature specimen of the tree is singularly picturesque, but although it is a very fast grower it looks rather gaunt and clumsy before it reaches that stage. The timber yielded by the tree is poor, but its value lies in the resin that can be produced from it.

Norway Spruce (Picea abies): a ripened cone 12.5–15cm (5–6in) long.

Resin (or rosin – the words are interchangeable), turpentine, tar and pitch are all either extruded from the living wood or produced from the timber of coniferous trees, particularly the *Pinus* species. In Europe the Maritime Pine, *P. pinaster*, and the Scots Pine, *P. sylvestris*, are used for this purpose, while in the United States the main source is the Longleaf Pine, *P. palustris*, the timber of which is known as Pitch Pine, and the Slash Pine or Cuban Pine, *P. caribaea*, both trees being native to the south-eastern states.

A Scots Pine (Pinus sylvestris) painted c.1903 by Ruth Brand at Invergarry.

Man has exploited this attribute for thousands of years, probably first in Asia, where the oldest word associated with all the substances, resin, derives from the Indo-European language. The sticky substances make a variety of gums, varnishes and paint thinners, as well as waterproof coverings, a recipe for which, before the invention of Wellington boots, included mutton fat, linseed oil, beeswax and resin, all melted and boiled together, and then brushed on dry and clean boots at the beginning of autumn.

Turpentine oil may be obtained either by distilling the exudates of the living pine, obtained by tapping into the tree – this is known as gum turpentine; or by shredding the timber and producing wood turpentine by steam distillation. Within the turpentine oil is the non-volatile resin, the two together being known as the oleoresins. Resin, when dried, is translucent, brittle and friable, and used mostly in soap, varnish, adhesive and paint manufacture. Dancers and gymnasts may recognize resin as the powder they press on the soles of their shoes to stop them from slipping on the stage or studio floor, and musicians with stringed instruments know that their bows and strings need to be treated regularly with it for, as described by an anonymous critic in 1642, 'Those who make musick with so harsh an instrument, need to have their bow well rosend before'. The substance was earlier known as colophony, from Colophon, a town in Lydia where the best resin was made. There are a number of other trees that extrude a viscous mixture from which turpentine oil can be produced. One is the European Larch, *Larix decidua*, introduced into Britain in about 1620. From this tree is produced a pale green substance known as Venice Turpentine, used for varnishes, in lithographic work and particularly to make sealing wax. *Abies balsamea*, the Balm of Gilead and a native of Canada, Nova Scotia and other parts of North America, yields from its cones and bark exudates from which is made a turpentine called Canada Balsam. This is used in the arts, and particularly in preserving microscopic objects. Strasburg Turpentine is made from the exudates extracted from the Silver Fir (*A. picea*).

Scots pine cones.

Because of their waterproofing qualities, tar and its derivative pitch were some of the most important ingredients of shipbuilding. Reed boats plying their trade on the Nile in 3000 BC were coated with the black sticky substance. However, man's ingenuity being what it is, tar and pitch became part of a terrifying liquid fire, eventually developed and refined for warfare by a Greek Syrian architect Callinicus during the seventh century and known throughout the Mediterranean as 'Greek fire'. A Russian chronicler records: 'The Greeks have a fire like lightning from the skies. They cast it against us and burned us so that we could not conquer them.' This early version of a flame-thrower or missile launcher, weighing anything up to 450kg (1,000lb), contained a mixture of pitch, turpentine, charcoal, sulphur, phosphorus, salt and quicklime, and spat fire and venom as it hurtled some 686 metres (750yd).

John Evelyn goes into great detail about how to extract tar from the Pine Tree. He draws from a presentation The Royal Society had received on the process of making tar and pitch in New England by John Winthrop, the son of the Governor of Massachusetts and later appointed Governor of Connecticut himself. Winthrop explained that wood was collected from two sources: one was

Barrels of resin awaiting export at the resin dockyards in Savannah, Georgia, 1903.

the detritus left following the annual firing of the undergrowth by the Indians, and the second naturally wind-blown trees. John Evelyn particularly emphasizes the gathering of 'knots' – 'that part where the bough is joined to the body of the tree' – left behind after felling and where the resin is strongest. The hearth for the firing was made of clay or loam, with channels and a gullet to allow the tar to run out freely, and built up to a height so that a cauldron or vessel could 'stand a little lower than the hearth to receive the tar as it runs out'. The wood, including the knots, was then piled on to the hearth and covered with a coat of loam or clay, 'leaving a small spiracle the top whereat to put the fire in' (much as in charcoal burning). Once the tar had been extracted, 'a kind of rude distillation' took place. The burned wood left behind was much prized as charcoal, particularly by smiths, as, having had all the resinous material removed, it did not spit. Another use for it was as candle wood: finger-thick pieces were burned to serve as candles, giving, so Evelyn was assured, a very good light, although producing 'much fuliginous smoke'. Candle wood was a familiar domestic item throughout New England, Virginia, and among the Dutch settlers as well.

So important to the navy were these different plant materials in building and maintaining wooden sailing ships that there were two distinct categories of naval storage. The turpentine and by-products collected from living trees were referred to as 'Gum naval stores'. 'Wood naval stores' were all derived from salvaged pine wood – timber, fallen bark, branches or extracted stumps or any last morsel, which was shredded and subjected to heat under pressure. Well aware of how important tar was to the navy, Samuel Pepys took the trouble, in 1662, to meet 'with old Mr Greene among the tarr-men', recording: '[I] did instruct myself in the nature and prices of tarr, but could not get Stockholme for use of the office [the naval yards] under £10 15s per last [a measure of tar, twelve barrels of 30 gallons each] which is a great price.' Cables and cordage were both manufactured from Hemp, *Cannabis sativa*, which was first spun into yarn and then slowly heated for about two days above a charcoal fire to soften it. After that the yarn was coated in tar to waterproof it, and transferred to the long sheds or ropeyards in the dockyard, where it was twisted into rope. During the winter of 1664 (while *Sylva* was being written) there had been a general shortage of rope throughout the navy, and the Naval Board, distrustful of buying in ready-made rope, was planning to construct both new ropeyards and stove-houses.

Scots pine
*(*Pinus sylvestris*).*

MASTS

Until the beginning of the seventeenth century masts for English ships and eventually the navy were usually felled from the huge Baltic forests. It had been discovered that coniferous timber was the most suitable for shipbuilding and masts in very early times. The Hebrew Prophet Ezekiel, writing in the sixth century BC, commented about the Phoenicians during the fall of Tyre: 'They have made all thy ship boards of fir trees of Senir: they have taken cedars of Lebanon to make masts for thee. Of the oaks of Bashan have they made thine oars.' Senir is now Mount Hermon, 2,814 metres (9,232ft) high, on the Lebanon/Syria border. It is often snow-capped (being the highest point on the eastern Mediterranean), so there would have been a plentiful supply of pines, fir and cypresses, for as John Evelyn says, the trees 'effect cold high and rocky grounds'.

The tree most suitable for manufacture into masts was the Scots Pine, *Pinus sylvestris*. It is indigenous over temperate Asia, and the whole of Europe, including Britain, where it is the single native coniferous species. Although home-grown pine would undoubtedly have been used on occasions, it had been discovered that both native Scots Pine and that grown further south in Europe lacked the elasticity of more northerly grown pine. Timber grown in northern latitudes has a higher resin content and therefore the required flexibility for masts.

The great northern forests stretching into Russia had been plundered for some 800 years for straight-trunked pines. As early as 1297 two ships sailed from Yarmouth to the Baltic and Norway to buy mast timber, and sailed again three years later. The *Cristofre*, also from Yarmouth, set forth in 1305 on the same quest. During a period of twenty years from 1600 over one hundred shiploads of mast timber were recorded as arriving from the Baltic. However, long before then, in the fifteenth century, single lengths of timber were becoming difficult to obtain and shipyards, as a matter of necessity, and at greater expense, had to manufacture masts. These 'made' masts were coaked and banded so that shorter lengths could be fitted together like some gigantic jigsaw, into a composite form to give the mast the required height. Nevertheless 'whole' masts were still being purchased by the navy; in Evelyn's time a huge, and complicated, contract was being negotiated by the Navy Board during 1662–63, for the delivery of 150 Gothenburg and 300 Norwegian masts by Sir William Warren, the greatest timber merchant of the era. Mast timber was used 'wet', unlike the more usual 'dry' timber. This wood was kept outside to age or season, generally over a period of years, planked up and kept dry in circulating air. Mast timber, on the other hand, was submerged in great mast docks, to help maintain its greatest asset, the flexibility of the wood.

The combination of the lack of suitable trees and the threat of the sea-borne Dutch harrying English ships in the Baltic (as in November 1664) finally made the Admiralty search for mast timber elsewhere. Across the Atlantic, along the richly wooded shores of New England, good naval timber could be found. The most suitable seemed to be a North American White Pine, *Pinus strobus*. It was considered by the naval authorities not to have the same strength as the familiar Baltic forest fir, but the weight of the wood was far less. Spruce trees – either the European *Abies alba* or the New England *Picea mariana* (syn. *Abies nigra*) – had also been considered but were found to be too coarse grained and under strength to be used as masts; however, shipwrights proved that they could be useful as topmasts and spars. The first shipload of masts arrived from Jamestown in 1609, but it was twenty-five years later, in 1634, before another such venture took place. In the 1650s the Navy Board began to place regular New England orders for its larger-diameter – 68 centimetre (27in) – masts.

Planks of White
Pine (Pinus
strobes), with
Frank Stenlund,
an employee at
Tozer's Sawmill,
Minnesota, 1912.

Although there was continual comparison between the measurements, price and value of Scandinavian and New England masts – it was usually the former that came out on top – both areas continued to supply the navy with masts. In 1662 both Sir William Warren, who was to deliver three shiploads of New England masts, and William Wood, a timber merchant and also mast-maker of Wapping, were negotiating with Samuel Pepys and the Board for the supply of 'masts of New-England'. Eventually the Wood family held a monopoly of the supply of masts on the Thames, with timber yards at Rotherhithe as well as Wapping. Pepys nearly always distrusted Mr Wood, and once spent a cold December morning at the Deptford Yard, measuring all Mr Wood's New England masts to make sure that they were of the correct size.

One ship that bore a New World mast was the *Royal Sovereign*, which Evelyn inspected on 9 April 1655. It had been launched at Woolwich in 1637 and was the finest ship of the line, a first rater and one of the earliest three-deckers, carrying between 90 and 100 guns. According to the traveller and merchant Peter Mundy (*c*.1596–1667), who kept an extensive diary and visited the ship just before Evelyn in the same year, her masts were made 'of one tree, the maine mast being 38 inches [1m] brought from New England that grew there'. This could have been one of the masts that arrived in 1634. The *Royal Sovereign* remained in service for about sixty years and, although much praised, had to be rebuilt twice before finally being consumed by fire in 1696.

Mast timber eventually became a highly prized war trophy, particularly if it came from America; the Spaniards, French and Dutch were all delighted to capture a 'mast ship'. So valuable were masts that, for protection, most ships sailed in convoy with an armed vessel as escort.

France was always as perturbed as Britain over the lack of mature timber in its homeland, and a hundred years after Evelyn, the explorer André Michaux (1746–1803) was charged by Louis XVI to travel to the United States with detailed instructions to search out – and return with – plants (both medicinal and ornamental), useful animals (the wild turkey, for instance) and, most important of all, trees that could be cultivated in France and specifically grown for their timber's use in shipbuilding.

Of the Larch, Platanus, Lotus, Cornus

Larix Pinaceae, *Platanus* Platanaceae, *Lotus* Ebenaceae, *Cornus* Cornaceae

COMMON OR EUROPEAN LARCH (*Larix deciduas*):

NATIVE TO MOUNTAINS OF CENTRAL AND SOUTHERN
EUROPE, 30–42M (100–140FT); DECIDUOUS; MALE
AND FEMALE FLOWERS OPEN MARCH, EARLY APRIL; BARK
IS GREY OR PINKISH-GREY WITH VERTICAL CRACKS AND
SCALY RIDGES

A S JOHN EVELYN POINTS OUT, although the Larch is a conifer, it behaves as if it is a deciduous tree, and in autumn the leaves of all the ten or so species turn brown and drop. He was writing about the European Larch, *Larix europaea*, now *L. decidua*, a tree familiar throughout the northern hemisphere but a native of the Alps, its habitat spreading eastward towards Poland.

There is some confusion about who first introduced the Larch into the British Isles, and it was probably not until the seventeenth century that it began to be planted here. It was first written about by William Turner in his *Names of Herbes* of 1548, in which he records that 'Larix or larex growth in the highest tops of the Alpes, higher than the firres do … it may be called in English a larche tree.' There is no indication that Turner knew of its existence in England. However, by 1629 John Parkinson in *Paradisus in Sole Paradisus Terrestris* could write that it was 'rare and noursed up … it growth both slowly and becommeth not high'. This date would fit in with the theory that John Tradescant senior had returned with the tree from his trip to Archangel in Russia thirty-one years before. There is a suggestion that it may have been a different tree, the Siberian Larch, *Larix russica*, a native of northern Russia and Siberia, although this seems unlikely as it was reputedly not introduced until much later, in 1806. Even today, 200 years later, it is a rare find and the tree has never made it into woodlands or forests, always remaining a planted tree within a planned landscape.

The fact that the Larch is not listed by Jacob Bobart in the Oxford Botanic Garden catalogue of 1648, or by the Tradescants at Lambeth in 1656, and that even John Ray in his *Historia Plantarum* of 1686 makes no mention of it, perhaps confirms the tree's relative newness in 1629. John Evelyn certainly made no mention of the Larch when he visited the Oxford garden in 1644 and again in 1675. However, in 1656, he journeyed to Chelmsford to view the old house and grounds of New Hall, and when writing about the Larch in *Sylva* eight or nine years later he remembered seeing a Larch there, describing it as apparently thriving and 'arrived to a flourishing, and ample tree'.

Evelyn is more discursive than usual about the Larch, although the chapter is very short. He writes of its weight-bearing qualities, and how slow it is to burn, but that it holds 'far better than any other for the melting of iron'. The quality of the timber was known about from earliest times and it has been discovered among Roman remains in England. While in Venice in 1645 Evelyn wrote of the abundance of larch timber used in the buildings there. He makes no mention of how the tree should be propagated or where to plant it – perhaps a further sign of its newness in Britain? Larches require a fairly good loamy soil, and should always be raised from seed, and planted out early – so, in 1914, William Bean of Kew recommended. From being a relatively unknown tree in Britain the Larch came to be planted prolifically during the nineteenth and twentieth centuries and in 1949 it was one of the top five most planted forest trees.

John Evelyn is equally discursive about the next tree in this chapter, the 'Platanus', as he calls the Oriental Plane, *Platanus orientalis,* which he clearly appreciates, describing it as 'that so beautiful and precious tree'. Before he gets down to explaining the intricacies of seed planting, he recalls two wonderful stories relating to the tree. The first involves 'Xerxes the King, King of Kings, King of all the land, son of Darius', as Herodotus called him, who in 481 BC gathered what Evelyn describes as a 'prodigious army of seventeen hundred thousand [1,700,000] soldiers' to fight the Greeks. The army included twenty-nine divisional generals, each commanding 6,000 men; there were also charioteers summoned from India and Libya, foot soldiers from Ethiopia, as well as the elite 10,000 'Immortals' of the Persian Empire – to quote Herodotus again, 'There was not a nation in all Asia that he did not take with him against Greece.' Even if the numbers were exaggerated, the army must have been like a swarm of locusts streaming for miles across the countryside. Xerxes took his time travelling from Sardis, where he had overwintered, halting at Troy to sacrifice 1,000 oxen to the Trojan Athene and stopping again at the Hellespont, where he held a review of his army and navy. By the River Meander, the King of Kings fell in love with an Oriental Plane tree and again brought his massive forces to a halt, 'so to admire the pulchritude and procerity of one of these goodly trees, and became so fond of it that spoiling both himself, his concubines, and the great persons of all their jewels, he covered it with gold, gems, necklaces, scarves and bracelets, and infinite riches'. So enamoured was Xerxes by the beauty of the tree that he dallied far too long, 'to the concernment of his grand Expedition'. When eventually he

ABOVE:
Oriental Plane
(Platanus
orientalis).

RIGHT:
London Plane
(Platanus x
hispanica)
*bark is distinctive,
smooth light grey to
reddish-pink with
peeling off in flakes.*

moved on, John Evelyn tells us, he had had created for himself an image of the tree made in gold, which he wore constantly around his neck. Over 2,000 years later the composer George Frederic Handel (1685–1759) brought the whole saga to life in his opera *Xerxes*. (It was not the operatic success he had hoped for, but one of the melodies from it, the Largo, has remained a musical favourite.)

The second story that John Evelyn retells apparently took place following the introduction of the Plane Tree into Italy by the Romans in the second century BC, and concerns the two orators Cicero and Hortensus, who, when conversing about the plants growing in their respective villas, said they would 'refresh their Platans which they would often irrigate with wine instead of water' – a strange habit, and one not usually recommended by horticulturists.

The Plane Tree is a sturdy doer, a long liver, and a tree that can withstand both the heat and the tremendously harsh winters in places like northern Iran. John Evelyn notes that Pliny suggests that it is because of the dense shade the tree gives during the heat of the summer months that it is so often planted in hot countries. The genus is small, with only about six species, and widely scattered across North America to southern Europe, Asia Minor and India. Known in the Middle East as the Chenar (a Persian word), it is a most distinctive tree, and looks not unlike a Maple (*Acer*) with its goose-foot-shaped leaves; however, these palmately lobed leaves grow alternately on the leaf stalk rather than opposite each other, as on the Maple. The shape of the leaf is so distinctive that, certainly in the past, it has been likened to a map of the Peloponnese. One of the characteristic features of the genus is the production of the seed vessels, which hang in spherical balls, either singly or strung up six together, and persist during the winter, falling only when new growth takes place the following spring.

The Plane Tree that is most usually planted in England is an intriguing hybrid, *Platanus* x *hispanica*, better known as the London Plane. It is thought to be a cross between *P. orientalis* and the American *P. occidentalis*, the Buttonwood of the southern and eastern United States. Botanists are unsure when or where the cross-pollination took place. Although the American tree can grow in Britain (it was introduced during John Evelyn's lifetime, in 1636) it does not thrive, needing hotter summers to ripen the wood and produce seed. Because of this, hybridization between the two species is believed to have taken place in Spain, where the Buttonwood was introduced some time in the seventeenth century. How the London Plane, or *Platanus inter et occidentalum media*, as it was first called, reached Britain no one is quite sure, but it was recorded in 1666 as growing in the Oxford Botanic Garden, where it had been planted three years before in 1663.

The sobriquet of the London Plane for *P.* x *hispanica* seems to have first been used during the nineteenth century, when it became one of the more familiar trees to be planted in the capital. Berkeley Square, where the nightingale famously sang its song, can claim to accommodate the oldest London Plane trees. They were planted in 1789, and there is a persistent rumour that they grew so vigorously because of the proximity of a well-matured plague pit. The oldest surviving Plane Tree in Britain is the one growing in the Bishop's Palace at Ely. There are also two gigantic specimens, each topping 46m (151ft) high, growing in the grounds of Bryanston School in Dorset.

Berkeley Square, London, with some of the eighteenth-century London Plane Trees.

John Evelyn gives the 'Lotus' and the 'Cornus' very few lines. Of the Lotus, he says that 'in Italy [it] yields both an admirable shade, and timber immortal'. He is referring to a member of the Ebony family, *Diospyros lotus* (not the exotic water plant of Egypt, *Nelumbo nucifera* (syn. *Nelumbo speciosa*). The tree, known as the Date Plum, is common throughout the Himalayas, China and Japan. It was a surprisingly early introduction, noted by John Gerard in 1597, and one wonders who it was who first brought the tree to England. The seed needs to be sown as soon as it is ripe, and the growing tree requires shelter from frost and drying winds. One of its cousins is the Persimmon, *D. virginiana*, which Evelyn could have seen, as it arrived about a hundred years later in 1699.

The Dogwood or *Cornus* genus is small, comprising about forty-five species of trees and shrubs, of which only two are native to Europe: the Dogwood, *Cornus sanguinea*, and the Cornelian Cherry, *C. mas*. As would be expected, both were being grown by the Tradescants in Lambeth, and by Jacob Bobart in the Oxford garden. John Evelyn makes the accurate statement that 'The Cornel tree though not mentioned by Pliny for its timber is exceedingly commended for its durableness', and that is indeed so, the merits of both species having been discovered centuries earlier. The wood was renowned for its toughness and, 'lasting like the hardest iron' as Evelyn says, was used to make pins, wedges, butchers' skewers and the like, all of which need to be highly durable. He does not relate any propagation details, or where or how to plant the shrub (seeds should be sown in the autumn, or in the spring, when they have been stratified – shocked into growth by exposing them to frost or refrigeration). Evelyn also asserts that 'the preserved and pickled berries are most refreshing and an excellent condiment'; however, today the Royal Horticultural Society warns that the fruits of some species may cause mild stomach upset and – something that Evelyn does not mention – that the tiny hairs on the leaf may also irritate the skin.

Dogwood
(Cornus sanguinea*).*

Of the Cypress
Tree and Cedar

Cypress Cupressaceae, *Cedar* Cedrus

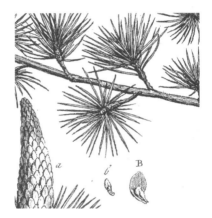

WHEN EVELYN EULOGIZES ABOUT the 'Cupress the cypress tree', he is writing of the Italian or Mediterranean Cypress (*Cupressus sempervirens*), whose native lands stretch from the eastern Mediterranean to Iran; few others had then been discovered. This is the tree that caught the imagination of the ancients; papyri and documents from Egypt, Persia (Iran), Turkey and Italy all refer to the tree, and references to its being cultivated in Moorish and Hellenistic gardens confirm its uniquely favoured position. The whole of Greek mythology is infused with the idea of the sacred grove or *alsos*, within which were often found oracles. Its concept

was a wonderfully effusive mixture of eternal spring, spirituality and symbolism. More than just a cluster of trees dedicated to a god, this earthly paradise could include meadows, countryside set aside for hunting and *al fresco* meals, as well as woodland and agricultural fields; in fact it is an early example of land fulfilling the requirements of the community. Its idealistic philosophy seeped deep into European culture, emerging much later into the monastic life of the Christian world. The trees that comprised the groves were themselves regarded as sacred and the Cypress – being associated with Dis, the god of the underworld – was therefore planted frequently. An ancient text from the Oracle of Trophonius in Boetia (Peloponnese) inscribed on gold leaf warned: 'In Hades, thou wilt find on the left, a spring, and near the spring a white cypress. Go not nigh'. Because of its connection with the underworld, the tree was gradually thought of as a tree of sadness and mourning. Later it became a frequent planting in early Greek cemeteries, where its very presence seemed to add a dignified aura.

The Cypress Tree was originally believed to have arrived in England in about 1500, but now scholars consider an earlier date of the late fourteenth century more appropriate.

During the course of the twentieth century, the tree gradually lost its reputation. The problem was twofold: its association with the fast-growing and thug-like Leyland Cypress (*Cupressocyparis leylandii*), which is a cross between

The Isle of the Dead, painted by Arnold Bocklin (1827–1901).

Chamaecyparis nootkatensis and *Cupressus macrocarpa*; and confusion about what is and what is not a Cypress. The *Cupressaceae* family, of which the Cypress is a member, is very large, consisting of eighteen genera, including cedars, *thujas* and junipers. Confusingly, the word 'cypress' seems to be used to identify members of other families, including 'false cypress' species such as the Hinoki Cypress (*Chamaecyparis obtuse*), a Japanese species, and the Swamp Cypress (*Taxodium distichum*), introduced by John Tradescant in about 1640 from the swamps of the Everglades and the southern USA.

With an eye for its visual appeal, John Evelyn describes the Cypress as 'most pyramidal and beautiful' and assures his readers that 'we see it now in every garden, rising to as goodly a bulk and stature, as most which you shall find even in Italy itself.' In fact his enthusiasm had carried him away, as this species is quite tender in the UK, and thrives only in sheltered spots in the south and west. He would have discovered this for himself when he was developing his own garden at Sayes Court, where he had problems in keeping the young plants alive and in maintaining the viability of the cypress seed through the winter; he had to send to Paris, asking his father-in-law for replacements. Of course, had Evelyn been writing about the ubiquitous Monterey Cypress (*Cupressus macrocarpa*), which arrived from California in about 1838, it would have been a different story, as this is the toughest of all cypresses.

The seeds, Evelyn explains, can be sown to make a hedge 'in a shallow furrow' and once germination has occurred he recommends 'plucking up the supernumeraries where they come to close and thick' about a foot apart. As usual with Evelyn, the planting instructions are as correct now as they were 300 years ago. When the trees reach 1 metre (3ft) in height, 'which maybe to the half of your palisade, cut off their tops … and keep the sides clipped that they ascend but by degrees, and thicken at the bottom as they climb'. In six or eight years the hedge will be incomparable, better in resisting the wind above all else, 'holly only excepted, which indeed has no peer'. Evelyn recounts how in 1663 and 1665, when the late March and April winds came 'accompanied with cruel frosts and cold blasts, for the space of more than two months night and day', of 1,000 cypress planted in his garden not more than three or four were lost, and then only because they had been trimmed late the previous season. A few others had their tops damaged; but they 'might have escaped all their blemishes had my gardener capped them with a wisp of hay or straw, as in my absence I commanded'.

The Italian Cypress produces a nut-like female cone which contains the seeds. As these cones seldom ripen under the sometimes watery sun of England, the seeds are difficult to gather and, as he explains, if there is enough sun they must be exposed to it 'till they gape', otherwise the nuts must be soaked in warm water; or warmed by a gentle heat, 'by which means the seed will be easily shaken out'. To propagate them, make a seed bed of fine earth – 'clap down with your spade, as gardeners do' – ready for planting in early April or 'before if it be showery'. Scatter the seeds thickly, cover with 1 centimetre (½ in) of sifted soil and water them 'after sunset'. Germination should be fairly swift – within a month, Evelyn reckons, you should have seedlings at least 2 centimetres (1 in) high. After a year, these can be transplanted 'where you please'. Demonstrating his taste for detail, he cautions against using the common watering pot, as it gushes too heavily; it is better to 'deaw them rather with a broom or spergatory [sprinkler] as they need water but sparingly.' The same, he says, 'may also serve you for your most tender and delicate seeds'.

Evelyn extols the virtues of cypress timber. It resists 'the worm moth and all putrefaction to eternity'. (He calls the wood very sonorous; it is used for making organ pipes, harps and other musical instruments, as well as chests.) He quotes Thucydides (*c*.460–*c*.400 BC) as saying that Athenians buried their heroes in coffins made of cypress. Citing examples of the longevity of the wood, he describes how the great doors of St Peter's Church in Rome were believed to have been fashioned from the wood some time in the eighth century and were still 'fresh and entire' during the reign of Pope Eugenius IV in the fifteenth century. Even earlier than that, parts of the Ark were supposed to have been made from cypress wood, as were ships for Alexander the Great in the fourth century BC and a vessel built in the first century AD by the Emperor Trajan – all good reasons for planting cypress trees. As an afterthought, he tells us not to forget that 'the very chips of this precious wood … gives that flavour to muscadine and other rich wines.'

Evelyn also describes what he calls 'the cedar', 'which grows in all extremes, in the moist Barbados, the hot Bermuda's, the cold New England, even where the snow lies as (I am assured) about half the year … it grows in the bogs of America and in the mountains of Asia'. In citing America Evelyn must be referring to the White Cedar (*Thuja occidentalis*), then known as *Arborvitae*, meaning Tree of Life. Although called a Cedar – indeed it is related – the species belongs to a different

family. It was introduced into France from North America about a hundred years before Evelyn was born, sometime in the 1530s. The tree is native along most of the eastern seaboard stretching from Canada to Virginia, and gives the best results when grown in a permanently moist position. Although the tree is believed to have been brought into England at about the same time, two specimens were purchased in 1611 – at the cost of one shilling – by Tradescant senior from a Haarlem nurseryman, for planting at Hatfield House, the home of his employer Robert Cecil, 1st Earl of Salisbury (1563–1612). It is interesting to note that *Arbor-vitae* is listed in 1648 by the Oxford Botanic Garden, but not included in the slightly earlier Tradescant list. A further confirmation that it is the American White Cedar that Evelyn is writing about is his description of the seeds: he says '[they] set like the bay berries, and we might have of the very best kind in world from the Summer Islands'. These islands are situated on one of the five Great Lakes, Lake Michigan, and the area is renowned for growing good specimens of the White Cedar.

The six species in the *Thuja* or *Aborvitae* genus are all hardy evergreens, with aromatic foliage. Without exception they all have the name 'Arbor-vitae' or Tree of Life' attached to them. All six can be grown with varying success in Britain. The White Cedar was the earliest to be introduced and there are now over sixty named cultivars in the *RHS Plant Finder*. It is a versatile tree, and can be trained

Cedar of Lebanon.

and clipped to form a good evergreen hedge. The second species arrived some time in the 1690s, thirty years after *Sylva* was first published, and was the Chinese Arborvitae (*T. orientalis*), a smaller tree or shrub native to north and west China. This too has a number of forms, several of which are small and slow growing enough to be suitable for the rock garden. There is also both the Japanese Arborvitae (*T. standishii*), collected by Robert Fortune (1812–80) in 1860 in Japan, and the Korean Arborvitae (*T. koraiensis*), introduced by E. H. Wilson in 1917. The largest *thuja* of all, growing to a height in the wild of 61 metres (200ft), is the Western Red Cedar (*T. plicata*) – note the 'cedar' name: it is a cousin of the White Cedar. Collected by the Cornishman William Lobb (1809–64) from California in 1853, this is the handsomest and best grower of all the *thujas*. It is also a good forest tree, and is one of the most important timber trees in North America.

There are only three true *Cedrus*: the Cedar of Lebanon, *C. libani*, which is frequently planted as an ornamental tree; the Blue Atlas Cedar, *C. atlantica*, a native of Morocco and Algeria, which was introduced into England during the middle of the nineteenth century; and the Deodar or Indian Cedar, *C. deodara*,

*Western Red Cedars (*Thuja plicata*), Vancouver Island, western Canada.*

indigenous to Afghanistan and the north-west Himalayas and also introduced to England in the mid-nineteenth century. The last two trees are both planted in southern Europe for their timber. Confusingly, there are several other trees that go under the name of cedar which, although related to the *Cedrus*, are not true cedars. Already noted from the American continent are the *thujas*, but there is also the Pencil or Red Cedar, *Juniperus virginiana.* In the southern hemisphere two trees from the genus *Athrotaxis* (*athroos* in Greek means crowded together and *taxis* refers to the arrangement of the evergreen leaves on the primitive conifers) are known as cedars: the Smooth Tasmanian Cedar, *Athrotaxis cupressoides*, and the Summit Cedar, *A. laxifolia.* These two and one other, *A. selaginoides* (King William Pine), comprise the family; all are native of western Tasmania. All three trees were introduced in about 1857 and because of their tenderness can best be grown in Cornwall and the west of Ireland. The 'cedar' name is also attached to a tree from Guiana, *Icica altissima* of the Myrrh family; Queensland in Australia has *Pentaceras australis*; and then there is one from India, this time in the Mahogany family, a native of the Bengal and Pegu forests, *Cedrela toona.* From Japan comes a further cedar, this time a single species and the nearest relative to the Tasmanian cedars, *Cryptomeria japonica,* the Japanese Red Cedar. This tree was first introduced by Captain Sir Everard Home in 1843, and has since become a favourite planting in European gardens.

The homeland of the Cedar of Lebanon, *Cedrus libani,* is a very restricted area in the north of Lebanon and its surroundings. It is not included in either of the Lambeth or Oxford plant lists of the time. This is not surprising, as the tree's date of introduction is variously given as between 1638 and 1680. Seedlings were first described accurately in Britain in 1659, although none of the introduced trees produced cones until 1732. The seeds are listed in the 1677 catalogue of the London seed and plant merchant William Lucas (d.1679). Evelyn certainly knew about the reputation of the tree, or at least its timber, as he had already cited the Old Testament prophet Ezekiel when he described the use of cedar for masts. Evelyn also tells of the 2,000-year-old timber discovered in the Temple of Apollo at Utica (now called Utique, and traditionally considered to be the earliest Phoenician settlement on the coast of North Africa); and cedar wood found further west on the eastern shores of Spain in an oratory dedicated to the goddess Diana at Sagunti (Sagunto), the timber having been transported across the length of the Mediterranean from the Ionian island of Zacynthus (Zante) some time in the mid-thirteenth century BC.

For thousands of years the tree and the timber were held in the highest regard. The Bible records several instances of its use: Moses (*c.*fifteenth–thirteenth century BC) directed the Israelites to collect the fragrant and resinous wood; the temple of Solomon, built some time during the eleventh or tenth century BC, and other famous buildings were constructed from the wood; Hiram, King of Tyre, presented Cedar Trees to David, King of Israel (d.*c.*993 BC). The stature of the tree in the landscape has earned *Cedrus libani* a reputation of aristocratic grandeur that few other species can match. Its massive tabulae form is very distinctive and, planted in a (large) lawn, adds gravitas to the surrounding area. The first really extensive planting of trees took place in Sussex at Goodwood, the estate of the Duke of Richmond. By that time 'Capability' Brown was using Cedar Trees in his landscapes – almost the only exotic conifer that he selected.

Cedar of Lebanon.

Of the Cork, Alaternus, Phyllyrea, Granad, Lentise, Myrtle, Jasmine, Etc.

Quercus Suber/Suber *var.* Occidentalis,
Alaternus Rhamnaceae, *Phyllyrea* Oleaceae,
Granad Lythraceae/Punicaceae,
Lentise Anacardiaceae, *Myrtle* Myrtaceae,
Jasmine Oleaceae

CORK OAK (*Quercus suber*):
NATIVE TO WEST MEDITERRANEAN
COUNTRIES; INTRODUCED TO ENGLAND
*c.*1699; HEIGHT TO 20M (65FT);
LEAVES DARK GLOSSY GREEN ABOVE AND
CLOTHED IN GREY FELT BELOW

J OHN EVELYN DISCOURSES ON TWO different Cork Oaks: *Quercus suber* and
what later came to be called *Q. suber* var. *occidentalis*. He recommends
growing the latter in England, as with its broader leaves and ability to
thrive in the cooler parts of south-west France and around the Bay of
Biscay, then known as 'Biscany', it should be able to tolerate the British climate,
at least in the south. It is interesting to note that he made a distinction between
two different types of Cork Oak as early as 1662, as it is usually the French
botanist Jacques Gay (1776–1864) who is credited with distinguishing between
the two in 1855. Both the trees produce a thick bark, which is harvested in the
Mediterranean countries to manufacture cork. However, *Quercus suber* produces
its acorns in one year, whereas the sturdier *Q. suber* var. *occidentalis* takes two
seasons to mature – although this only happens in Britain following an
exceptionally hot summer. According to the records, the Cork Oak arrived in
Britain in 1699, thirty years after Evelyn wrote *Sylva*, but it is possible that he
admired the tree during his travels in southern Europe, especially Italy, during
the 1640s, and his enthusiasm for the species could have led to its later
introduction.

Evelyn challenges Pliny's statement that the Cork Oak was not grown in France
or Italy during his lifetime (the first century) and had to be 'transplanted thither'.
John Evelyn relates how, when he was in Italy, admittedly 1,500 years later, he

*Harvesting cork
bark in Portugal.
Commercial cork
bark production
takes place in Spain
and Portugal, and
in California and
other southern states
of the USA.*

'travelled through vast woods of them about Pisa, Aquin [Aquino] and in divers tracts between Rome and the Kingdom of Naples'. He singles out the 'Spanish Cork' for the thickness of its bark – 'frequently four or five inches thick' (10–12cm) – and gives examples of its uses, including among more usual ones, such as floats for nets and corks for bottles, the shoe soles of light-footed Grecian ladies. More interesting, to fashionable cognoscenti in the twenty-first century, is his assertion that 'Venetian dames took it up for their monstrous chopines affecting or usurping an artificial eminency above men, which nature has denied them'; chopines – the word was first used in 1577 – were very thick-soled shoes raised above the ground, pre-dating platform soles and shoes by several hundred years. Evelyn relates that the Egyptians made coffins of cork, lined with a resinous composition to 'preserve their dead incorrupt'. The Spanish poor 'lay planks of it by their bedside to tread on (as a great person use turkey and Persian carpets) to defend them from the floor'. Cork was also used as insulation in beehives, and in Spain in 'leather cases, wherein they put flasquera's with snow to refrigerate their wine'.

After felling a Cork Oak there are two further parts of the bark, which Evelyn calls the 'libri'. One of these, reddish in colour, was useful in the tanning industry, for which, as the ever-practical Evelyn points out, a good price could be obtained. It also provided excellent firewood, and 'many other uses', including one which the Navy Board experimented with in 1666 when it purchased 'four or five Tons of Corke, to send this day to the fleet, being a new device to make Barrecados with, instead of Junke'. The cork was to be fashioned into fenders (the 'Barrecados'), replacing old rope (the 'junke'), for use around the quarter-decks. Presumably this was because the supply of hemp, used to make rope, was always expensive and usually in short supply. However, the experiment proved not to be satisfactory.

Following the Cork, Evelyn writes of another southern European tree, the 'Alaternus', now known as the Italian Buckthorn. It was named by Linnaeus as *Rhamnus alaternus* and is one of about 125 buckthorns, some of which are evergreen. The hardy species are widespread across northern temperate latitudes, with a few in the southern hemisphere. Despite its name, the Italian Buckthorn is a native of Portugal, Morocco and the whole of the Mediterranean, stretching into the Crimea. Evelyn states quite clearly: 'I have had the honour to be the first who brought it into use and reputation in this Kingdom'; presumably he

collected it during his travels on the Continent. Alas for Evelyn, the shrub is listed as being grown in the Lambeth garden of John Tradescant senior in 1634, when Evelyn was aged only fourteen. How many of us though have had the same thought on returning with seeds or cuttings from abroad? An 'Alaternus' was also included in the catalogue of plants listed for sale by William Lucas in about 1677. Evelyn considered 'his' shrub a most useful hedging plant, but it has since lost favour, as keeping it neat and trimmed requires the hedge to be clipped at least three times a year.

Next John Evelyn describes another good hedging shrub, 'yet more hardy'. It is *Phillyrea angustifolia*, which with *P. latifolia* is native to southern Europe. They are part of a very small genus of four species native to the Mediterranean and south-west Asia. The two small trees arrived in Britain together, and were first recorded in 1596 by John Gerard. Both the Phillyrea and the Italian Buckthorn can be 'raised of seed … Plant it out at two years growth and clip it after rain in the spring', Evelyn instructs. The Phillyrea was known in England as the 'narow-leafed mock Privet' or 'Clusius his mock Privet'. This suggests that the Flemish horticulturist Charles de l'Ecluse (1526–1609) may have been responsible for its

English-grown Cork Oak at Mamhead, near Exeter, Devon, photographed c.1903.

introduction into cultivation when he explored southern France, Spain and Portugal in the mid-1550s. Clusius was influential in encouraging the garden cultivation of a large number of botanical discoveries throughout northern Europe.

British gardeners at this time had very few evergreen shrubs to choose from, so the introduction of one that can tolerate being clipped and acts as foil for other more glamorous plants was most welcome. John Worlidge, the Hampshire agricultural writer, remarked in his *Systema Agriculturae* of 1675 that the Phillyrea could be used 'for the raising of Espalier Hedges and covering of Arbors, being always of incomparable Verdure'. It became quite a fashionable plant and Thomas Hanmer, Evelyn's gardening friend from Flintshire, considered the shrub to have replaced the Pyracantha as a hedge plant. Evelyn must have thought otherwise, as he makes only a passing reference to it when discussing hedging and fences. Phillyrea remained in favour for about another hundred years, into the eighteenth century, but gradually, because of a change in garden design and an influx of other more interesting plants, the shrub drifted into obscurity. Yet looked at closely it is quite lovely, particularly *P. latifolia*, which makes a small, rounded, tree or shrub and has oval glossy, dark green leaves; the white-greenish flowers, which admittedly are not of a flaunting nature, are fragrant; the berries begin red and then turn blue-black as they ripen. Planted in well-drained, fertile soil, it prefers a sunny disposition, but must be protected from cold, dry winds. Its nature is of a maiden aunt, always there and impeccably behaved, but in the background, never drawing attention to herself.

Pomegranate (Punica granatum) makes a large shrub or a small bushy tree, with deep shiny green oblong-shaped leaves. It is naturalized in south-eastern Europe, where it can make a dense hedge.

The fourth shrub to be recommended in this chapter John Evelyn calls the 'Granade of which there are three sorts'. A little detective work reveals that this is what Pliny knew as *Malum Punicum* and we now call *Punica granatum*. The species name forms the second part of its common name, the Pomegranate. Jacob Bobart at Oxford recorded it as *Malus Granata*; it had earlier been noted by John Tradescant senior, who called it 'pomgranet'. When he travelled to Paris in 1611, he had included the purchase of pomegranate plants for Hatfield House in Hertfordshire on behalf of Robert Cecil.

There are only two species of this shrub. One is a native of the Yemen; the other is indigenous to south-east Europe and south-west Asia and the Himalayas. It is a variety of this, *P. granatum,* which Evelyn recommends, and which has been cultivated from very ancient times. The earliest representation of its fruit was discovered in the Egyptian tombs of the Middle Kingdom (*c.*2040–*c.*1786 BC) and the New Kingdom (*c.*1570–1085 BC), when it was known as *inhemen.* The remains of real fruit have been found in other tombs. The fruit needs a hot, dry summer to develop, and both the jewel-like seeds and the sweet syrup made from the juice, called granatine or grenadine, are used in cooking, particularly in the Middle East. From the lower Himalayas the seeds of the wild Pomegranate are collected, dried and ground into *anar dana,* a condiment useful in Indian cooking.

This takes us a long way from the possibility of planting pomegranate as a shrub in an English hedgerow, and it was probably the double wild variety that Evelyn was recommending. Tradescant senior had collected it in the year of Evelyn's birth – 1620 – when he found himself in the Mediterranean, as one of fourteen gentlemen who were part of a punitive expedition endeavouring to rid the area of the harassing Barbary pirates. The assault was unsuccessful, but on the return journey, the pinnace *Mercury,* to which Tradescant was attached, anchored off Formentera, one of the Pitiusas Islands, where it is known he botanized. The party made at least two other stops along the Spanish coast. John Parkinson, who later visited the Canterbury garden of Tradescant's employer, recorded that Tradescant had collected a number of plants, including some 'greater or double blossomed wilde' pomegranate trees, saying 'the wilde I thinke was never seene in England, before John Tradescante my very loving good friend brought it from the parts beyond the Seas.' This variety is *Punica granatum* var. *flore plena.* It bears no fruit, but is floristically superior to the species and it is recommended today for growing in a shrubbery or as hedging.

John Evelyn's next recommendation is another Tradescant introduction, which he collected at the same time as the Pomegranate: Evelyn lists it as 'Lentiscus the Lentise'. This is *Pistacia lentiscus,* often known as the Mastic Tree. The shrub is in a genus that includes the pistachio nut; in all there are eleven species, which are widely dispersed. The tree Evelyn recommends is a native of southern Europe from Portugal to Greece, Morocco and the Canary Islands. Others in the genus are indigenous to Central Asia, Japan, Malaysia, Mexico and the

The Mastic Tree (Pistacia lentiscus), an evergreen shrub or small tree reaching 4.6–6.1m (15–20ft). The red fruit gradually ripen to black and are the size of peppercorns.

southern USA. The Mastic Tree exudes a fragrant sap, which is renowned for its usefulness in dentistry – already known about by Evelyn, who writes that the tree makes 'the best tooth pickers in the world, and the mastic or gum is of excellent use, especially for the teeth and gums' – and as a varnish. He rates it for more than just its practical qualities, though, describing it as 'a very beautiful evergreen' that 'will thrive abroad with us with a little care and shelter'.

Evelyn's 'vulgar Italian wild Myrtle (though not indeed the most fragrant)' is the Common Myrtle, *Myrtus communis*, or as Tradescant recorded it in 1632 *Mirtis florence.* The shrub is indigenous around the Mediterranean and into west Asia. The Common Myrtle shows great variability – its leaf-shape alters, as do its floristic qualities, height and habit, as Bobart shows when in the Oxford Botanic Garden list he records a 'Double flowered myrtle', both a broad and narrow-leaved variety, and a 'Wild Spanish myrtle'. These differences were considered enough to justify naming them, and many others, as species. The structure and composition of the known myrtles were later examined and the nomenclature subsequently altered. Some were amalgamated under the name of *Myrtus communis*; others were moved to a different genus. In the twenty-first century the situation is changing again. For a long time it was believed that apart from the European species there were only two other myrtle species and both of them were native to Chile. The first was *Myrtus luma*, now known as *Luma apiculata,* which was originally introduced in 1844 by William Lobb, the collector who worked for Veitch and Sons' nursery. The second was introduced into cultivation in the 1920s by the plant collector Harold Comber (1897–1969) and was named *Myrtus lechleriana*. Similarly, this too has had its name changed and has been re-classified as *Amomyrtus luma*. These two shrubs are familiar to British gardeners, but there are believed to be a further twenty-five myrtle species in Chile.

*The Common Myrtle (*Myrtus communis*) in full flower during July and August.*

The whole of the ancient world knew the Common Myrtle. Traditionally the Arabs believed that when Adam was sent from Paradise, he took with him a sprig of Myrtle (as well as a date stone and a grain of wheat). In the Old Testament there are two mentions of the Myrtle Tree in the Book of Zachariah. The oil from the leaves and the berries was one of the ingredients of perfume in ancient Egypt. There are a large number of references to the shrub in classical literature; it is mostly associated with Aphrodite (goddess of love), and her attendant Hours, who preceded her with garlands of Myrtle leaves. This is how the Myrtle came to be associated with love and weddings; a sprig of Myrtle is still sometimes included in a bridal bouquet. Strangely, the shrub also came to signify war and death; in Greece a victorious general would be crowned with a myrtle wreath, and the hardness of the wood, from which spear shafts were made, confirmed its warrior symbolism. Myrtle wreaths were also the *de rigueur* accoutrement of Athenian magistrates; so many were needed that part of the market place in Athens was known as the Murrinae, or myrtle market. In Italy at the end of 299 BC, when Rome finally subdued the Sabines, the weapons were ritualistically laid under a Myrtle shrub, and the armies 'purified' themselves with its branches. Later the Myrtle became the symbol of the Roman Empire.

The shrub could have been an import into Roman Britain, although there is no direct evidence of this. The earliest written record is contained in a letter written in 1562 by Lord Burghley to Mr Windebank, who was acting as travelling companion to his son Thomas, 1st Earl of Exeter (1542–1623), in Paris. Lord William Burghley, statesman of the Elizabethan period and founder of the formidable Cecil family, built both Theobalds in Hertfordshire and Cecil House in The Strand, London, and was enhancing their grounds and gardens. He asked Windebank to purchase a Lemon, a Pomegranate and a Myrtle Tree, giving instructions on their upkeep. Windebank's reply duly notes that 'a lemon tree and two myrtle trees, in two pots' had been packed and sent off; he says '[they] cost me both a crown, and the lemon tree fifteen crowns … it is the best cheap we could get it, and better cheap than other noble men in France have bought of the same man'. Later, Burghley's son Robert Cecil, 1st Earl of Salisbury, employed John Tradescant to help him create the great garden at Hatfield House. Included in the huge continental purchases Tradescant made during 1611 were 'myrtill trees 7 at halfe a croune the peece' and again 'for on pot of mirtill trees 3 in it'. These ten Myrtles must have been special, as fourteen years previously, in 1597, there is a record of no fewer than six varieties being cultivated in England.

As has been noted by John Evelyn, Myrtles can grow quite tall, and are able to withstand most of the weather that occurs in England. The shrubs thrive in situations similar to Camellias: both enjoy being planted in dappled shade, in a shrubbery or on the edge of a woodland or grove, although, like the Camellia, the Myrtle can be fashioned into a hedge, providing there is some shelter from cold, drying winds. The wood is hard and mottled and often knotty, and is still much used in turnery. Culinary use may be made of the aromatic leaves for flavouring meat, especially pork. The Myrtle's extracted oil can be one of the ingredients used in the perfume industry, although in Sardinia it has been recorded by the cookery writer Elizabeth David as being particularly good for frying fish. Around the Mediterranean the edible berries are sometimes made into an aromatic condiment, and in France the sweet *tarte aux myrtilles* is a speciality of *pâtissiers*; these, though, will in all probability contain bilberries, *Vaccinium myrtillus*, rather than myrtles, as *myrtille* is the French name for the bilberry.

John Evelyn finishes this chapter by listing five other plants which, he says, are 'fittest for the shrubby part and under furniture of our evergreen groves, and near our gardens of pleasure'. The first is *Lignum vitaea*, from the West Indies, later called after its native South American name of *Guaiacum officinale*. This shrub or tree, which grows to about 9 metres (30ft), is one of about eight species in the *Guaiacum* genus, which is in the

Bilberry or Whortleberry (Vaccinium myrtillus) leaves are deciduous and oval, and bright green. It does not grow on limestone, but thrives on moorland, heaths and in open woods.

*Laurustinus
(Viburnum tinus).
A very useful
winter-flowering
evergreen, tolerant
of shade and of salt
spray.*

Zygophyllaceae family, all of which flourish in warm regions. Although Evelyn mentions the tree, significantly it is not listed as growing either in the Lambeth garden of the Tradescants or in the 1648 list of the Oxford Botanic Garden. To survive in England the tree needs some indoor warmth and protection. It must have been the timber that Evelyn was writing about, as it is known to have been a familiar wood in England during the seventeenth century. In 1660, Samuel Pepys was presented with a 'Cupp of Lignum vitae' by his cousin 'as a token'. Three years later he received a second drinking vessel fashioned from the same wood. The timber is renowned as being rock-like in its hardness and because of this it was used to make ship's pulleys and blocks for the printing industry.

Listed next is something John Evelyn calls *Aethiopic seseli* and later in what he had begun and hoped would become his *magnun opus, Elysium Britannicum*, he records it as *Aethiopicum frutex*. The plant was first recorded in Britain in 1596 by John Gerard and again in 1632 by Tradescant, who listed it as *Sesely Ethiopicum*. All these names suggest a North African origin; however, the plant is a native of southern Europe. Linnaeus renamed it *Bupleurum fruticosum*, Hare's Ear. It is a member of the Umbelliferae family and an evergreen glabrous shrub that reaches a height of 1.5–3 metres (5–10ft). The plant has another word associated with it, Thorow-wax. This comes from a word coined in 1548, 'thoroughwax', and is the botanical description of the way the branches of the plant appear to grow through the middle of the leaf, giving the shrub a rather surreal look. Evelyn says that growing it 'added to ornament and pleasure'.

Halimus latifolius was another plant that Evelyn believed would add a touch of brightness to a shrubby area. Now known as the Tree Purslane, *Atriplex halimus*, it is another native of southern Europe, believed to have been first collected by John Tradescant senior in about 1632, when he called it *Hulimus* (which means a maritime plant). Although it is called a tree, it only reaches a height of about 2 metres (6ft), and has silvery grey leaves, and bears insignificant greenish-white flowers in the summer.

The fourth of this small list of shrubs is *Viburnum tinus*, known in John Evelyn's day as *Laurus tinus*. It is a large although compact evergreen shrub, and again a native of the Mediterranean region, and has perhaps made the most impact as a hedging and sheltering plant. Tradescant senior grew it in

Lambeth, as did Bobart in the Oxford Botanic Garden. The shrub also featured in the 1677 catalogue of William Lucas. It is as popular and useful in the garden today as it was then.

The last shrub mentioned by Evelyn is what he calls *Celastrus*. This is now the name given to the thirty species of Bittersweet, mostly twining, woody climbers from the warmer parts of the world. John Tradescant junior, in his plant list of 1656, records *Celastrus alaternus* as growing in the garden at Lambeth, describing it as 'ever-green Privet', but this turns out to be *Rhamnus alaternus*, which Evelyn has mentioned earlier. Jacob Bobart lists an '*Amara dulcis*', literally meaning Bitter-Sweet, a name which does not seem to be in modern use. In the seventeenth century, confusion of identification often reigned (quite naturally) over newly arrived plants, and it is difficult to unravel what plant John Evelyn could have meant. The word 'Celastrus' comes from the Greek for evergreen, and according to the records, the first of the Celastraceae family, *C. scandens*, the Climbing Bittersweet, arrived in England from America (via Peter Collinson) in 1736. The different plant names used by Evelyn, as well as the earlier Tradescants and Bobart (not to mention John Gerard and John Parkinson), all highlight the confusion that existed prior to the work of Linnaeus in the eighteenth century.

Tradescant's mention of Privet is a reminder that although he lists *Ligustrum vulgare* – as does Jacob Bobart eight years earlier – John Evelyn does not include it in this short list of shrubs, even though it is a British native. It seems a strange omission, when it is both easy to propagate and useful – although critics dismiss it, preferring the more distinctive and later nineteenth-century introductions from China and Japan.

It is interesting to consider the choice of trees John Evelyn wrote about in this chapter and his statement that 'they added to ornament and pleasure'. It shows that, although coming back time and time again to the practicalities of planting and growing trees to produce timber and wood, Evelyn realized that a balance could be achieved between utilitarian and aesthetic planting.

The only tree in this chapter of *Sylva* that could be considered a forest or woodland tree is the Cork Oak. But it has never become naturalized in the English countryside; instead it has been decoratively maintained in England as part of a planned landscape. None of the other trees and shrubs which John Evelyn recommends here can be grown with any success in a woodland. Neither are they particularly useful producers of timber. John Evelyn's recommendation for them is to be grown in copses, planted on the edge of fields or boundaries, or as hedging plants. This idea of planting trees and shrubs 'for ornament' is at the core of the philosophical idea that, a hundred years later, sparked off the English landscape movement.

Cork Oak
(Quercus suber*)*.

Of the Acacia, Arbutus, Bay, Box, Yew, Holly, Juniper and Laurel Trees

Acacia Leguminosae/Mimosaceae, *Arbutus* Ericaceae, *Bay* Lauraceae, *Box* Buxaceae, *Yew* Taxaceae, *Holly* Aquifoliaceae, *Juniper* Cupressaceae, *Laurel* Rosaceae

STRAWBERRY TREE (*Arbutus unedo*):
4.5–9M (15–30FT) IN HEIGHT; NATIVE TO
SOUTH-WEST IRELAND AND SOUTH-WEST
EUROPE; EVERGREEN; DARK GLOSSY GREEN
LEAVES; FLOWERS AND FRUIT PRODUCED
SIMULTANEOUSLY IN LATE AUTUMN

OF THE EIGHT TREES in the title of this chapter, most of them are native; one is a chance import of the post-Ice Age in Ireland; and the first was a seventeenth-century arrival from the New World, via France.

John Evelyn describes the import as *Virginia Acacia*, but we know it by the name *Robinia pseudoacacia*. Before Linnaeus gave it that name, it was also known as *Acacia Americana*; in 1635 in France it was *Acacia Americana Robini,* and a year later it was recorded as *Acatia Africana*. Tradescant senior's first cataloguing of it, in 1634, was as *Locusta Virginiana arbor*.

Evelyn rightly remarks, 'The French have lately brought in the Virginia Acacia, which exceedingly adorns their walks.' The tree had been collected originally from Canada, at about the beginning of the century. Its later Linnaean name commemorates the French Royal Gardener of the time, Jean Robin (1550–1629). In about 1586 Henri III granted Robin the title *Arboriste et simpliciste du roi*. He had qualified as an apothecary in Paris, and was also a botanist and herbalist. In 1597 Robin was invited to draw up plans for the projected Jardin Royal des Plantes Médicinales (later to become the Jardin des Plantes). A friendship sprang up between the French Royal Gardener and John Tradescant senior, when the latter visited Paris in 1610 and 1611, and as is usual between gardening friends, exchanges of horticultural delights – new and old – took place. One of the gifts Robin gave Tradescant was a small plant or seed of *Robinia pseudoacacia*. So by the time Evelyn was writing *Sylva* in 1664 the Robinia (as it came to be called) had been established here about fifty years – barely long enough for it to be recognized for its forestry potential.

It is a fast-growing tree and quickly became a favourite. 'Acacias' were planted during the work that André Mollet advocated for St James's Park in the 1660s; Evelyn observes, 'They thrive well in his Majesties new plantation.' Unfortunately the trees were all brought down by a great storm during the autumn of 1703 (when it is reckoned over 8,000 people died). This highlights a recurring problem pertaining to the tree, and it is interesting to note that both Evelyn in the seventeenth century and the *RHS A–Z Encyclopedia of Garden Plants* in the twentieth century use the same word to describe its branches, Evelyn saying 'our high winds, by reason of its brittle nature it does not so well resist'. Or as the RHS, in more modern language, alerts us, 'Shelter from strong winds, as the branches are brittle.' Evelyn goes on to say that the roots 'which

insinuate and run like liquorice underground are apt to emaciate the soil'. He recommends planting the trees for walks and shade rather than as part of a garden.

By the time Evelyn came to write about the Arbutus, it was well known among gardeners, having first been described by the Reverend William Turner in 1538. The Common Arbutus or Strawberry Tree, *Arbutus unedo*, may be grown as a tree or a shrub. However, John Parkinson says it 'groweth but low, or rather like a shrub tree then of any bignesse'. John Gerard remarks how large the trees were in the valleys around Mount Athos in Greece, 'where being in other places but little, they become great huge trees' (presumably he saw *Arbutus* x *andrachnoides* which can reach to about 12.19 metres (40ft), about twice the height of *A. unedo*). Like thirty-eight other species of plants that are indigenous around the milder southern margins of England, the Arbutus can be traced to its original home of the Mediterranean. All these plants slowly followed the warmer post-glacial period as the ice slowly retreated northwards. They grew and seeded over thousands of years, gradually increasing their range of habitation, until they

ABOVE:
A Strawberry Tree, Killarney, Ireland, showing how it withstands gales in coastal districts.

RIGHT:
Strawberry Tree: flowers and fruit.

eventually settled permanently all along the fringe of England and Ireland. *Arbutus unedo* was one of these slow travellers which found even the climate of south-western England not quite to its liking and discovered the conditions more agreeable in southern Ireland. When the climate was somewhat warmer, the plant spread through western Europe to Brittany and then to Ireland.

Somewhat less scientific is the legend that the Strawberry Tree miraculously appeared to help comfort Bresal, the monk who yearned for the Spanish monastery where he had earlier been sent to teach the Irish style of choral music. Sometimes known as the Killarney Strawberry, it grows wild in the counties of Cork, Kerry and Sligo, and is the only tree native to Ireland that has no counterpart in Britain. Although it could easily have been brought to England in early classical times, the first record of its appearance was in 1586, when both Robert Dudley, Earl of Leicester (*c*.1532–88), and Sir Francis Walsingham (*c*.1530–90) requested plants to be sent to them from Ireland. Sixty or so years later the inventory taken of Henrietta Maria's palace, the Manor of Wimbledon, records 'one very fayre tree, called the Irish arbutus, standing in the middle parte of the sayd kitchen garden very lovely to look upon'. However, Evelyn makes no mention of the tree a few years later, in 1662, when he visited Wimbledon with the then owner, 'my Lord of Bristoll'.

There are about fourteen species in the *Arbutus* genus, all of them evergreen, and they are part of the huge Ericaceae family. As well as the Mediterranean, members of the family can be found growing from western North America to Mexico and Guatemala. All of them enjoy rocky habitats; most of them are frost hardy, once they have reached maturity. Evelyn never missed an opportunity to recommend a plant for its hedging attributes and noted that they 'may be contrived into most beautiful hedges'. On the Continent arbutus timber was recommended for use as charcoal in goldsmiths' work. The fruit of the Arbutus develop as strawberry-like clusters (with numerous seeds) during September through to November, and can be used in making jam or jelly. Perhaps more interestingly, the fruit may be distilled into wine and a liqueur. Both the leaves and the fruit are used in herbal preparations, the leaves having antiseptic qualities. Evelyn says the seeds are difficult to germinate, although the RHS makes no mention of that, recommending that they should be sown as soon as they are ripe in the autumn; alternatively, semi-ripe cuttings can be taken during late summer.

The third shrub John Evelyn writes about is what he calls 'bay' – that is, the Sweet Bay or Bay Laurel, *Laurus nobilis*. In classical times, long before Linnaeus brought order to the botanical world, there was a crude system of classification based on the shape and morphology of leaves. Under this, all evergreen plants with leathery, oblong or lanceolate leaves were included in the Daphne or Laurel genera, so Daphne was originally called the Sweet Bay. As more and more trees and shrubs with similar leaf characteristics were known by the same name, confusion reigned; six at least, including two Oleanders, *Nerium* spp., and a Broom, *Ruscus*, bore the name bay or laurel.

Now the *Laurus* genus is very small, and the Sweet Bay, *L. nobilis*, a native of the Mediterranean, reigns supreme under that name. Growing in the garden it appears a genial giant; it is an accommodating shrub and if desired it may be clipped and prinked into different topiary shapes. Historically the whole shrub was held in great esteem. Its leaves have long been used to add an aromatic flavour to cooking. The ancient Greeks used it to make crowns for heroes (a practice revived for the 2004 Olympic Games in Athens). Fruiting sprays were made into wreaths for distinguished poets – hence the title Poet Laureate. In seventeenth-century France the Latin *bacca-laureatus*, laurel berry, became the French word *baccalaureate*. This in turn has developed into what every child in France knows as 'Le Bac' or the Baccalauréat, the exam taken by most schoolchildren to qualify them for higher education. The English word 'bachelor' also derives from *bacca-laureatus*; so receiving a Bachelor of Arts degree, or passing 'Le Bac', is still a reminder, however faint, of the reverence the Greek world had for the Sweet Bay, *Laurus nobilis*.

By the time John Evelyn came to write of it, the Bay was a familiar plant in England. He chose it to mark the very centre of the Grove he designed in his garden at Sayes Court. Having been classically educated, he would have been well aware of the shrub's ancient Greek associations with poets and heroes, and it would have seemed entirely natural to him to mark the very heart of his Grove with this plant. There is some debate as to whether the Romans were responsible for introducing the tree during their sojourn in Britain, as by 995 Abbot Aelfric included it in his Latin-Anglo Saxon grammar of that year, under the name *Laurus domestica*. Evelyn recounts how Pliny made sure seed germination was successful by gathering 'the berries in January and spreading them till their sweat be over, then he puts them in dung and sows them'; Pliny rejected the idea of steeping them in wine, but suggested bruising the berries so that the seeds could be washed in water to rid them of their mucilage. Evelyn writes confidently that for 'a competent scattering, so as you would furrow peas', adding: 'Both this way and by setting them apart (which I must comment) I have raised multitudes.' The RHS recommendations differ both in preparation and planting of the seeds. There is no helpful advice as to whether you should use wine or water in cleaning the seeds, and as to time scale, the Society advises they should be planted during the autumn, in containers and placed in a cold frame. Evelyn says 'Bays are increased … of their suckers,' but the RHS says, as with the arbutus, semi-ripe cuttings may be taken in summer.

Box, *Buxus sempervirens*, was another well-known evergreen shrub, although according to Evelyn it was beginning to be rejected as a garden plant because of the 'unagreeableness of its smell … and indeed bees are no friend to it'. It is a common native in northern Europe but a rare native in Britain. Despite its not being bee friendly, Evelyn urges the planting and cultivation of it because of the excellent wood it produces. Lest there is any mistake about what he is recommending, he says: 'I mean the taller sort, for I meddle not here with the dwarf and more tonsile.' Here he is referring to *B. sempervirens* 'Suffruticosa', the Dwarf or Edging Box that was then becoming familiar in gardens. It was a relative newcomer to the British garden, having been developed possibly in Holland, although no one is quite sure. It was considered by some 'a mervailous fine ornament' and was first remarked upon by John Gerard in his *Herball* of 1597.

*Box (*Buxus sempervirens*).*

Box wood is the only timber to be sold by weight rather than in lengths; this is because it is such a heavy wood – it sinks like a stone in water. Evelyn lists the turner, the engraver, the carver, the mathematical instrument-maker, comb- and and pipe-makers, carpenters, as well as the musical instrument-maker as among those who relied on a steady flow of the wood. The range of items that could be manufactured from it was the widest of all woods, ranging from axles for carriages, to rulers, rolling pins, pestles, nutcrackers, weaver's shuttles and, the newest use of all in Evelyn's time, mall balls, for playing the game pell mell (the driving of a ball, with a mallet, through an iron ring). One could have boxwood chessmen, bobbins for lace-making, pins, pegs and screws. The stem wood, when cross cut, gives the most wonderful surface for wood engravings and printing, for which about 600 tons each year was imported from Turkey. Box Hill, near Dorking in Surrey, is one of the most famous sites that produce naturally growing trees; in 1815 the area produced timber worth some £10,000.

No other native tree has so embedded itself in the history of Great Britain as Evelyn's next tree, the Common Yew, *Taxus baccata*, or, as he spells it, the 'Eugh'. Within the genus there are somewhere between five and ten species; the botanical differences and varietal nuances that occur across its huge geographical range – it is a native of Europe, and an area spreading from North Africa to Iran – make it difficult for the nomenclature to be agreed upon. Even Evelyn writes: 'we have two sorts, and other places reckon more.' Nowadays there are about fifty different varieties of the native tree, the most popular being the Irish or Florence Court Yew, *T. baccata* 'Fastigiata', named for its place of discovery in 1780, when it was found

Sprig of Yew (Taxus baccata).

growing on the moors of County Fermanagh, near Florence Court Farm. With its columnar habit and dark green leaves, the Irish Yew was a favourite for planting in churchyards. Yews are very long-lived and have the same aged look that cedars have. In 1880, a tree believed to be over 1,000 years old and growing in Buckland Churchyard, Dover, in Kent, had to be moved as it was threatening the church. It was only a matter of a few feet, and the task was successfully accomplished by William and John Barron, a father and son team who specialized in the Victorian equivalent of a garden makeover. William Barron (1800–91) had earlier written *The British Winter Garden: a Practical Treatize on Evergreens*, and had had a variety, *T. baccata* 'Barroni', named in his honour.

John Evelyn would no doubt have been interested in all these developments, but he did know that yew wood was hard, strong and yet elastic – eminently suitable in the manufacture of the earlier long bows, for hundreds of years the main British fighting weapon. Evelyn recommends that all the uses he has listed for boxwood may be replicated in yew, as they share the same qualities. Cogs for millwork, posts for moist ground, lutes, theorbos, wheels, pins, bowls and tankards are all among the items he says can be made of yew. Propagation by seed is easy, he remarks, once they have been 'washed and cleansed from their mucilage and buried in the ground', but germination can take two or more years – 'it will commonly be the second winter ere they peep'. Nowadays some authorities suggest mixing the seed with sand in the autumn (to keep it dry) and sowing out of doors in spring, others sowing the seeds as soon as they are ripe. Summing up the 'Eugh's' qualities, John Evelyn writes: 'In all which works they succeed marvellous well and are worth our patience fore their perennial verdure, and durableness.' It is surprising that Evelyn does not mention that Yew makes a good hedge, as it was one of the attributes of a tree or shrub he found most useful. There were certainly Yew hedges for him to admire, for in a diary entry for 1658 he notes seeing a handsome hedge of the shrub when visiting Sir Edmond Bowyer at Camberwell.

St Andrew's Churchyard, Buckland-in-Dover, Kent, in 1880. The Yew survived and may now be seen in its new position.

There is no doubt about the hedge-making quality of the next tree John Evelyn describes, the Holly. 'Is there under Heaven a more glorious and refreshing object of the kind, than an impregnable hedge of one hundred and sixty foot in length seven foot high and five in diameter, which I can show in my poor gardens at any time of the year.' Evelyn is writing of the Holly, *Ilex aquifolium*, which he calls *Agrifollium* or *Acuifolium*. He had already described it as a superb boundary hedge when writing about fences and quicksets; now he expands, noting especially its beauty – he writes lyrically of the berries, for instance, when describing 'the taller standards at orderly distances blushing with their natural coral'.

Evelyn says there are two kinds of hollies, 'the prickly and the smoother leaved or as some term it the free-holly, not unwelcome when tender to sheep and other cattle'. In fact the *Ilex* genus is very large, containing some 400 species in the Aquifoliaceae family, spread across the world; some are evergreen, others deciduous. The genus includes shrubs, trees and climbers, which occur in all regions, hot, warm and cold. The leaves may be spiny (the typical holly leaf), spiny-toothed or smooth-edged. Hollies are remarkably tolerant; for example, Evelyn points out that 'At Dungeness in Kent they grow naturally amongst the very beach and pebbles,' and they still thrive there, in the great mounds of noisy shingle.

Holly timber is smooth and white, and has always had an appeal for use in decorative work. The inlayer, Evelyn relates, places it 'especially under thin plates of ivory to render it more conspicuous'. More prosaically, its sturdiness was of use to the millwright, and to the carpenter who fashioned handles and stocks for tools, riding rods and carters' whips.

*Holly (*Ilex aquifolium*). Century-old yew and variegated holly hedge at Wakehurst Place, West Sussex.*

The bark of the Holly, so Evelyn informs us, is used to make birdlime, a viscous substance smeared on to boughs of trees to ensnare birds. He gives detailed instructions on how it is made. The peeled bark must be taken during midsummer, covered with (spring) water, and boiled for about twelve hours, until the grey and white bark separates from the green bark. Drain away the water; lay the green bark in a cool dark place such as the cellar, covering it

thickly with rank weeds – docks or thistles would be suitable; and leave it to rot for about two weeks, 'by which time it will become a perfect mucilage'. After which it must be pounded into a paste, and the resulting mash rinsed thoroughly in running water. During the following fermentation, remove the scum that rises to the surface. Now add clarified capon or goose grease, or, even better, walnut oil, stirring the birdlime over a low heat until it is well mixed, after which it should then be ready for use.

Birdlime, as Evelyn reports, was used and made throughout Europe and, as he goes on to explain, the Italians made it from the berries of mistletoe – so not much kissing there. Spain's was a whiter mixture, but was considered to have the most disgusting smell; birdlime from Syria was of a yellow hue. Great quantities of green birdlime were imported from Turkey and Damascus. Evelyn believed this was made from sebestens, a fruit obtained from a small tree of *Cordia myxa* or *C. latifolia*, natives of India. Both these trees were widely cultivated in the Middle East, and the sebestens (an Arabic word) were eaten as well as being used in the manufacture of birdlime.

Not recommended today, but used as a medicine in the seventeenth century and written about by Evelyn in *Sylva,* was mixing dried and powdered holly leaves with white wine as a cure for kidney stone. More terrifying, and definitely not recommended, is his suggestion of swallowing 'a dozen of the mature berries … to purge phlegm without danger'.

Juniper (*Juniperus communis*) is Evelyn's next tree, an ancient, native small tree or shrub, and a member of the Cupressaceae family. It is a variable species, and has possibly the widest distribution of any tree, being a native of eastern North America, and occurring throughout Europe eastwards to Asia, Korea and Japan. The genus has between fifty and sixty species, all spread over the northern hemisphere, and a large number of them are prized for their aromatic oil and long-lasting timber. It is surprising that Evelyn does not mention the juniper that had been introduced to Britain in 1548, the Savin, *J. sabina*, which is a native across central Europe to northern China. One which has already been discussed and that is probably familiar to us all is the Pencil Cedar, *J. virginiana*, the wood of which, as the name suggests, makes one of the best casings for lead pencils. In the twentieth century the wood was sometimes employed for making railway sleepers.

'I have raised them abundantly of their seeds (neither watering nor dunging the soil) which in two months will peep', Evelyn says. This is one of the rare occasions when his advice differs sharply from modern-day thought: seed germination is now considered to take up to five years.

John Evelyn believes the berries taken in various forms to be a veritable panacea. Swallowed whole they relieve wind; soaked in water they are a marvellous cough cure. 'They are of rare effect being steeped in beer. The water is most singular specific against the gravel in the reins [kidney stones].' A medicine called Venice treacle, an electuary composed of many ingredients including juniper berries, Evelyn considers helpful in relieving rheum, physic, dropsy, jaundice, gout and even the Plague. The Evelyn family enjoyed Wotton-brewed juniper-berry ale as well; so good was it that it was often sent to Sayes Court by river, either for collection at the Whitehall Steps in London or taken all the way to Deptford.

The extracted oil of the juniper berry, he says, can be made into a varnish that is useful for preserving pictures and woodwork, and for keeping polished iron from rusting. Evelyn also recommends that juniper gum can be rubbed on parchment 'to make it bear ink'. The dried berries were a (poor) substitute for pepper, or so Evelyn thought, and this idea leads him into a polemic about Jamaican pepper. This is not pepper at all but Allspice, the delicious aromatic spice that comes from *Pimenta dioica*. The tree was not brought to England until 1759, and since then has only ever been a rarity; it was the berries that were of interest. During 1662 Jamaica was in the news as the newly appointed Governor of Jamaica, Thomas, Baron Windsor (d.1687), had launched an attack on Cuba, but had then subsequently left his post after only ten weeks, citing ill-health. Samuel Pepys was among those who were not amused by his dereliction of duty; and it is possible that the Governor brought back the berries, along with other seeds, to help assuage the annoyance caused by the quickness of his return.

Discussing allied spice trees, Evelyn urges 'his Majesty and the planters there to think of procuring Cinnamon, Cloves and Nutmeg trees … from the East India's … and to plant them in Jamaica'. This novel idea concerning economic horticulture again illustrates the importance of *Sylva* and the inventiveness that John Evelyn showed in his belief that Britain could become an international

Holly bark is smooth grey with some dark markings.

trader in plants, combining both welfare for a country and profit and prestige for Britain. It precedes the ideas and work of the later Sir Joseph Banks (1743–1820) at Kew by a century, when one of his earliest initiatives was the transfer of the Tahitian Breadfruit, *Artocarpus communis*, to the West Indies by Captain Bligh. Continuing his innovative line of thought, Evelyn goes on to speculate whether any of the trees could be grown for timber in England, saying they 'may be of improvement amongst us … since we daily find how many rare exotics and strangers with little care, become endenizoned … to live amongst us'.

He lists a large number of foreign imports, including the 'Constantinople chestnut' or Horse Chestnut, *Aesculus hippocastanum*, introduced in about 1616, and 'Glandferos Ilex', the Holm Oak, *Quercus ilex*, which has already been noted, was an introduction during the sixteenth century. Both these trees have fulfilled John Evelyn's belief in them, becoming well established in Britain's countryside and contributing significantly to the beauty of the landscape. John Evelyn next writes of the 'Styrax' or Storax, *Styrax officinalis*, which entered Britain some time in the latter part of the sixteenth century. It is a native of southern Europe and south-west Asia, but unlike either the Horse Chestnut or the Holm Oak, the Storax really only thrives in a warm sheltered situation so has never made any significant impact in the landscape. What Evelyn does not mention is that on the Continent the dried gum taken from the tree was burned as incense at Mass, and the seeds were used to make rosaries: in the religious unease and the proclivities of the time, perhaps he considered it too sensitive to write of in *Sylva*.

Evelyn furthers his argument by giving examples of what could be gained by opening up new markets and by the growing of economically viable plants. 'The Orange of China being of late brought into Portugal, has drawn a great revenue every year from London alone.' This would have been the Sweet Orange, *Citrus sinensis*, which was being imported into England from at least the beginning of the 1600s if not earlier. Its availability can be confirmed by Samuel Pepys, who bought a 'box of china oranges' during the winter of 1660; also during the Plague years of 1665 and 1666, when it seems that the price of oranges rose and

The Breadfruit Tree (Artocarpus communis).

they became a luxury purchase, Pepys records paying 3d each for them (equivalent to the price one would pay today for a white truffle). The fruit was in short supply not only because of the war with Holland but also because of the restrictions placed on merchant shipping. There was, of course, the added pleasure (particularly for Pepys) of buying the fruit from orange-sellers, the most well known being Nell Gwyn, who later became an actress. (Evelyn heartily disapproved of her, calling her 'Mrs Nellie … an impudent comedian'.)

The first record of orange trees growing anywhere in England was in 1595 at Beddington in Surrey, the home of the Carew family. In 1664 Pepys went 'to walk … in the physique garden in St James park', which had been designed by André Mollet, and where he 'first saw Orange-trees'. When in 1666 Pepys visited Brooke House in Hackney, owned by the Greville family (and coincidentally formerly owned by the Carews), he recorded seeing them again and describes how he 'pulled off a little one by stealth … and eat it; and it was just as other little green small oranges are; as big as half the end of my little finger.' This would probably have been the Seville Orange, *Citrus aurantium*. In September 1679, at Sayes Court, when Evelyn entertained his friend the Master of the Mint, Henry Slingsby (*c.*1621–*c.*90), and the Italian painter Signor Antonio Verrio (*c.*1640–1707), he gave them as dessert 'China oranges off my owne trees, as good, I think as were ever eaten'. These could have been picked from the citrus fruit he had planted in the 1650s – in which case no wonder he was so delighted with their taste.

The exedra and orangery of Chiswick House, London, c.1780.

Another plant that was proving itself in economic terms abroad, and which Evelyn cites, was 'The vine of the Rhine [which] taking root in the Canaries, has produced a far more delicious juice, and has made the rocks and sunburnt ashes of those islands, one of the richest spots of ground in the world.' It is difficult to establish the exact variety of grape that Evelyn was writing about, but it could well have been the German 'Malvasier'. This was one of the numerous varieties of Malvasia Grape, *Vitis vinifera*, which by the seventeenth century was well established on the Canary Islands (particularly Lanzarote) and made a much admired sweet wine. John Evelyn had become interested in the vine on his Continental journey. On almost the first day, in November 1643, he recorded seeing his first vineyard (near Beauvais, France); and the following June (near Tours) he was intrigued by 'a Vineyard, which was so artificially planted and supported with arched poles that stooping downe one might see from end to end a very greate length, under the vines, the bunches hanging down in abundance'. English viticulture during the seventeenth century was hardly flourishing and in much the same situation as it had been when recorded by the Domesday survey in the eleventh century, when only thirty-eight vineyards were cultivated. In 1610 John Tradescant senior was supervising 'works done aboute the vineyard' at Hatfield House; fifty years later, in 1661, it was still there, as Samuel Pepys records on one of his rare journeys out of London. In 1630 Tradescant was appointed 'Keeper of the Gardens, Vines and Silkworms' at Oatlands Palace in Surrey. On 1 May 1665 Pepys records visiting another vineyard, this time at the home of Colonel Thomas Blount of Wricklemarsh, south of Blackheath.

Evelyn also reckons that the 'profit will be inexpressible' if silkworms in Virginia were to thrive; the colony had 'already given silk for the clothing of our King, and it may happen hereafter to give clothes to a great part of Europe'. However, unlike the wine trade of the Canaries, which became of major economic importance to the islands, unfortunately, as we have seen, the experiment to manufacture silk in the American colonies failed, as it did in England.

Grape vine.

The last tree in *Sylva* that Evelyn refocuses on is what he calls the 'laurel' and again there are problems as to which species it could be. By the time he was writing *Sylva* there were two evergreen shrubs commonly known as 'laurel'. Both were indigenous to Europe. One was the Cherry Laurel, *Prunus laurocerasus*, which had been introduced from eastern Europe in 1576, and the other had arrived about 1648, and was the Portugal Laurel, *P. lusitanica*, a native of the Iberian peninsula. This was the larger, and possibly is the more handsome of the two – it has lustrous shiny leaves. However, the Cherry Laurel is an accommodating shrub; a quick grower, it is well able to be used as an undergrowth plant in thin woodland or as a sheltering shrub for game. The two plants were confusingly named in the Tradescant lists, eventually being given their present names by Linnaeus. While Evelyn presumably would have known the two laurels, it is probably the Portuguese Laurel that he was discussing, as he writes familiarly of using it for hedging or growing as a standard. It is a familiar shrub in modern gardens and parks, having about thirty different varieties listed. As Evelyn says, 'They are raised of the seeds or berries with extraordinary facility or propagated by layers, and cuttings where ever there is shade and moisture.' Autumn is the time to sow the seeds, and the semi-ripe cuttings should be taken in summer, with a recommendation to give them some bottom heat.

Evelyn finally returns to his brief 'that of trees and plants, the industry we have recommended …Yet I would be glad to encourage the carpenter and the joiner and rejoice to see that their work … do daily improve and that by the example and application of his Majesties Universities and Royal Society the restoration and improvement of shipping, mathematical and mechanical arts, the use of timber grows daily in more reputation'. John Evelyn then sounds a word of warning about society itself drifting away from these practical notions, and becoming too self-indulgent; he found it hard to reconcile the sometimes hedonistic behaviour of the post-Restoration Court and its 'tapestry damask, velvet, and Persian furniture' with his own discreet and more modest behaviour, 'when it will be very difficult if not impossible to recover ourselves from a softness and vanity which will in time not only effeminate, but undo the Nation'. This statement is at the very core of Evelyn's book, where he makes clear his determination to encourage not only self-sufficiency in home-grown timber production but also the efficiency and hard work of the artisan.

CHAPTER IV

Arboreal Husbandry

JOHN EVELYN USES the concluding eight chapters of *Sylva* to support his arguments for the importance of trees and the need for their planting, both for timber and for the improvement of the natural world. The first five concentrate on practicalities. At the heart of his narrative remains his concern that timber in all its forms should be produced to the highest standard, but being eclectic by nature and infectiously passionate about his subject, he explores every aspect of a tree's husbandry: its growth, use, production and ailments; but also the history, myth and legend.

'Of the Infirmities of Trees'

Evelyn begins by listing, in what he calls 'the Rustick Rhyme', the diseases to which trees are susceptible:

The Calf, the Wind-shoc and the Knot,
The Canker, Scab, Scurf, Sap and Rot.

The catalogue of ailments has hardly changed and he alerts us to other familiar problems that may harm a tree: 'weeds, suckers, fern, wet, mice, moles'. He lists 'Sideration', which in the seventeenth century meant the sudden, unexplained death or blasting of a tree or plants, and even cites the Plague as bringing about the death of a tree. 'Tumors, Distortions, Lacrimations [weeping], Tophi [stones], Goutes, Carbuncles, Ulcers, Crudities, Fungosities [fungal growth], Gangreen and an Army more' sound more like the complaints in a medieval hospital than diseases of trees. Most are still relevant today, but with a few additions: pollution, acid rain and the chainsaw.

Worms, snails, earwigs – he deals with each problem in turn. Ant hills, or 'pismires', as he calls them, are to be destroyed – then as now – with scalding

*Coppiced Hazel
under standard
Oak Trees,
Dorset.*

water. Traps are to be used to eradicate mice, as well as moles, on which subject Evelyn adds, 'every woodman knows, It is certain that they are driven from their haunts by Garlick for a time, and other heady smels buried in their passages'. Alas, garlic probably proved as ineffective then as it does now in creating a mole-free zone. He mentions the teredo and other boring worms that 'poison that passage to the great prejudice of some Trees … and the Woodpecker and other Birds often pitching upon the stem, as you may observe them … is a mark that the Tree is infected'.

Evelyn complains about conies (rabbits) and hares 'barking' trees during a hard winter – the surest way to kill a tree unless you 'anoint that part which is within their reach, with Stercus humanum [human excrement], tempered with a little water or urine, and lightly brushed on'. Another of his solutions, sprinkling tree trunks with 'Tanners liquor', was no more salubrious, as hides were – and are – steeped in week-old urine, the stench of which has to be smelled to be believed.

Hornet and wasp nests are to be destroyed by stopping up their entrances with tar and goose-dung. Reassuringly he tell us that earwigs and snails 'seldom infest Forest-trees', but are a nuisance on trees that bear fruit. Earwigs must be destroyed by 'enticing them into sweet waters', and snails need to be picked off in the morning and during 'rainy evenings'. Evelyn insists: 'I advise you to visit your Cypresse Trees on the first Rains in April [when they will be] covered with young snails no bigger than small pease.' Caterpillars are to have their webs cut from the twigs 'before the end of February'. If you are too late and the caterpillars have hatched, he recommends washing them off with a mixture of squashed caterpillars and garlic in water.

Rooks, pinching off the buds and tips of trees when building their nests, 'cause many Trees and Groves to decay'. Cattle and particularly goats break in and cause a 'conclamation' (a clamour) among the trees, and their 'mouths and breath is poison to Trees; they never thrive well after'. Evelyn tells us that according to the first-century Roman scholar Marcus Varro, 'if they but lick the olive tree, they [the tree] become immediately barren'.

Anyone experiencing storms today would do well to follow Evelyn's wise advice: 'in case any goodly trees chance to be prostrated by some impetuous and extraordinary storme; you be not over hasty to carry him away, or despair of him'. He cites examples both in England and on the Continent, where, once polled, 'many vast trees have raised themselves by the vigour only of the remaining roots, without any other assistance'. This happened following the great storms of the autumn of 1987 and the winter of 1989–90.

To end this chapter, Evelyn shares with his readers a secret formula to keep felled timber healthy. This includes using 'Aqua fortis', a modern word in Evelyn's day for nitric acid, and still in use today. He recommends we mix it with common yellow sulphur in a 'cucurbitt-glasse', a long glass tube to help ripen and keep cucumbers straight, dry it by distillation, whereupon it will become 'of a blackish or sad red colour', and then tip the powder on to a marble top or into a glass, where it will dissolve in oil. This mixture, Evelyn says, is a marvellous remedy, and could be used not only for preserving wood but on ropes, cables, fishing nets and so on. He also recommends linseed oil, which 'has proved very effectual, it was experimented in a Wall-nut Table, where it destroyed millions of worms immediately … oyl of wall-nuts will doubtless do the same, is sweeter and a better Vernish, but above all is commended Oyl of Cedar, or that of Juniper'. A good husbandman, rather like a good Boy Scout, should 'be prepared'; at least this is the motto that Evelyn recommends for ensuring the good care of a tree and its timber.

'Of Copses'

Today the very word copse conjures up a tranquil image of a traditional English landscape, with clumps of trees, hedgerows and perhaps sunlight filtering through them on to a spring-like scene. However, for hundreds of years the copse was part of the working woodland, and an essential ingredient in the economy of England. By Evelyn's time copse had come to mean a small wood or thicket grown for the purpose of periodical cutting. The word is a shortened version of coppice, or coppice wood, or even encoppice. It has its roots in Roman Latin, although in Latin it meant underwood. The Anglo-Saxons used the word *hris* for underwood. The Norman-French word, sounding similar, was *tailz*, the equivalent in modern French being *taillis*.

'There is not a more noble, and worthy Husbandry than this, which rejects no sort of Ground,' writes John Evelyn. Practical as ever, he points out that the copse should be securely fenced, but the pasture (the land between the trees) 'will lye both warm and prove of exceeding delight to the Owner. These spaces likewise useful and necessary for Cart-way, to fetch out the wood at every Fall'. The usual planting seems to have been of Hazel or Birch, but Evelyn recommends Ash, Chestnut and Sallow (Willow); in particularly boggy ground, Alder, Poplar, Sycamore and Willow should be considered.

Exploit. des Bois. Pl. IV. P. 250.

Preparing faggots for use in the making of charcoal, and fascines for artillery batteries.

Copse wood was an important and essential local facility, and to be of long-term service it needed to be properly husbanded. When felling, Evelyn says, 'you are to spare as many likely Trees for Timber as with discretion you can'. An early statute laid down what growing material should remain per acre following a felling. Both the number and the scantlings (the size) of felled wood were listed. There were four different categories and these started with 'Firsts' or 'Bests', of which only three or four would probably remain; there had to be at least fourteen 'Seconds', twelve 'Thirds' and eight 'Wavers'. This was on top of the twelve oaks per acre decreed by a statute of Henry VIII. Coppice laws regarding enclosure and fencing were reinforced during the reign of Elizabeth I; for example, if a copse was to be felled within fourteen years of its last coppicing there had to be a four-year period of fencing; if growth was to continue for more than that length of time, a further two years had to be added. The extraction of wood at regular intervals was also controlled, as were all the types of material. There were 'billets' or 'billet-wood'; originally a Celtic word for a sacred tree, by Evelyn's time billet had come to mean a legally prescribed bundle of ten or fourteen sticks for fuel, cut into approximately 1m (3ft) lengths and 19m (7$^1/_2$in) in diameter. A 'stack of wood', 'which is the boughs and offal of the Trees to be converted to Charcoal', was to be 3.66m (12ft) long.

These measures, set in place to ensure the renewal of the wood and approved by Evelyn, are sound environmental practice by today's standards. Such attention to detail about a piece of land, which today we might notice simply as being attractive in its setting, was then crucial to the cycle of timber production.

'Of Pruning'

The pruning of trees and shrubs – essential for controlling and regulating their well-being, growth, flowering and fruiting – is the third in Evelyn's series of practical skills. 'Tis a misery to see how our fairest Trees are defaced and mangled by unskilful Wood-men, and mischievous Bordurers, who go always armed with short Hand-bills, hacking and chopping off all that comes in their way; by which our Trees are made full of knots, boils, cankers and deformed bunches to their utter destruction. Good Husbands [husbandmen] should be ashamed of it', he complains. In the twenty-first century, despite supposedly superior equipment, the hacking and mangling of trees is unfortunately still

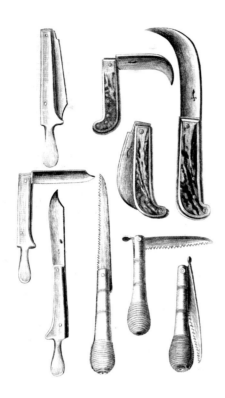

with us. Today complaints about shoddy pruning are made usually on aesthetic rather than on utilitarian grounds, but when Evelyn was writing, the growth, felling and dressing of timber were all vital for meeting the manufacturing, domestic and naval requirements of the age. It was therefore most important that when pruning, husbandmen or foresters attained the highest level of professional competence, and Evelyn goes into great detail about what they should accomplish.

As *Sylva* focuses on woodland and hedgerow trees, the 'pruning' Evelyn discusses is mostly what we would now call tree surgery: a much more advanced (and sometimes dangerous) technique for promoting the well-being of fully grown trees. But when he was writing there was no distinction made between the two skills and the key to ensuring a tree reached and maintained its full growth was to begin pruning at a very early stage. Evelyn lists the tools required for doing a good job: a hand bill, a hatchet, hook, hand saw, pruning knife, axe, broad chisel and mallet, 'all made of the best steel and kept sharp'. He stresses that when pruning a tree, clean, smooth and close cuts are to be made, with no tearing away of the bark as the upward stroke is made. Work should be undertaken during the winter months; the more mature the tree, the earlier in the winter the work should be carried out, whereas the younger and more immature trees should be left until later. Boughs that do not allow the light and air 'are cumbersome', and 'Sucker, Water-boughs, Fretters [branches rubbing one with another]' should all be removed. Amongst all this practical advice Evelyn slips in a reminder about the decorative uses of trees, warning that 'such trees as we would leave for Shade and ornament, should be seldom cut.' He criticizes the treatment meted out to the 'branchy' elm trees growing in both St James's Park and Pall Mall, which had recently taken place, and feared that 'the remedy comes too late to save their decay'. In fact later the elm trees were replaced by fashionable lime walks that, as he points out, 'will sooner accomplish their perfection'.

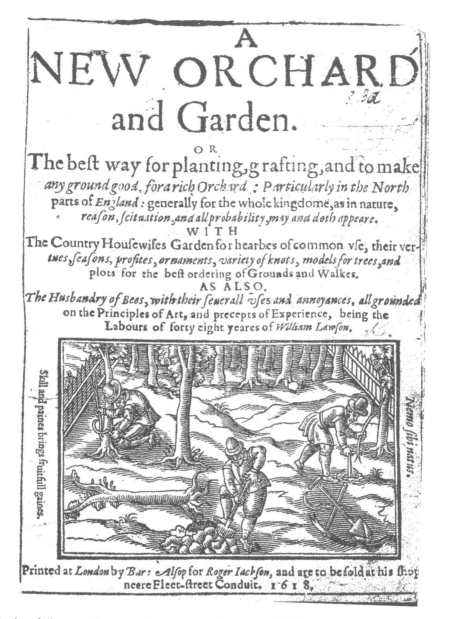

A
NEW ORCHARD
and Garden.
OR
The best way for planting, grafting, and to make
any ground good, for a rich Orchard : Particularly in the North
parts of *England* : generally for the whole kingdome, as in nature,
reason, scituation, and all probability, may and doth appeare.
WITH
The Country Housewifes Garden for hearbes of common vse, their ver-
tues, seasons, profites, ornaments, variety of knots, models for trees, and
plots for the best ordering of Grounds and Walkes.
AS ALSO,
The Husbandry of Bees, with their seuerall vses and annoyances, all grounded
on the Principles of Art, and precepts of Experience, being the
Labours of forty eight yeares of *William Lawson.*

Skill and paines brings fruitfull gaines.

Nemo sibi natus.

Printed at *London* by *Bar: Alsop* for *Roger Iackson*, and are to be sold at his shop
neere Fleet-street Conduit. 1 6 1 8.

Evelyn follows with quotes from the earlier work of William Lawson
(*fl.*1570s–1610s). Born in Yorkshire, Lawson published two books, both in
1618: *The Country Housewife's Garden*, the first book to be directed towards
women working in the garden, and *A New Orchard and Garden*, in which the
author, drawing on 'eight and forty years experience concerning timber-trees',
explains that from the trunk of the tree (or as Evelyn calls it the 'boal' or bole),

William Lawson's
A New Orchard,
1618.

the arms, branches, scions (twigs) should all be free, and 'not touch his fellow'. The tree should be made to spread outward and upward equally, and the undergrowth lopped up as it matures. As Evelyn says, 'Thus shall you have handsome, clear healthful, great lasting trees.'

To maintain the health of the trunk of the tree, and to speed its growth, 'there is not a more excellent thing than the frequent rubbing of the boal or stem, with some piece of hair-cloth, or ruder stuff, at the beginning of Spring.' Sealskin or, for more rugged bark, 'a piece of Coat of Maile, which is made of small wyres' could also be used. A brisk rubbing down following heavy rain to open the pores, frees a trunk of moss, kills worms, and produces 'a wonderful and incredible improvement'. Nowadays a quick scrub with water to enhance the look of our silver birch trees is about all that takes place.

Finally, Evelyn reminds the husbandman that it is his continual duty to walk about and 'survey his young Plantations dayly; and to see that all gaps be immediately stopped'. Once again he shows that his interest is not exclusively practical by declaring that if all pruning rules are followed, not only the value of the timber but also the beauty of the forests will increase.

'Of the Age, Stature, and Felling of Trees'

In this chapter Evelyn allows himself the indulgence of including everything he has ever discovered about the particulars and peculiarities of trees – especially ancient specimens. Looking to far-flung lands for ancient writings, myths and legends, he offers a wonderful miscellany of tree wisdom with some occasional misinformation and one intriguing mystery.

He begins, logically enough, by saying: 'For there is certainly in Trees (as in all things else) a time of Increment, or growth; a Status of season when they are at best (which is also that of Felling) and a decrement or period when they decay.' He is more fanciful when he goes on to discuss the age to which trees live. Fruit trees, he believes, 'may possibly arrive to a thousand years'; and he cites Pliny's conviction that there were Oaks growing in the 'Hercynian Forest' in mid-Germany that were contemporaneous with the beginning of the world, and that their roots had raised mountains. Evelyn mentions a Turpentine Tree of

Idumea (Israel) – possibly *Pistacia lentiscus* – that was supposedly as old as time. A ruined sepulchre 'somewhere in Persia' helped to shelter an ancient Cypress thought to be about 2,500 years old. In Jerusalem an aged 'sycamore', probably *Ficus sycomorus*, the Sycamore or Mulberry Fig, was believed to have been growing when Our Lord rode in triumph through the city on Palm Sunday. Pliny, as Evelyn notes, marvels not only at the great age of trees but also at their stupendous size, citing that the Congo could supply 'trees capable to be excavated in vessels that would contain two hundred men a piece'. 'Punti' (canoes) large enough to hold some forty people were made from great trunks of German oak. Evelyn notes the Vatican, Cyprus, Athens, Nicaragua and India were among many places distinguished for having trees of great bulk. He says that there was also 'a certain Fig in the Caribby Islands, which emits such large buttresses, that great planks for tables and flooring are cleft out of them'. Could this be the Banyan Tree, Ficus *benjamina* or *F. benghalensis* – both produce great aerial roots? Although of Asian origin, the trees could have been introduced via sixteenth-century Portuguese or Spanish traders. There is also the possibility

Ficus benjamina *can grow to 30m (100ft). It is used as a conservatory or house plant in Britain.*

that they were introduced by the Chinese during their great world exploration of 1421. Recent research into this remarkable period of Chinese adventuring has thrown up evidence that plant material may have been exchanged between Asia and both South and North America much earlier than previously believed.

From China Evelyn cites two examples of enormous trees: 'a certain Tree called Ciennich (or the Tree of a thousand years) in the Province of Suchu neer the City Kien, which is so prodigiously large, as to shrowed 200 sheep under one onley branch of it ... and a greater wonder ... in the Province of Chekiang whose amplitude is so stupendiously vast as fourscore persons can hardly embrace'. In fact 'Ciennich' – or in its modern (pinjin) spelling, Quiannan – means Ten Thousand Years. Both Roy Lancaster and his Japanese associate Mikinori Ogisu, the two foremost experts on Chinese flora, believe that the tree Evelyn could be referring to is the Maidenhair Tree, *Ginkgo biloba*. If so, this is the earliest reference to it that has so far been found in England. It is possible that by the seventeenth century the Ginkgo was known about in Europe. The Portuguese had traded with the Chinese from 1557, when their vessels made a permanent base in the port of Macao. There is definite evidence that by Evelyn's time the Chinese were growing maize, and that the peanut was also being cultivated; both may have been introduced to China by the Portuguese, the peanut presumably having been collected from Brazil. There was at the very least some horticultural talk between the Chinese and the Portuguese and an exchange of flora is possible. John Evelyn, having travelled abroad and maintained good contacts in Europe when he returned to England, may well have been aware of discussions there about foreign flora. The Ginkgo's long history of medicinal use in China and Japan and its ancient lineage made it a much-revered tree. It was often planted adjacent to monasteries; during the 1980s Lancaster recorded seeing at Hongchunping or Spring Crag Monastery in the region of Emei Shan, Sichuan Province, 'two magnificent ginkgoes of about 30m (100ft) reputed to be 1,500 years old'. A first-hand account of the Ginkgo appeared in *Amoenitates Exoticae*, written by the German physician and botanist Engelbert Kaempfer (1651–1715) in 1712. An employee of the Dutch East India Company for two years from 1690, he was in Japan, where he studied the flora. Kaempfer recorded initial descriptions of many Japanese and Chinese plants, including several varieties of camellia and lilies, as well as aucuba, hydrangea and chimonanthus. The seed of the Ginkgo Tree seems to have first arrived in Europe in about 1730, but it was another twenty years before it arrived in England, from Holland. It is of course unique, not only for its ancient lineage, healing properties and usefulness in the kitchen, but for its qualities as a street tree; it is widely planted throughout several provinces of China, including the cities of Shanghai and Beijing. The Ginkgo has been used in London street plantings too, as well as putting in an appearance in various supermarket car parks from Cornwall to Cumbria.

Having scoured the world for its silvicultural wonders, Evelyn turns his attention nearer home. He describes 'an old and decayed Chestnut at Fraiting in Essex' (now Frating Green) whose stump yielded thirty sizeable loads of logs; a stately Lime Tree at Depeham in Norfolk (now Deopham); a 'most stupendous' Willow Tree in Berkshire; great Elms growing on the Evelyn family estate in Surrey; and a 'superannuated Eugh-tree growing now in Braburne Church, not far from Scots-hall in Kent'. Evelyn had visited Brabourne, near Ashford, and measured the Yew, and later in 1663 had it measured 'more exactly'. According to local accounts, the circumference measured 17.98 metres (59ft); Evelyn records it as 17.67 metres (58ft). When it was felled around 1800, the tree was reputed to be 3,000 years old. There was 'Such another monster … to be seen in Sutton Churchyard, neer Winchester'.

Henry, Lord Howard of Norfolk (d. 1684) – whose family had been friends with Evelyn's for several generations, and who had previously invited Evelyn to design the gardens at Albury in Surrey – supplied detailed information to John Evelyn about trees and land he also owned in the north of England. From the Sheffield Lordship of Rivelin (now almost consumed by the western development of Sheffield) Evelyn relates the story of how, when a certain oak was felled and laid flat, 'Sam Staniforth a Keeper and Edward Morphy both on horse-back could not see over the tree one anothers Hat-crowns'. He praises other oak trees in 'Worksopp-Park' (now Worksop) in Nottinghamshire, owned by the Norfolk family, for their beauty and great girth or standing.

Eager to inform his readers about the inside of a tree too, Evelyn explains the concentric rings that can be seen on a cross-section of a tree trunk 'from the centre of the Wood to the inside of the Bark'. He distinguishes the different type of rings observed on the different trees: fast-growing ones, such as Fir and Ash making larger and thicker rings, whereas slower-growing species, such as the native Holly and Box, together with the introduced Quince, Lignum-vitae and Ebony, all hardwoods and slower to mature, making smaller or less distinct rings. The 'Tree gains a new one every year' and in the northern hemisphere the rings develop better on the southern and therefore sunnier side of the tree than they do on the northern, colder side.

So to felling; 'a felling should be celebrated', Evelyn says enthusiastically. Although trees that are 'perceive to decay are first to be picked out for the Ax', ideally you should choose a tree full of 'vigour and perfection'. To test the soundness of a tree, he recommends 'Lord Bacon's Experiment', which involved piercing the trunk of the tree with an auger, 'as those who bore the Earth to explore what Minerals the place is impregnated with, and as sound cheeses are tasted'. Augers are still used by, among others, cheese-makers, although nowadays foresters and geologists use other methods as well. Francis Bacon, 1st Baron Verulam (1561–1626), was a philosopher and statesman; Evelyn and he could not have met but they both held the same belief that man was

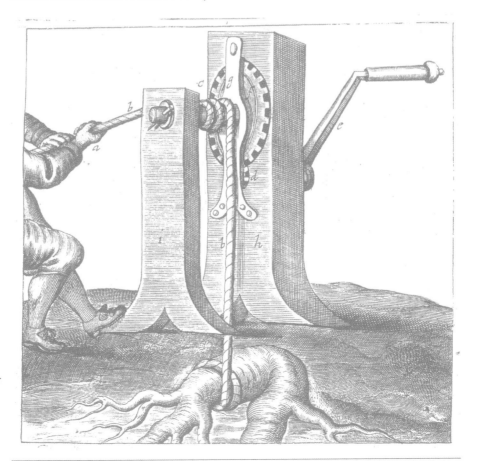

A proposed machine for the extraction of tree roots. Evelyn calls it the 'German-devil'.

the servant and interpreter of Nature. Unfortunately, while stuffing an eviscerated chicken with snow in order to measure the time of putrefaction, in an experiment to test the effects of extreme cold on flesh in the winter of 1626, Bacon caught a chill and died.

The time of year for felling a tree, Evelyn remarks, 'is not usually till about the end of April'. (Today's readers must remember that Evelyn was writing before the adoption of Gregorian calendar, when all dates moved forward by eleven days.) However, timber to be made into 'plows, carts, axel-trees, naves, harrow and the like husbandry-tools, do frequently cut in October.'

Evelyn highlights the writings of Gervase Markham (*c.*1568–1637), who in *Farewell to Husbandry*, published in 1620, writes that immediately after Christmas a forester should survey the woods, list the various species to be felled and make a catalogue of the items to be fashioned from the timber – wheel spokes, naves (central rings into which spokes and axel tree fit), pales (stakes), spares, all to be made by the wheelwright – as well as the cooper's needs (wood for making or repairing tubs, casks, barrels, buckets and so on), not forgetting 'scantlings for the ploughs' and the brush (bundles of faggots or twigs) for firewood. Sale of the wood and timber should begin at about Candlemas (2 February) and continue till spring.

Eighteenth-century French methods of cutting timber without a sawpit.

As to the actual felling, 'the most principal thing is the skilful disbranching of the boal of all such arms and limbs as may endanger it in the Fall, wherein much forecast and skill is required of the Wood-man'. The only difference today is that now the chainsaw is used. The cut, Evelyn says, should be as close to the ground as possible. Once the tree is down, the bark should be stripped off, so that it can dry. Then the trunk must be cleared of all its remaining branches; it is then ready to be sawn into lengths for squaring the timber.

Regarding measuring timber and estimating its girth and length, he scorns the 'divers Country Gentlemen, Stewards, and Woodmen' who had on their rulers something called Gunter's line, saying 'few of them understand how to Work from it'. Edmund Gunter (1581–1626) was a mathematician and astronomer who, in about 1610, invented the unit of measurement known as the chain. This comprises four poles or 20.15 metres (66ft), a pole being 5^1/$_2$ yards length, for the chain. The distance between the two wickets on a cricket pitch is a chain and the measurement is still used in land surveying today. Gunter's line was a logarithmic calculation for multiplying and dividing measurements mechanically. Evelyn implies that it was quite complicated to use. Pepys probably used the same system; when calculating timber bought for naval use, he too had difficulties in computing the measurements, and had to spend time practising.

A steam tree-feller in action in 1878, watched by Prime Minister William Gladstone.

Concluding the chapter, Evelyn gives advice for the sawing up of timber. He recommends employing the 'Norway Engine', a sawmill that could be turned by either water or wind power. There was also an engine for the mechanical making of timber pipes, aqueducts and columns, powered in the same way.

*Of Timber, the Seasoning
and the Uses, and of Fuel*

Emphasizing the 'universal use of that precious Material', and how crucial timber was to the economic life of the country, Evelyn begins this chapter: 'We had better be without gold than without timber'. For the seasoning of timber the site requires to be out of the wind and sun if possible, but in an airy place. The planks should be dry and laid lengthways, and, so that air can circulate, stacked up with space between each plank 'to preserve them from a certain mouldinesse'. Evelyn explains this is not the only way of preserving the raw material. There are some 'who keep their Timber as moist as they can, by submerging it in Water'. Certainly this was the way mast timber was kept, and in 1667 one of the first mast docks along the Thames at Woolwich was constructed on behalf of the navy. Elm felled for immediate use could be plunged into salt water. Another way was to bury the wood in earth, while others used wheat to cover it. To harden timber it could be fired, ready for use as piles to be dug into earth, or it could be kept continually wet, for building locks or bridges, or riverbank work perhaps. Sir Hugh Plat (or Platt), who had had a house and gardens in Bethnal Green and in St Martin's Lane, London, described in *Jewell House of Art and Nature* (1608) how he had witnessed the Venetians burning and scorching their timbers 'till they have gotton upon it an hard, black, coaly crust'. From his own travels on the Continent, Evelyn observes: 'I myself remembering to have seen Charcoals dug out of the ground amongst the ruines of antient Buildings, which have in all probability lain covered with earth about 1500 years.' Thus, all the elements – earth, fire, air and water – can contribute to the making of usable timber.

He also points out that certain woods acquire different properties according to the time of year when they are cut. Button mould-makers had noticed the differences: pear wood is at its hardest if cut in the summer; box is at its hardest when cut in the spring, and conversely if sawn in the summer the wood appears mellower; winter is the time when holly is at its hardest.

Green timber, which is unseasoned (or raw) wood, clogs the teeth of a saw with too much sawdust and is best kept for use in carving and turning work. For joiners' or close work, green timber must never be used, as it is unstable and has not dried out; doors, windows and floors should always be made from seasoned wood, especially 'where walnut-tree is the material, which will be sure to shrink'.

Hewn timber (wood cut by an axe or chisel) is easier to use than split or cleft wood, particularly when making 'huge and massif columns'; Evelyn suggests 'let them be boared through', as this 'is an excellent preservative from splitting'. Split timber lasts longer than hewn and is therefore recommended for making fence posts. To prevent timber from drying and splitting, he recommends rubbing it with a wax cloth or painter's putty. Before beginning work, and to lessen 'the effects both of Sun and Air upon it', smear the timber with cow dung. To keep green timber supple, try soaking it twice in 'fat of powdered beef-broth'; an alternative method, which some carpenters used, was to mix grease and sawdust together and coat the wood with this mixture, but Evelyn is rather dismissive of this and believes the first suggestion is the best. To preserve wood exposed to the elements, once it had been fashioned into gates, sluices, drawbridges and so on, the Dutch used 'a certain mixture of Pitch and Tar, upon which they strew small pieces of cockle and other shells, beaten almost to powder, and mingled with Sea-sand or the scales of Iron'.

Although he seemingly did not play an instrument, Evelyn appreciated listening to music. He recorded on 20 November 1679, for instance, dining with 'Mr Slingsby' and hearing music 'which was exquisitely performed by foure of the most renowned masters, Du Prue, a Frenchman on the lute; Signor Bartholomeo, an Italian, on the harpsichord; Nicolao on the violin; but above all for its sweetnesse and novelty the viol d'amore of 5 wyre-strings plaied on with a bow, … by a German'. It is perhaps not surprising, then, that he describes the use of wood in musical instruments. The soft but close-grained European spruce, *Picea abies*, which he calls 'German Fir', was used to fashion viols and violins – as it still is – and the rim of the viol as well; 'the finest grained fir' was saved 'for the Bellyes'. The back of the instrument and the thin ribs required the harder fine-grained maple, *Acer* spp. yew and pear wood were used for making fingerboards, back and ribs. By the time Evelyn wrote *Sylva*, recorders and other woodwind instruments were made from several pieces of wood, rather than a single piece – although Mozart's 'magic flute' was reportedly fashioned out of one piece of

Strawberry tree

1,000-year-old (unnamed) wood – and this increased their range of play and popularity (Pepys had a recorder made for himself during 1665). Evelyn notes that they could be made from hard or soft wood.

To achieve a smooth high polish, it is the hardest woods of all which 'are best to receive politure', and he lists woods that glow when polished, such as ebony, box, terebinth, cornus and yew. Linseed oil, from flax, *Linum usitatissimum*, or a sweeter nut oil are his suggested 'politure'. He quotes Pliny's belief that a decoction of crushed walnut shells and wild pears would help to bring up a shine.

Oak is not included in the list of easily polished wood, being reserved 'for Ships and Houses'. For shipbuilding Evelyn says that the keel should be of oak, and advocates walnut for the stern, and elm wood for the pumps. He goes on to enumerate a series of experiments to test the strength and suppleness of oak, ash and fir that were undertaken for The Royal Society during 1663 and 1664. He also discusses subterranean or fossilized wood, noting in particular 'that it might be observed how far any kind of Wood bends before it breaks'. Fossilized wood seems to have been a source of great interest in the seventeenth century. Pepys records that during the enlargement of the Thames in 1665 'perfect trees overcovered with earth' were found at Blackwall Dock on the north bank. He describes hazel trees 'with the branches and the very nuts upon them … black with age'. Evelyn's close associate and fellow member of The Royal Society, the chemist and physicist Robert Hooke, carried out a number of trials on the fossilized wood, reporting that the sample 'retained the exact shape of wood … and … it resembled wood.' But Evelyn noted that it would not burn in the fire, but was brittle (like flint) and felt colder than wood usually does, being 'much like other close Stones and Minerals'.

Evelyn acknowledges that one of the principal uses of wood was as fuel. For the best-quality underwood, 'for the use of our Chimneys', Evelyn recommends that felling should take place between 'Martle-mas' (Martinmas, 11 November) in one year and 'Holy-rood' (Holy Cross Day, 14 September) the following year. Oak should not be cut after May, and ash 'twixt Michael-mas and Candle-mas' (29 September and 2 February), with the proviso that if cattle are to browse the ash, it must be cut on a daily basis. Cutting for fuel when the sap is up, Evelyn warns, 'is a mark of improvident husbands, besides it will never burn well'. He even explains the best way to stack logs: by alternating courses of end-on and side-on logs. Today owners of wood-burning stoves will recognize these instructions. In Brittany, where the use of wood as fuel has never really died out, the stacking of the winter logs has almost reached the status of high art; it is fascinating to view the patterns different owners employ. However, being concerned to address shortages of wood, he makes a plea to 'all ingenious persons studious of the benefit of their Country, to think of wayes how our Woods may be preserved, by all manner of Arts which may prolong the lasting of our fuel'; to them, he 'would give the best encouragements'. Remarking how careful and ingenuous the 'Hollanders' are in their abstemious use of fuel, making do with 'dung of beasts, and Peat and Turf', he reproduces a fuel recipe given by Sir Hugh Plat, who believed it was 'generally used in Mastricht'. This consists of a third part coal (pit, sea or char coal), mixed with loam, moistened with beast or human urine – whichever is available – and formed into balls, about the size of goose eggs, or any other shape that takes your fancy. Air dried, these will 'burn very clear, give a wonderfull heat, and continue a very long time'. For cooking, particularly the baking of bread, he recommends the energy-efficient invention of Dr Keffler, whom he subsequently met in July 1666, whose 'iron ovens, made portable for the Prince of Orange's army … would be an extraordinary expedient of husbanding our fuel'.

Showing a frugal turn of mind, he extols the merits of using seaweed or wrack (some of which comes as packing in oyster barrels) to help kindle a fire 'and maintain a glowing luculent heat without wast'. It should, he says, be gathered in summer, from the rocky shore, or if need be, by boat, after which it should be spread out and dried or 'fully cured'. (Damp seaweed, unless spread as a fertilizer or hung up to tell the weather, eventually becomes stinking and mucilaginous.) He believes 'It makes an excellent fire alone, and roasts to admiration.' As a bonus, the ash left behind makes 'one of the best manures for the land in the world'.

Evelyn goes into great detail about the size and shape of bundles of wood made up to sell for fuel, examining billets and faggots, which were almost the same length (just over and just under 1 metre – 3ft 4in and 3ft respectively). A faggot, though, had a stick 'one foot in length to harden and wedge the binding of it. This to prevent the abuse (too much practised) of filling the middle part, and ends with trash, and short sticks.' He also quotes the antiquarian and scholar William Camden (1551–1623), who noted in his book *Britannia* a faggot that had fused together and grew at Hall, on the banks of the Fowey River in Cornwall; it was complete even to the band around the middle and 'carefully preserved many years'.

He also considered that it would be helpful to 'know how to Stop, Prime, and Paint their Timber-work'. First, he says, rough wood must be smoothed and filled with putty, made of white and red lead, which is derived from lead carbonate and hydrated oxide (a lethal substance, not now in use). White lead had been in use since Egyptian times, and was known to the Greeks and the Romans. Evelyn recommends mixing the putty with a little Spanish white (a fine powdered chalk) and linseed oil to make it into a paste. Then give the timber three priming coats: 'Oaker and Spanish-white, very thinly ground. The second is the same, a little whiter; but it matters not much. The third and last, with White-lead alone.' Ochre or ocher is a mixture of hydrated oxide of iron mixed with varying proportions of clay and produces a colour anywhere between pale yellow and deep orange, or brown. And to finish, 'if you desire it exquisite, instead of Lin-seed-oyl, use that of Wall-nuts'.

Of paint colours, 'Blew', Evelyn writes, was obtained from *Indigofera tinctoria*, and a few other allied trees. There are over 700 species in the genus, distributed widely in mainly tropical and subtropical regions. Although several species of the tree can be grown in Britain, *I. tinctoria* is not one of them, as it cannot survive northern winters, and when it was brought to Europe in 1731 it required stove treatment or raising in a heated greenhouse. The extracted blue pigment was an expensive import from India. Such was the intensity of the colour that Sir Isaac Newton called it one of the seven prismatic or primary colours. A cheaper option was to use oxide of cobalt, which after various processes was finely pulverized to produce the blue pigment called Byce (or bice). But as Evelyn points out, it was a dull blue identified with azure rather than the clear blue from India. Blue could be made greener by adding orpiment or King's Yellow. This is a bright yellow mineral substance; its other name is yellow arsenic; this was the arsenic of the ancients. Green itself was derived from verdigris, the 'Green of Greece', which could be made artificially by putting dilute acetic acid on thin plates of copper. The resulting encrustation was ground with linseed oil 'pretty thick, and then tempered with Joyners Vernish'. Brushes had to be washed in 'sope' to keep them clean and supple, and oil (linseed oil in particular) stored in bladders (probably pigs' bladders).

Oak galls.

To keep the various pigments in tip-top condition these, in their containers, were to be plunged into 'fair water'.

Evelyn provides an all-weather recipe for a black paint that could be used either indoors or outside, for instance 'to a Coach with perfect success'. The mixture includes oak galls boiled in white wine vinegar and ground up. The timber has to be rubbed over twice with this concoction. Next stir aqua-vitae (a form of undistilled alcohol) and lamp black (soot collected from oil lamps) together with some of the black dye used in the silk industry, which Evelyn recommends as it was 'cheap and easy to be had', and mix well. The paint should be of a thin consistency, 'enough to passe through a Strainer'. This concoction, he says, will not only stain the timber but 'if at any time it be stained or spotted with dirt, rubbing it only with a Wollen cloth dipped in Oyl, it will not onely recover, but present you with a very fair and noble polish'.

Lastly, take a polishing brush, made of short stiff boar bristles, fastened with wire, and 'labour it till the lustre be to your liking'. Other ways of bringing up a shine include using a woollen cloth or a felt duster, which we might do today, and some that would now be considered a little more esoteric, such as using a brush made of 'bents' (stiff reedy grasses) or a hog's-hair rubber.

Evelyn discloses what he calls 'that imcomparable Secret of the Japon or China-Vernishes'. This was then a new way of decorating furniture, and in describing it he shows the modernity of his outlook, and that he was keen to use everything at his disposal to encourage the enjoyment of timber products. Apparently brought to Europe by an Augustine monk, Father Eustachius Imart, lacquer and japanning were just beginning to become popular, although consignments of lacquer screens, chests and cabinets had been brought to Europe, mainly by the Dutch East India Company, from *c.*1600. Later, in 1688, two Englishmen, John Stalker and George Parker, wrote *A Treatise of Japanning and Varnishing*, which further helped to popularize the process.

To make the varnish was complicated, but Evelyn describes how to achieve the very best results: 'Take a Pint of Spirit of Wine exquisitely dephlegmed'. 'To dephlegmate' was to distil the alcohol. The term was used in old chemistry, meaning to extract a spirit or an acid from phlegm or watery matter; derived from Latin, it was first recorded in 1664, when Evelyn was writing *Sylva*.

Other ingredients of the varnish were 'Gum Lacq', to be broken up and sticks and rubbish in it removed, spring water and 'Castle-sope', which is a hard soap made with olive oil and soda, which originated from Castile in Spain. Then add a little alum (a mineral salt), plus a small amount of Sandarac. This was a gum extracted from *Tetraclinis articulate*, a tree of North Africa and Malta, the wood of which was much in demand for cabinet work. Place all the materials in a matrass (glass phial), warm it for two days so that all can be dissolved (although some may heat it more), then strain it through a linen cloth into a glass, after which it is ready for use.

When applying the varnish, the wood should be 'very clean and smooth and without the least freckle or flaw'. Evelyn recommends four coats within two hours of each other, and then much polishing with 'Dutch-Reeds', a species of Horsetail, *Equisetum hyemale*, which could be used wet or dry (and which Grinling Gibbons used – see page 123). After that, he says, 'rub it with Tripoly and a little oyl-olive or water'. A particular grade of fine silica earth was found at Tripoli, now the capital of Libya but earlier an area of North Africa (as well as a town in Syria), and this was made into a polishing powder for furniture. Finally, after a two-day rest, repeat the whole varnishing and polishing process again. Various colours could be used with the varnish, including a rich vermillion, applied in three or four layers 'with a swift and even stroke', after which the surface should be polished and more plain varnish applied, followed by yet more polishing. Though the process was lengthy and painstaking, this method of furniture decoration would have had a lasting effect.

In case 'it may be any service', Evelyn also mentions 'Coloured Woods, I mean such as are naturally so'. Coloured woods were always in demand for decoration and marquetry. He lists the yellow wood of the Barberry, *Berberis* spp., and the white wood of the Holly, both native trees; *Rhus cotinus*, known as Fustic (an Arabic word), which produces a yellow dye, as does the Carob tree, *Ceratonia siliqua*; and Rosewood, which could have been any one of a number of fragrant, close-grained tropical timber trees. He also refers to Brazil wood, which produced a reddish timber; this would have probably been the East Indian tree *Caesalpinia sappan*, although later a similar timber was imported from South America. The country Brazil gained its name from the 'Brazil' tree, and not the other way round.

John Evelyn does not forget to mention 'Glew', although he says, as ''tis common and cheap', 'I need not tell you it is made by boyling the sinues and so on of sheeps-trotters, parings of raw hides to a gelly and straining it.' Finer and more delicate cabinet ware would have required the use of fish glue. The practical section of *Sylva* then concludes with a short paragraph in which Evelyn describes what he calls 'the modern Art of Tapping Trees in the Spring, by which doubtlesse some excellent and specific Medicines may be attained'. Birch sap was used to help dispel kidney stones; this was a common complaint in the seventeenth century and one from which Evelyn's brother Richard suffered, and from which he died in 1670. Drinking the sap taken from the Elm, according to Evelyn, could be used to alleviate fevers. The Elder, the Vine and the Oak could all be used in the same way, and 'even the very bramble'.

Above all else, these chapters of *Sylva* demonstrate that Evelyn's philosophy was remarkably in line with twenty-first-century environmental thinking. Each aspect of the tree, timber production and use is considered with sustainability in mind. Evelyn wanted his country to meet the arboreal needs of the seventeenth century, at the same time ensuring that later generations would also benefit from his policies.

Tapping a tree for sap; note the inserted barle funnel.

CHAPTER V

The Dawning of Conservation

THE THEME THAT DOMINATES the last chapters of *Sylva* is conservation. John Evelyn does not use the word conservation in its modern sense, but in these pages he encourages his readers to understand why the tree made such an impact on the ancient world and why the planting and preservation of trees is almost a moral obligation. Here is the summation of all he has striven to express; the ethos and essence of what has gone previously.

'Of the Laws and Statutes for the Preservation and Improvement of Woods'

Writing with his usual passion and confidence, Evelyn begins with a wide-ranging discourse on some of the arcane byways of silviculture, stating that 'the very first Law we find which was ever promulgated, was concerning trees'. To leave us in no doubt, he quotes the exhortation given in the Bible (Deuteronomy 20:19, 20) on behaviour when besieging a city: 'do not lay waste the whole countryside with thy axe, and destroy the trees that yield food. Trees are not men … Spare the fruit trees, and be content to cut down such wild trees as are fit for other use.'

Writing about laws concerning trees generally, he cites 'Civil Constitutions of great Antiquity', mostly of Roman emperors, which he believed were the foundation of the laws of his time – some of which are still pertinent in the twenty-first century. For instance, there was a law 'that none might so much as Plant Trees on the Confines of his Neighbours Ground, but he was to leave a space of at the least five foot [1.52 metres] for the smallest tree, that they might not injure him with their shadow.' If branches hung over a boundary, the trunk of the tree was to be stripped of its branches up to a height of 4.6 metres (15 feet). Trees were not permitted to grow near aqueducts for fear 'the roots should insinuate into, and displace the Stones'. Nor should they line the banks of navigable rivers, in case boats or vessels were hindered and 'because the falling of the leaves corrupted the water'. In ancient times trees planted beside a road had to be a specific distance from the highway. Ever practical, Evelyn points out that without overhanging trees the road would dry better after rain, and a highway clear of wayside trees would 'less cumber the Traveller'. However, in most of the Roman world they would have required the shade from the sun that roadside trees provided.

In England, from the thirteenth century onwards, various laws were enacted regarding trees in relation to highways and verges so as to provide a safe open area between the highway and the surrounding countryside. In 1285, to protect travellers a statute decreed that 'the high roads from merchant towns [were to] be widened, where there are woods or hedges, or ditches, so that there be no ditch, underwood, or bushes, where a man may lurk to do evil near the road for two hundred feet [61 metres] on one side and for two hundred feet on the other side'. Shortly afterwards, following an event sometime in the 1290s when two merchants, travelling along a heavily wooded section of the road near Longstowe in Cambridgeshire, were attacked, pulled from their horses and murdered, Edward I (1272–1307) had an edict drawn up 'that all woods through which there was a common right of way should be cut down to a width of sixty ft [18 metres] on either side of the king's road.' An exception was made for oak trees and other great trees, as long as all the brash and underwood was cleared from beneath them.

Despite such laws, 400 years later, in 1653, Evelyn was attacked on a journey. He had been to the coast to meet his wife on her return from France with her mother by coach; they were going to stay in Tunbridge Wells for a short while as Sayes Court was not yet in a fit state to receive a young bride, and Evelyn was alone, travelling by horseback from the Kent coast to Deptford . He had ridden as far as Bromley when, near a place called the Procession Oake, 'two cut-throates started out, and striking with long staves … haled me into a deepe thicket some quarter of a mile from the highway.' The miscreants stole two rings, one emblazoned with emerald and diamonds, and the other carved in onyx, and a pair of 'bouckles' set with rubies and diamonds, and escaped, leaving Evelyn bound and gagged (most of the stolen property was later recovered). 'I told them if they had not basely surprised me they should not have had so easy a prize, and that it would teach me never to ride neere an hedge, since had I ben in the mid-way they durst not have adventured on me.'

He returns to the theme of conservation when discussing laws designed to protect growing trees. There were 'many excellent Laws for the Planting, securing, cutting and ordering of Woods, Copses, and Under-woods … together with several penalties upon the Infringers'. In addition, Evelyn explains that 'Severer punishments have lately been ordained against our wood stealers, destroyers of young trees.' He rails against 'those royotous Assemblies of Idle People' who, under the pretence of celebrating May Day, often cut down a straight-limbed tree and hauled it away to 'some Ale-house, or Revelling-place, where they keep their drunken Bacchanalias'. In 1645, when visiting Rome as a young man, he had complained of witnessing the 'setting up a foolish May-pole in the Capitol' – it was 'very ridiculous' he says.

A number of laws were promulgated from medieval times onwards, all aimed at restricting animal intrusion and grazing – usually cattle, but sometimes colts or calves (Evelyn does not mention sheep) and, as he points out, 'less than a 14 or 15 years enclosure is, in most places, too soon'. There were many laws regarding grazing in woods and copses, as well as different decrees that applied to trees in parkland and chases. Evelyn cites Germany, where if a single tree is 'observed to be extraordinary fertile' it could not be cut down without special leave.

However, his main concern in England was the 'increase of devouring Iron-mills'. He describes a number of statutes made in Queen Elizabeth's time which prohibited both the felling and burning of young timber for firing iron works; for instance, timber was not to be cut if it was growing within fourteen miles of the coast or navigable rivers, and the extraction of underwood, 'as well as great trees … was prohibited within 22 miles of London'. Nevertheless, iron-manufacturing remained a problem, both because it depleted timber reserves and because it had a destructive effect on the countryside (as did glass works). Evelyn suggests removing it to Virginia rather 'than thus to exhaust our woods at home'. Ireland was also considered 'better' for iron smelting and Evelyn said that it would be much better and cheaper to purchase iron from 'Forreigners'. This would improve the countryside and 'we [would] prove gainers by the timely removal'.

Evelyn points out, though, that heavy timber usage does not necessarily mean de-afforestation; it is all a question of balance: properly managed woodland should mean the steady supply of timber and the steady maintenance of trees. He cites as an example the estate of a wealthy iron master living in Surrey, Christopher Darell, whose woodland, despite heavy use, was thriving. He also praises the well-wooded land surrounding his family home of Wotton, which had been managed for industrial use earlier in the century. (Sadly, when he retired to live at Wotton he would decry the poor state of the woodland.)

Taxation is a source of aggravation and cause for concern in any age and the seventeenth century is no exception, so it is no surprise that Evelyn turns his attention to a particular tax, that of tithes. He gives them careful scrutiny since the tax was charged on the type of trees grown and so impinged directly on landowning families who were the bulwark of timber production. Tithes were a tax on the produce of land. Their history goes back to pre-Christian times, but they were adopted by the Church as a means of financial support. Tithes were not a tax collected by the state. The name tithe derives from the Old English word *teogothian* or tenth, which explains the nature of the tax. In England they evolved into payments made by the inhabitants of a parish for the support of the church and its incumbent. By the tenth century, payment was obligatory and tithe law had become complicated. Following the Reformation, tithes were also collected by private individuals and by the universities of Oxford and Cambridge.

There were two categories of tithes, known as the 'Greater' and the 'Lesser'. They divided roughly between goods that could be stored in a barn and had a long-term future, such as hay and corn; and more perishable produce, such as meat and dairy. No tax was imposed on timber trees so that landowners would be encouraged to plant and grow them, but it was not clear what should or should not be considered a 'timber tree'. As early as 1541, in a case relating to tithes due to the vicar of Stansted Mount Fitchet in Essex, the judge, Sir William Shelley, said, 'What shall be called great trees? It seems that they are trees used for timber which have not been used to be felled for coppice wood and firewood, and kept to grow back again.' Evelyn lists several trees upon which tithes are not to be paid, unless they are felled before they reach twenty years of age. These include the hornbeam, maple, and aspen, while the beech 'in countys where it abounds, is not tythable, because in such places 'tis not accounted Timber'. However, it all seems to be a matter of interpretation. If a wood was mainly composed of underwood and bushes, with beech trees scattered thinly, then a tithe was collected, but when it consisted mainly of timber trees, with a small amount of brushwood and bushes, no tithe need be paid. Trees were not charged if they were lopped before they were twenty years old, then allowed to re-grow and were re-lopped later. If a parson received the tithe on a fruit tree that was then felled in the same year, and the timber used for fuel, then no second tithe was applicable. However, in Buckinghamshire cherry trees were classed as timber trees and so were not liable for a tithe. Hop poles cut on titheable land were exempt, as was wood cut from hedges for fuel. But acorns and beech mast, if collected and sold, 'must be answered by the tenth penny'. If the mast was eaten by pigs, then the pigs became subject to the tithe. Parsons at a village near Boston in Lincolnshire claimed payment of Tithe Ale from the local ale-house.

The complications and confusion endured long after Evelyn's lifetime. In 1874 the Victorian judge and Master of the Rolls, Sir George Jessel (1824–83) – also an amateur botanist and a Fellow of The Royal Society – gave a legal definition of timber trees when giving judgement in the case of Honeywood v Honeywood:

> By the general rule of England, oak, ash and elm are timber, provided they are of the age of twenty years and upwards, provided also they are not so old as not to have a reasonable quantity of useable wood in them, sufficient . . . to make a good post. Timber, that is the kind of tree which may be called timber, may be varied by local custom. There is what is called the custom of the country; that is of a particular county, or a division of a county, and it varies in two ways. First of all you may have trees called timber by the custom of the country – beech in some counties, hornbeam in others, and even whitethorn and blackthorn and many other trees are considered timber in peculiar localities – in addition to the ordinary trees. Then again in certain localities, arising probably from the nature of the soil, the trees of even twenty years old are not necessarily timber, but may be of twenty-four years or even to later period, I suppose, if necessary; and in other places the test of when a tree becomes timber is not its age but its girth.

N. OZANNE F,

The different local regulations for timber have never been completely rationalized. Tithes remained extant in an attenuated form until they were finally abolished in 1962.

Evelyn goes international to compare silvicultural practices in England with those in Europe. In Spain an officer of the Crown marked trees that had to be left for ship timber. In the province of Vizcaya (Biscay – part of the modern Basque country), which included Bilbao, by law three saplings were to be planted for every tree felled. Although copses were not favoured in Spain, most trees were pollarded or lopped. However, the acres of coppiced wood that existed in the Vizcaya area could be used for the extraction of fuel wood for the iron works. In Germany and in France, the woods (and forests) were divided into eighty partitions, 'every year felling one of the divisions so as no wood is felled in less than fourscore years'. Mature oak trees, 'good fair sound and fruitful', were to be left standing. Royal forests in France had their own surveyors and officers to mark wood that was to be felled. No cattle were permitted to graze within them until the seedling acorns were large enough to be out of danger. Evelyn finishes by remarking that all ideas concerning the production of timber have been considered 'particularly as they concern the Forest of Dean'.

Eighteenth-century French shipbuilding surveyors inspecting woodland for suitable timber.

'The Paranesis and Conclusion, Containing some Encouragements and Proposals for the Planting and Improvement of His Majesties Forests'

While laws helped maintain existing trees, planting was 'the main Design of this whole Treatise': this was the solution to the shortage of timber facing the nation – the problem that The Royal Society, in commissioning *Sylva*, aimed to address – and here Evelyn sets out his tree-planting proposals, and argues how economic this planting could be.

There is not a more efficacious, cheaper and easier expedient in the production of 'Ship timber' in the royal woodlands, he writes, than combining mature trees and arable land. He is of the opinion that using trees 'to enclose would be an excellent way'. As he points out, this was already established practice for the growing of walnut trees in Burgundy (and it still is).

However, before that could happen, foresters, borderers (those living around the periphery of the royal land) and workers involved in the Royal Forests would have to be obliged to toe the line: 'his Majesty must assert his Power, with a firm and high Resolution to reduce these men to their due Obedience'. *Sylva* was dedicated to Charles II, whom Evelyn flatters by suggesting he 'will leave such an everlasting Obligation on his People, and raise such a Monument to his fame as the Ages for a thousand years to come, shall have cause to celebrate his precious Memory and his Royal Successors to emulate his Virtue'. To achieve this the King must give the borderers long-term tenancies at low rents and reversions by copy-hold (an inferior form of freehold abolished in 1922) 'or what other Tenures and Services his Majesty shall please to accept of '.

Turning to the creation and planting of new woods, Evelyn puts forward ideas about where best to grow trees: while rough ground and hills will do, 'rich fat vales' are best. Fencing, enclosures, hedges, trenches and vallations (earthworks associated with double hedging) are all explained, as is the Devon method, which is 'frequently practised in divers places' – the practice of growing oak trees very near a bank or stone wall boundary, so that over the years the roots would grow into it, supporting and maintaining the bank, and if the bank crumbled or tumbled away, a boundary of trees remained.

THE ROYAL FORESTS

From earliest times, Royal Forests grew up around royal palaces and on Crown land. These were not necessarily forests as we understand the term today; they were areas of land set aside for the pre-eminently royal pursuit of hunting. From the beginning, their boundaries and legal status were complicated. The one constant was ownership of the deer (usually fallow), which always belonged to the monarch; the land, on the other hand, did not necessarily always belong to the Crown. The King did not own the land in Waltham Forest (later Epping Forest), for example, but in the Forest of Dean he owned the land and the trees, as well as the mineral rights, swine, fallow and red deer, all the timber and underwood. The loss of such rights was one of the principal reasons why barons and earls always objected to the declaration of Royal Forests. (Nowadays it is the making of National Parks that can cause similar difficulties.) Commoners (the local farmers) had rights that predated the Royal Forest and included pasturage, woodcutting and coppicing, and these had to be accommodated. Stealing deer (or anything else that moved) and encroachment of boundaries, either by grazing or by grubbing up land, were among offences that were subject to fines – and worse. The laws differed for each Royal Forest, depending on the circumstances.

By the thirteenth century those Royal Forests not wholly owned by the Crown were beginning to drift out of Crown focus; they would eventually revert to control by the landowners, almost by default, with the commoners continuing to exercise their ancient rights. The management of Royal Forests wholly owned by the Crown declined and they contributed little to the manufacturing requirements of the kingdom. This state of affairs continued for the next three to four hundred years until Samuel Pepys' began his insistent railing against the mismanagement and corruption.

In 1803, during the reign of George III, Sylvester Douglas, Lord Glenbervie, was appointed Surveyor General of Woods and Forests. His work developed a sense of urgency when, the following year, during the winter, the First Lord of the Admiralty, Lord Dundas, wrote to him setting out the serious deficiencies in the provision of timber suitable for naval use, particularly the non-availability of oak. This was no wonder, given the paucity of timber enclosures in the Royal Forests: enclosures covered a mere 762 hectares (1,883 acres), which was less than one per cent of the total area of the forests – 273 hectares (676 acres) in the Forest of Dean, and the remaining 488 hectares (1,207 acres) in the New Forest. In response, Lord Glenbervie worked vigorously to improve and plant the land, and to take the political and legal measures needed to enable the Office of Woods to carry out its duties in an efficient manner. In finding the impetus to restructure the department, Lord Glenbervie must have been influenced by Edmund Burke (1729–97); the economic reforms Burke had expounded gave specific remits to government departments. During the eleven years of Lord Glenbervie's tenure, about 16,188 hectares (40,000 acres) were drained, enclosed and planted with trees.

This regime continued through the nineteenth century until it became clear that what was required was a national woodland policy. Several official committees and boards examined every aspect of forestry, including the training required for forest workers, and the different species of trees to be grown. The great dream remained for England to be self-sufficient in timber production. During the First World War, although a vast quantity of wood was felled, Britain still had continual problems meeting its timber requirements. In 1916 a Forestry sub-committee was formed within the Ministry of Reconstruction. One of the outcomes was the recommendation that all forestry areas should be centred under one authority. The Forestry Act of 1919 allowed the setting up of the Forestry

Commission, which assumed responsibility for all woodland throughout the United Kingdom, as well as Northern Ireland. All Royal Forests, with the exception of Windsor Forest, were transferred to this commission. Thus land that had been in the same royal ownership and management (or mismanagement) for almost 1,000 years was brought into the modern world. John Evelyn might have mourned the passing of the royal connections, but by acknowledging the importance of planting and maintaining forest trees the formation of the commission achieved some of the ideals he had set out in *Sylva*.

Another way of increasing the standard of timber would be to make what we would call a conservation area, which Evelyn calls 'a good Act to save our … trees from the Ax of the Neighbourhood'. His recommendation is to leave trees growing for between thirty and forty years, adding 'who would not preserve Timber, when within so few years, the price is almost quadrupled?' He also cajoles all landowners to plant limes, firs and elms 'and other shady and venerable Trees as adorn New-hall in Essex'. In 1656 Evelyn had visited New Hall, near Chelmsford, and in his diary described the garden as 'a faire plot, and the whole seate well accommodated with water', adding 'but above all I admired the faire avenue planted with stately lime-trees, in 4 rowes, for neere a mile in length.' In the sixteenth century New Hall had been acquired by Henry VIII and renamed the Palace of Beaulieu. In 1622 it was bought by the Duke of Buckingham, whose gardener was then John Tradescant senior. He was probably responsible for overseeing the planting of 'one thousand timber trees of Oake', a gift from King James I, and later another 500 donated by Charles I; elm and walnut trees – 2,000 of the latter – were also received from the Earl of Northumberland. By 1660 New Hall was owned by General George Monck (1608–70), the architect of the restoration of Charles II and newly created Duke of Abermarle. Since 1799 the estate has been an independent Catholic girls' school, the oldest in the country.

Comparison is made between the delight and pleasure of planting trees and owning dogs and horses 'for Races, and Hunting, neither of which Recreations is comparable to that of Planting'. As so often, when reinforcing a point, he draws on examples from abroad. He had heard of a nobleman in Italy, who, on the birth of his daughter, planted 'Oaks, Ashes, and other profitable and Marketable Trees, to the number of an Hundred thousand, as undoubtedly calculating, that each of those Trees might be worth twenty pence before his daughter became Marriageable' – a noble idea and one also practised in Flanders. While these numbers may seem overwhelming, the practice is still current today: many of us like to commemorate a significant event by planting a tree in our garden – though perhaps without a financial investment in mind. In Germany, at the beginning of the seventeenth century, the Prince Elector IV sowed 'the most barren Heath of Lambertheim [near Mannheim] with acorns, after plowing … and is now likely to prove a most goodly Forest'. Evelyn explains that the calculations of a Captain Smith supported the idea of bulk planting as a profitable investment; he worked out that on 405 hectares (1,000 acres) of land with trees planted at 30-centimetre (12-inch) intervals and divided into 7,201 rows, over 51 million plants or seeds could be sown, and that after 150 years the remaining great trees would be worth 'an immense and stupendious Summe', which he reckons to be £13,516,660.00 (about twelve times the parliamentary provision made for Charles II to govern the country). Even then it was recognized that it was advantageous to spice preservation of the environment with commercial benefits.

Beech leaves.

Turning his attention to the removal of hedgerows – a very modern cause – Evelyn points out 'that it is a shame that Turnip-Planters should demolish and undo hedgerows neer London where the mounds and Fences are stripped naked to give Sun to a few miserable Roots'. He also encourages the growing of trees in some of the most inhospitable places, particularly ash, but also oak, beech and elm, which will 'prosper in the most flinty Soils'. Bringing Germany into the equation again, calling it 'a small and wretched country', he remarks on the number of oak trees that farmers would plant as a matter of course in Westphalia: because of the need to feed acorns to the swine, oaks were planted around every farm.

'An Historical Account of the Sacredness, and Use of Standing Groves'

For Evelyn the planting and conservation of trees was not just a practical matter for the good of the individual and the country. Turning his back on the practical themes of planting trees and harvesting timber, he ends his book by exploring, at length, the ancient world of the sacred grove, determined that his readers should understand that the growing of trees would also enhance the spiritual life of a nation's people. His reputation as a horticultural authority was already in place by the time he came to write *Sylva*, and the classical knowledge and passion he brought to bear in the book – becoming almost a custodian of the nation's arboreal conscience – certainly helped to popularize the idea of tree conservation.

Discoursing on many ancient myths and legends, he describes what he interprets as the almost mystical association trees had for the ancients. Near trees 'intire and never violated with the Ax', deities, heroes and patriarchs could 'Compose their Meditations, and celebrate Sacred Mysteries, Prayers, and Oblations'. He cites the Bible to support the ideal of the 'Arboreous Temple', and explains that a number of writers believe the Burning Bush described by Moses was not just a single shrub but 'an intire Grove'. (There are several shrubs which bear the sobriquet 'burning bush'; the most likely fit seems to be Dittany, *Dictamnus albus*, a member of the rue family, native to Europe, including Britain, and Asia; it has a pungent oil and may burst into flames if a match is put to it.) In the Christian era, sacred groves are for the worship of God, and 'an impure Grove on Mount Libanus, dedicated to Venus was by Imperial Edict of Constantine extirpated.'

For John Evelyn, Paradise itself was a sacred grove, 'Planted by God himself, and given to Man'. This phrase, slipped into the book without any real preamble, expresses Evelyn's deepest-felt belief – a belief that lies at the core of his writing, and indeed his life. It explains his idealism, his love of nature and his almost religious fervour regarding the planting and nurturing of trees. Paradise – that seemingly unobtainable and achingly beautiful landscape – is as important to us now as it was to the people of Evelyn's day. It is indeed a fundamental and largely unexpressed ideal of the whole of humanity. At times of intense happiness, or great stress, depression or grief, the consolation of the sunlit 'sacred grove' can give us inexpressible joy and serenity.

A painting in the style of the picturesque, c.1800, by William Gilpin (1762–1843). He believed that round-headed trees were easier to place in a Romantic landscape than columnar-shaped trees.

CHAPTER VI

A Lasting Legacy

'From early times trees have afforded man shelter, food and clothing, and have exercised a tremendous influence over his daily life.'

ERNEST WILSON, 1930

John Evelyn, carved in relief sculpture, possibly by Grinling Gibbons.

'BUT I HAVE DONE, and it is now time for us to get out of the Wood, and to recommend this, and all that we have proposed to His Most Sacred Majesty, the Honourable Parliament, and to the Principal Officers, and Commissioners of the Royal Navy.' So Evelyn ends *Sylva*. None of The Royal Society Fellows who had assembled during that autumn afternoon in 1662 to listen to Evelyn's 'Discourse concerning Forest-trees' could have realized how long-lasting and influential the book that resulted from it would become.

When *Sylva* was published, with its *Kalendarium Hortense* appendix, in 1664, it became an immediate success. Over 1,000 copies of the first folio were sold in less than two years. By 1666 Evelyn was considering a new edition and appealing to Fellows for additional information that he could include. In 1669 the second edition was published, enlarged by the addition of a second appendix – *Pomona, concerning fruit-trees in relation to cider*, several engravings, and a poem composed (in Greek) by Evelyn's fourteen-year-old son John.

Ten years later, in 1679, a third edition of *Sylva* was published. This was quite different from the first edition, in that Evelyn added some disparate parts to the original core. In many ways this edition takes on the mantle of his unfinished work *Elysium Britannicum*. Two poems were included: one, entitled 'Nemus' (the Park), was written by Renatus Rapinus in 1673 and was taken from a longer verse about various aspects of the garden; written in Latin, it had been translated by John Evelyn junior. The second poem, entitled 'The Garden', had been composed by Evelyn's old friend Alexander Cowley. Evelyn also included his own *Terra, a Philosophical Essay of Earth, being a Lecture in Course*, which under its original and snappier title *A Discourse of Earth* had first been published in 1676.

This edition of *Sylva* was the last to be published in Evelyn's lifetime. Evelyn was working on a new edition when he died in 1706, making many changes and yet more additions; the fourth edition was published posthumously in the year of his death. The appendices included *Acetaria: a Discourse of Sallets*, about salad plants, which Evelyn had first published as a separate book in 1699. There was also a newly written essay entitled *Dendrologia*, a cogent argument for the ornamental use of trees in the landscape that reinforces Evelyn's position as a progenitor of the landscape movement. A portrait of the author appeared, albeit of a much younger Evelyn; it was taken from a drawing made of him in Paris in 1651 when he was thirty-one. In the light of Evelyn's modesty, which made him refuse numerous royal honours and appointments, it seems most likely that it was either Mary, his widow, or his son John who decided to include the portrait as a tribute. This edition also saw a change in the spelling of the title, from the old-fashioned *Sylva* to the more modern *Silva*.

Twenty-three years later, The Royal Society still considered *Silva* a worthwhile commercial proposition. It was again re-issued, this time without the author's portrait, but otherwise with few alterations to the text. However, advances had been made in printing and the whole book was re-set and repaginated. This fifth edition, which appeared in 1729, would last for nearly half a century. By 1775 *Sylva* was both botanically outdated and very old-fashioned. The book, in its various editions, had been in print for more than a hundred years and much had changed in that time. The new Linnaean system of plant nomenclature established by Carl Linnaeus and published in 1736 had been accepted. There had been advances in the breeding and propagation of plants and trees, and an avalanche of recently introduced trees that could be planted in the landscape. Many of these newcomers were being used by 'Capability' Brown and (later) Humphrey Repton when creating great parks around equally magnificent houses. Such use for both practical and artistic purposes was, of course, absolutely in accordance with the ideas Evelyn had first promulgated a century before.

In view of these changes in the arboreal and horticultural world, The Royal Society decided to review the situation. It invited Dr Alexander Hunter (1729–1809), a Scots Fellow from Edinburgh, to undertake a thorough revision of the text. He himself had recently written *Georgical* [Agricultural] *Essays in which Food of Plants is particularly Considered*. Published in four volumes over a period of two years from 1770, this had earned him a certain reputation. Hunter undertook to examine Evelyn's original text and then update it. He incorporated the latest ideas, not only from the work of Linnaeus, but also material from other botanists such as the Finnish Peter Kalm (1715–79), a colleague of Linnaeus who, on behalf of Sweden, travelled to America from 1748 to report on the natural history of the continent. Dr Hunter also included – as Evelyn had done – information regarding English estates and their planting plans. This revised edition, including forty illustrations, was published in 1776 in two volumes. A further four editions of this fundamental revision were published between 1786 and 1825, no doubt enhancing John Evelyn's reputation.

*

In the years following *Sylva*'s publication, Evelyn became convinced that his clarion call to plant trees had been heard. In 1690, when he was seventy, he wrote to a young friend, Lady Ann Spencer, the eldest daughter of his long-time friend the Earl of Sunderland: '[The book] has been the occasion of propagating many millions of useful timber-trees throughout this nation as I may justify (without immodesty) from the many letters of acknowledgement received from gentlemen of the first quality and others altogether strangers to me.'

The fact that the book was continuously in print for so long, and that The Royal Society considered its revision in 1776 to be a commercial proposition, demonstrates that it had become standard reading for anyone involved in estate management or simply wanting to plant trees in the landscape. While there were numerous other writers on the subject, both before and after Evelyn, none had such a distinguished and long-lasting reputation. Evelyn was considered to be the most widely read man of his age. As was the custom of the time, he drew freely from the classical writings of Pliny (the 'Natural History') and *The Georgics* by Virgil, and Columella, Cicero and Ovid were all plundered for quotations and interesting 'facts'. Later Stephan Switzer (1682–1745), the landscape gardener and horticultural writer, praised Evelyn, saying he 'wrote like another Virgil'.

A precursor of Evelyn with an outstanding reputation in many fields was Francis Bacon, 1st Baron Verulam. Statesman, philosopher, and essayist, like Evelyn he wrote about the pragmatic and philosophical side of gardening and in 1625 had published his essay *Of Gardens*, which was hugely influential. It begins with the oft-quoted phrase, 'God Almighty first planted a garden'. Two years later Bacon followed this with his huge essay on the natural world, *Sylva Sylvarum or A Naturall Historie in Ten Centuries*.

Contemporaneously with Evelyn, in 1653 Ralph Austen (d.1676), Proctor of Oxford University, wrote an essay entitled the *Spiritual Use of an Orchard*; in the same year he also published his *Treatise of Fruit-Trees*, a second edition of which appeared in 1657. Both of these publications would surely have appealed to Evelyn. There was the nurseryman John Rea (*fl.*1620s–81), who, just as *Sylva* was being published, produced *Flora: seu De Florum Cultura* (when reprinted later, it was retitled *Flora, Ceres and Pomona*) and was aimed at those who gardened on a 'less grandiose scale'. Moses Cook, who had been involved in the design of the gardens at Cassiobury, near Watford, for the Earl of Essex, wrote two books, in the 1670s and 1680s: *The Manner of Raising Ordering and Improving Forrest Trees* and *How to Plant, Make and Keep Woods, Walks, Avenues, Lawns, Hedges*, both of them highly influential – the latter reprinted three times, the last time in 1724.

Francis Bacon and the title page of his Sylva Sylvarum.

An irregular base forming bays & promontories.

The summit regularly varied.

All these books (and more) presented new and modern ideas which would pave the way for the seminal change that was to take place during the eighteenth century: a countryside to please the eye, planted with trees to decorate the scene, rather than with the utilitarian purpose of providing building material. The landed gentry had been commanded or inveigled to plant for the nation's needs for such a long time that the idea of growing trees just for looking at must have seemed almost revolutionary. An early manifestation of the change in style was the 'ornamental farm' – or what came to be known as the *ferme ornée* (despite the fact that the idea had originated in England). This was first promulgated by Evelyn's admirer Stephan Switzer in his 1715 book *The Nobleman, Gentleman and Gardener's Recreation,* which states 'both Profit and Pleasure may be agreeably mix'd together'. The essence of the *ferme ornée* was the ornamentation of hedgerows, something that Evelyn had referred to specifically in *Sylva.* Exploratory early plantings took place at Woburn Farm, Chertsey, and at Painshill (both in Surrey) and contained an exuberance of newly introduced foreign trees. The idea proved impracticable and was current for only a short time but it did lead the way to more permanent alterations and these would evolve into the landscape movement, ultimately being epitomized by the designing genius of 'Capability' Brown and his followers.

*

Illustrations by William Gilpin showing the effect of different ways of planting trees in the landscape.

In freeing trees from the straightjacket of control in favour of a more natural style of planting, the landscape movement acknowledged for the first time the different silhouettes and shapes made by trees – rounded, columnar, spreading –

effecting a radical and long-lasting change to the gardened landscape. Since Evelyn's time much of the farmed and countryside landscape has altered almost beyond recognition. The distinctive landscape of an area depends on many things, and much of the change in the countryside is due to different (and sometimes alien) use of land. In both cases, however, some of this dramatic visual alteration has been brought about by the planting of non-native trees.

The widening choice of so many new and different trees that could eventually be grown in Britain would have pleased Evelyn immensely. When he wrote in *Sylva* 'we might have ample encouragement to denizen other strangers amongst us', little did he know how prophetic his words of welcome were to be, and that a whole forest of tree introductions were to find a home on British soil in the following centuries.

In Evelyn's day opportunities for planting anything evergreen in the landscape were few, and in particular very few pines or firs were available. Even in 1813, a century after Evelyn's death, the second edition of *Hortus Kewensis* compiled by William Aiton (1766–1849) recorded only seventeen *Pinus* species. This would change dramatically within fifty years. The earliest impact on the landscape was made by evergreens from the western seaboard of North America, introduced via Captain George Vancouver (*c*.1758–98) following his voyage at the end of the eighteenth century with the surgeon-botanist Archibald Menzies (1754–1842). However, it was David Douglas (1799–1834), under the auspices of the Horticultural Society (later the Royal Horticultural Society), who has

Prior Park, Bath, created c.1750. The landscape and bridge are believed to be the work of 'Capability' Brown.

turned out to be the instigator of the most momentous changes. He first travelled to the west coast of America during the 1820s. Of the eighteen or so trees which he is credited with introducing, at least five were found to be very useful timber trees and are now used extensively in forestry planting: *Abies grandis,* the Grand Fir; *Abies procera,* Noble Fir; *Picea sitchensis,* Sitka Spruce; *Pinus radiate,* Monteray Pine; and *Pseudotsuga menziesii,* Douglas Fir.

Today some eighty or so *Pinus* species are available. They are all native of the northern hemisphere, the greatest numbers being indigenous to the American continent. Europe can boast thirteen or so species, and about twelve belong to the Asian world, including Japan and China. Nothing has altered the balance of the British countryside more than the arrival, planting and growth of these dark green heavyweights. Pre *c.*1850 most trees were native, broad-leaved and deciduous; only the Yew, Juniper, Holly and the Scots Pine held their leaves through the winter, and autumnal colour was usually muted and creamily golden. Now with *Abies, Pinus, Picea* and other evergreens imported from around the world the range has increased. As W. J. Bean succinctly wrote in 1914, 'In no class of outdoor plants is our indebtedness to the floras of other countries so evident as in the case of hardy evergreens.'

*

Despite the impact of *Sylva,* and the strictures of Evelyn and others to plant and replant trees throughout the land, the parlous state of the supply of home-grown timber remained a matter of concern. During the eighteenth century the need for available timber dominated thinking, as building material was required for an increasingly industrial Britain and, in particular, there continued to be a pressing need for timber for shipbuilding. Over forty years Britain was engaged in three major wars – the war with Spain (1739–48), the Seven Years War (1756–63), against France mainly, and the American War of Independence (1775–83). All of them required new, modern and up-to-date ships.

The Royal Forests, which should have been one of the major sources of naval and commercial timber, were both ill-managed and lacking any form of forward planning. When timber was urgently needed – particularly for shipbuilding – the Royal Forests were continually found wanting. It was not until 1787, after the American War of Independence had ended, that a Parliamentary Commission was asked to report on the state and management of them. With a nice sense of juxtaposition, an admiral was made the principal commissioner. Admiral Sir Charles Middleton (1726–1813) was a man of great vision and integrity, and over sixty when he was appointed. (Much later, in April 1805, shortly before the Battle of Trafalgar, he was enobled as Baron Barham and Pitt appointed him First Lord of the Admiralty at the age of eighty-five.)

Middleton's comprehensive report left no stone or historical fact unturned, and it disclosed a disgraceful history of corruption and incompetence. Many of his pertinent conclusions are as relevant to forestry today as they were in the eighteenth century. Two examples might suffice. First: 'Commerce and industry seek for, and are supported by, speedy returns of gain, however small; and the more generally the commercial spirit shall prevail in this country, the less probability is there that planting of woods, for the advantages of posterity, will be preferred to the immediate profits of agriculture.' And second: 'It is true that there is no kind of property that requires the protection of laws more than timber, which may easily, and in very little time, be hurt or destroyed, but requires a century to come to perfection' – an observation that is probably even more relevant today than it was when it was first written, bearing in mind the frequent use of the ubiquitous chainsaw.

Seventeen further reports followed, dealing with every aspect of the Royal Forests. The last, dated 28 March 1793, dealt with the 'present and future management of Crown lands, woods and forest'. It was, however, another ten years before anything began to happen and more than likely this was prompted by the reopening of the war with Napoleonic France in 1803. Even the great Lord Nelson is supposed to have enquired why Evelyn's recommendations had not been carried out in respect of the supply of ship timbers.

It was all too little too late, but to promote the national planting of trees, the British did what they are best at and formed a committee. In fact it was was the Society for the Encouragement of Arts, Manufactures, and Commerce, founded in 1754, which first took the initiative. This remarkable body eventually became, in 1845, the Society of Arts, and in 1908 the Royal Society of Arts, by which name it is still known. One of the original founders was Henry Baker (1698–1774), a Fellow of the Society of Antiquaries and of The Royal Society. Baker had served as apprentice to a London bookseller, wrote poetry, was a naturalist – he is credited with introducing the ornamental

Silver Fir.

Chinese Rhubarb, *Rheum palmatum*, into Britain – and devised a system of instruction which could be understood by deaf and dumb people. In 1728, under the pseudonym Henry Stonecastle, he initiated, with Daniel Defoe, *The Universal Spectator and Weekly Journal*, which ran for almost twenty years. A year later he married Defoe's daughter Sophia. Baker acted as secretary, for a short while, to the newly founded Society, and in 1754 presented to one of its meetings a pamphlet by Edward Wade. The pamphlet was written 'to promote the planting of timber trees in the commons, and waste ground all over the kingdom, for the supply of the navy, the employment and advantage of the poor, as well as the ornamenting of the nation'. Influenced by Wade's ideas, the Society established a scheme whereby enticements, in the form of gold and silver medals, were offered to encourage the planting of Oak, Chestnut and Elm, and later Scots Pine and Larch – all fundamental to timber production. The scheme continued for over seventy years, from 1758 until 1835. It has been estimated that some 15 million oaks were planted during that time, and some 20 million pines and larches; in all a total in excess of 50 million trees were planted.

There were separate developments in tree planting in Scotland. Thomas Hamilton, 6th Earl of Haddington (1680–1735) was a soldier and an agriculturalist, whose estate of 5,700 hectares (14,085 acres) was on the east coast of Scotland, at Tynningham House. He developed an interest in the growing of trees, and planted more than fifty different species in the woods on his estate. The Earl kept notes about the experiment and a quarter of a century after his death the details were considered important enough to be made public. The subsequent book, entitled *Treatise on Manner of Raising Forest Trees*, was published in 1761.

At about the same time in the Highlands, the Dukes of Atholl had started what was to become an almost manic 'larchfest' at their estate at Dunkeld in Perthshire. Between 1740 and 1750 John Murray, the 2nd Duke of Atholl (1690–1764), planted some 250 Larches, *Larix deciduas*, syn. *L. europaea*. His son, the 3rd Duke, John Murray (1729–74), increased the pace and began experimenting with mixed planting on land that was agriculturally worthless and over 183 metres (600 feet) above sea level, exactly the sort of land that Evelyn had envisaged being used. Although the 3rd Duke was only forty-five when he died, in his lifetime he was responsible for the planting of almost 10 million larch. John Murray, the 4th Duke (1755–1830), continued the enterprise of

Larch.

planting marginal land with larch. By 1819, some fifty years or so after the first planting, he was beginning to reap the reward of his enterprising grandfather; larch timber was being felled on the estate for commercial use, in particular steamboat building.

In 1861 the Japanese Larch, *L. kaempferi*, was introduced into Britain by John Gould Veitch (1839–70), and was sent as seedlings to Dunkeld. Some thirty or so years later, in 1895, a hybrid larch developed there, a cross between *Larix decidua* and *L. kaempferi* and now known as *L.* x *marschlinsii*. This first seeded in 1904 and the healthiest and most vigorous cross became known as the Hybrid or the Dunkeld Larch. It is a vigorous large tree, of great commercial value throughout the forests of Britain. The original early plantings on the estate have now been joined, in the twenty-first century, by a new wave of tree planting at Dunkeld. The whole undertaking – a continuing enterprise over several generations, using marginal land and thus laying the foundation for a steady supply of timber – was just what Evelyn had urged landowners to undertake in the seventeenth century.

It did not escape the notice of other estate owners that the experiments taking place in Scotland could be transferred to their own land – in particular those estate owners who had a surfeit of land which would not support sheep or cattle. One of those to take up the challenge was Thomas Johnes of Hafod, in Cardiganshire, who demolished an old house to build a modern Gothic mansion (later destroyed by fire on Friday, 13 March 1807 and rebuilt) and planted over 5 million trees of various species on his otherwise unusable land. He was three times the recipient of the gold medal of the Society of Arts. (After various vicissitudes, this estate was taken over by the Forestry Commission in 1951 and the vast majority of the trees, having reached maturity, were felled.) In County Durham, an earlier recipient of the gold medal was Thomas White of Batsfield who received the award in 1786 for his enthusiastic planting of larch.

Interest in growing 'firs' on marginal land was nurtured by the botanist Aylmer Lambert (1761–1842), who wrote *The Genus Pinus*, which first appeared in 1803, twenty years before Douglas set off for the west coast of America. This two-volumed, illustrated opus included not only pines but other allied species as well. It was so popular that over forty years it went into five editions. Nearly thirty years later, in 1831, a catalogue appeared, compiled by Charles Lawson,

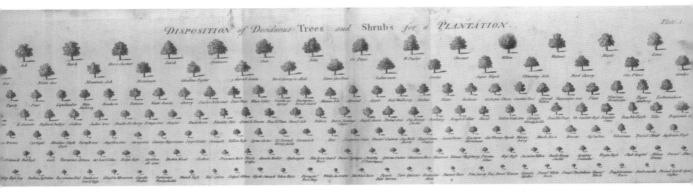

who owned the famous Seed and Nursery Company in Edinburgh, which listed all the known exotic conifers then in cultivation. Later, with the help of Edinburgh-based printer and publisher Edward Ravenscroft (1816–90), Lawson began to publish his three-volumed *Pinetum Britannicum*, which appeared between 1863 and 1884. This again helped to keep the interest of forest trees before the public.

Throughout the nineteenth century there was tremendous interest in the planting and growing of conifers. Evelyn would have been delighted by the new craze for growing every new 'pine' or 'fir' which arrived in England to make what from 1842 came to be called a pinetum. Perhaps the most grandiose of makeovers took place in Derbyshire at Elvaston Castle, the seat of the Earls of Harrington. In 1830 William Barron, who had been a student at the Royal Botanic Garden, Edinburgh, was appointed head gardener. If ever there was a case of creating an instant garden, this was it: Barron began moving and transplanting very large trees, mostly conifers, hardly any of which perished. He and his son John (1844–1906) experimented with digging up a tree with an immense soil ball, placing it in its new position on top of the ground, and then building up a great mound of earth

From The Planters Guide, *published in 1779 by James Meader, gardener to the Duke of Northumberland at Syon House, Isleworth, and later to the Russian Empress Catherine at St Petersburg.*

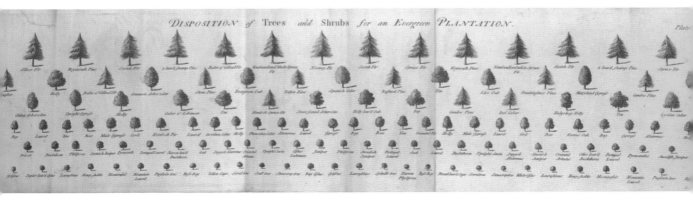

around it. This was a method promulgated originally by Evelyn in *Sylva*, and later developed at the beginning of the nineteenth century by Sir Henry Steuart of Allanton (1759–1836) in his *Planter's Guide* of 1828. Twenty-three years later, when the craze for conifer planting and altering gardens was at its height, William Barron wrote *The British Winter Garden: A Practical Treatize on Evergreens*.

*

The last updated edition of *Silva* was finally published in 1825 and coincided with the publication of the works of John Claudius Loudon. Like Evelyn, Loudon was a born communicator and teacher, and the fellow authors would have had much in common. Both were eclectic in their taste for gardens and their love of the natural world. It would have been interesting to compare Evelyn's monumental *Elysium Britannicum* with Loudon's own *Encyclopaedia of Gardening* (1822) and *Encyclopaedia of Plants* (1829). But Loudon's eight-volumed *Arboretum et Fruticetum Britannicum*, published in 1838, is the closest that he comes to reflecting the work of Evelyn. It shows just what a potent and iconic force Evelyn had become over the years.

The same influence can be seen in *Trees of Great Britain and Ireland*, a massive undertaking written by the Irish-educated Dr Augustine Henry (1857–1930) with Henry John Elwes, seven volumes of which appeared privately between 1903 and 1913. Henry had trained as a doctor at Queen's University, Belfast and, with a facility for learning languages, he was appointed an Assistant Medical Officer in the Chinese Imperial Customs Service (although this was a Chinese governmental service, it recruited mainly Europeans). He travelled to China in 1891, being posted first to Shanghai and then the following year to the remote outpost of Ichang. He gradually developed an interest in botany and dendrology, and this eventually became the main thrust of his career. By the time he returned to Europe in 1900, he had sent over 150,000 herbarium specimens to the Royal Botanic Gardens at Kew. His

Henry (standing) and Elwes.

change of career became complete when he decided to study forestry. He became Reader in Forestry at Cambridge, from 1907 to 1913, and from then until 1926 (when he was nearly seventy) he was Professor of Forestry at the College of Science, Dublin (now University College). Elwes was a keen naturalist and arboriculturist, who, during 1907 when he was President of the Royal English Arboricultural Society, founded the *Quarterly Journal of Forestry*.

Two years after the publication of Henry and Elwes's opus, during the inauspicious year 1914, *Trees and Shrubs Hardy in the British Isles* appeared. It was written by William (W. J.) Bean, who was at that time the Curator of the Royal Botanic Gardens at Kew. Despite the First World War, within two years there was a second edition, which was reprinted in 1919, with further editions in 1921 and 1925; in the 1930s a third volume was added, and the latest, three-volume eighth edition is dated 1970. This book is not so much to do with forest trees and their utility as with the ornamental planting of trees, sometimes in the garden and sometimes in the surrounding landscape. In his historical notes the author does not mention John Evelyn and *Sylva* (although he does mention a number of other forestry writers, including Augustine Henry and Elwes), but the influence of the seventeenth-century book is clear. Like Evelyn, Bean includes detailed information on pruning, transplanting and propagation, as well as the selection and hybridization of species and varieties.

In the latter part of the nineteenth century and early in the twentieth century, there slowly developed the idea that a career could be made in forest husbandry. It was driven originally by the demands and challenges of the Empire, particularly in India. The Royal Indian Engineering College in Surrey was founded in 1873 to train candidates for work in the subcontinent. Eleven years later a Chair of Forestry was established there. This was followed by university acknowledgement in the form of Chairs of Forestry in Edinburgh (1887) and later at Cambridge and Oxford. In 1904, the government-appointed Commissioners of Woods and Forests instituted a School for Woodmen and Foremen in the Forest of Dean.

The Royal Scottish Arboricultural Society, formed in 1854, and the equivalent English Society, formed twenty-eight years later, encouraged landowners to plant trees. Contemporary with Henry, Elwes and Bean was a fourth influential 'man *Holly.* of trees', the German born arboriculturist (Sir) William Schlich (1840–1925), who spent nineteen years in the Indian Forest Service, eventually attaining the position of Inspector-General of Forests, before returning to England and the University of Oxford's Chair of Forestry. With a colleague, William Fisher (1846–1910), with whom he had shared experiences in India, Schlich published *Manual of Forestry* in nine volumes. Another Indian link was with Professor John Nisbet (1853–1914), who had earlier been employed by the Indian Forest Services and later became Conservator of Forestry in Burma. Nisbet wrote *British Forest Trees* and *Essays on Silviculture*, both in 1893, *Studies in Forestry* in 1894, *The Forester* in two volumes in 1905 and *Elements of British Forestry* in 1911.

It was not only in Great Britain that forestry planting developed. In Germany, early anxieties had been voiced about the balance and maintenance of woodland versus arable clearance, and by the end of the Thirty Years War (1618–48) rules were in place to control timber felling throughout the German forests, regardless of who owned them. The first teaching of systematic forestry principles began over a hundred years in advance of Britain, with William Gottfried von Moser's *Principles of Forest Economy*, published in 1757, followed by *Forest Calendars*, which laid down the work to be done month by month. The science of forest management was developing a life of its own with something of an industrial feel about it, slowly diverging from the artistic planting of the landscape and garden and progressing John Evelyn's original arguments about economic timber production. About the same time as Elwes and Henry were producing their opus on the trees of Britain, the similar *Deutsche Dendrologie* was published in Stuttgart by Emil Koehne. France had earlier produced the wonderful volumes of Duhamel du Monceau's work of 1755, *Traité des Arbres et Arbustes*; and at the end of the nineteenth century Pierre Mouillefert wrote his *Traité des Arbres et Arbrisseaux Forestiers*. In North America the botanist Charles Sprague Sargent (1841–1927) took on the massive undertaking of cataloguing the native trees of North America, publishing his work in fourteen volumes between 1891 and 1902. Prior to that, in 1872, the Arnold Arboretum in Massachusetts (part of the campus of Harvard University) had been founded. Today it operates on two sites, consisting in total of 150 hectares (371 acres) with some 6,000 shrubs and trees planted from all around the world.

In Britain, out of the chaos of the First World War came the recognition that timber production should be rationalized and brought under state control. The Forestry Commission of 1919 was given the brief to develop a unified strategy of afforestation to ensure a steady supply of timber and eventually to hold a reserve. Grants would be made available to private landowners to assist in the planting of trees. Within ten years the Commission had purchased and was managing over 150 woodlands – 242,820 hectares (600,000 acres). Private estates were slow to respond, and about 21,854 hectares (54,000 acres) of grant-aided planting had taken place by then. By 1934 the Commission owned some 367,872 hectares (909,000 acres). Even so, of the 1,443,300 cubic metres of wood (51 million cubic feet) Britain used during the Second World War, only 10 per cent came from Forestry Commission land, much of that from two of the Royal Forests – the Forest of Dean and the New Forest; the vast majority was felled on private estates as it had been in Evelyn's time.

Following the war, the Forestry Commission continued to develop its planting policy and, for the first time, forestry became an industrial and more mechanized process, with use of the chainsaw, aerial spraying of insecticide (1954) and the spreading of fertilizer (1959). There was powered ropeway extraction of the felled timber, as well as helicopter use for load lifting, extraction and delivery to the lorries. All this seemed a far cry from the good husbandman practice that Evelyn, and many others (including Pepys), had advocated as being all that was necessary for good forest management.

Modern machine-felling of Corsican Pine, showing both the head and the stump being extracted.

There was a huge amount of disquiet, not only about the felling practices with which the Commission was experimenting but also about its planting policy: blanket conifer growing – a monoculture of stifling darkness – was seemingly choking glorious landscapes to death. Eventually, in the 1960s two things happened that helped defuse the situation; one was the Forestry Commission allowing public access to all its sites, and the other was the appointment of a landscape consultant to help improve the Commission's conservation and amenity policies. Many conservationists, professional foresters and members of the general public were relieved to learn of the change of policy. However, it has to be remembered that the organization was born during the aftermath of the First World War, when aesthetic considerations had had to yield to finding a way of producing enough home-grown timber for Britain's manufacturing needs.

*

Since the 1970s there has been a growing awareness of the vulnerability of trees, beginning perhaps with the sudden death of our Elm Trees and followed by the Great Storm of 1987. While the vast majority of us are able to plant only one or two trees in our gardens – and usually these are not British natives – at least it makes us aware of their development, and the length of time it takes for a tree to mature. Observation is all – as John Evelyn endeavoured to demonstrate with *Sylva*.

Evelyn would have been delighted to learn of the creation of the National Forest at the beginning of the new millennium. Two hundred square miles of 'ancient woodland and new planting' are being developed in the neighbouring counties of Derbyshire, Staffordshire and Leicestershire. Within the National Forest the charity the Woodland Trust owns and administers nineteen individual woods – some mature woodland and others newly planted. Towards the south-west corner, at Alrewas near Lichfield, is the site of the National Memorial Arboretum. This is the Royal British Legion's focus for remembrance of all who lost their lives or were affected by the wars and conflicts of the twentieth century; it is a lyrical and soothing reminder of the true essence of what a tree can be in our lives. In Britain trees and tree planting have become fashionable; there are 'Tree Weeks' and tree-planting schemes – some locally based and others, such as Future Forests, urging individuals and companies to participate in international plantings to 'help neutralize the effect of global warming'. All of these measures are the most recent in a line that can be traced right back to John Evelyn's enthusiasm and clear thinking.

Three hundred and more years ago the requirements for trees and their timber were very different to ours today. Then wood was a crucial raw material which powered the western world. Now it is oil which holds sway, but the anxieties, powerful manoeuvring, bribes, inefficiencies and national pride which are characteristic of the oil-rich nations today can be seen at play – if to a lesser extent – in the high-profile, powerful timber-producing countries of the seventeenth century. Every developed nation in the world has, at some time or other, suffered from a lack of timber, and as a consequence has traded with or raided its neighbours to satisfy its needs. All over Europe the timber and fuel supplies of all nations have been topped up by wood extracted from the great northern forests of Scandinavia. The Italian Alps, southern France, the sierra of Spain, the Caucasus, the coastal strip of North Africa, have all been denuded of trees to the point of almost total deforestation. China and Vietnam, the foothills of the Himalayas, Ethiopia, the Rockies in western America, even the great Canadian forests are all going through a similar crisis. Worst of all is the destruction of the great rainforests in Africa and South America.

As the worldwide devastation of forests continues, and the sound of the tocsin is now being heard alarmingly loud and clear, our support for tree-planting initiatives is imperative for the earth's very survival. No longer can we take trees for granted. Perhaps sheer terror, caused by the thought of what is likely to overtake the world without the great reservoir of trees to help us live, will at last make us understand that. The principles involved in the management and planting of trees are exactly the same as they were in 1664. What better, therefore, could we do than follow the advice of *Sylva*? The planting of trees is an essential element of life, and conservation is as necessary as it was when John Evelyn argued for it over 300 years ago.

Beech woodland in mid-Wales.

Tree Introductions

Some of the Trees & Shrubs Introduced during John Evelyn's Lifetime 1620–1706

1620 *Rhus glabra* Smooth Sumach; eastern North America

1620*c. Larix decidua* Common/European Larch; mountains of central/southern Europe; *c*.1730 brought to notice as forest trees by 3rd/4th Dukes of Atholl, Dunkeld

1623*c. Prunus x amygdalo-persica* (*P. dulcis x P. persica*) hybrid between Peach and Almond first recorded this date

1629 *Diospyros virginiana* Common Persimmon; central/southern USA where fruit much eaten
Malus rubra Red Mulberry; eastern/central USA
Prunus serotina Black/Rum Cherry; eastern North America /Mexico / Guatemala; fruit used for flavouring rum/brandy, timber cabinet-making
Pyracantha coccinea; southern Europe/Asia Minor

1629*c. Carya ovata* Shagbark Hickory; eastern USA; edible crop of hickory nuts
Rhus typhina Stag's Horn Sumach; eastern North America

1633 *Juglans cinerea* Butternut/White Walnut; eastern North America
Sassafras albidum Sassafras; eastern USA; aromatic/medicinal

1636 *Platanus occidentalis* Buttonwood/American Sycamore; South Ontario (Canada), eastern USA/north-eastern Mexico; parent of *P. x hispanica* London Plane

1638 *Cedrus libani* Cedar of Lebanon; Mount Lebanon/Syria/south-eastern Turkey
Liriodendron tulipifera Tulip Tree; Nova Scotia to Florida; grown by Bishop Compton; timber called white wood used for interiors in USA

1640 *Hypericum hircinum*; central/southern Europe, now naturalized in the British Isles
Taxodium distichum Swamp Cypress; swamps of southern USA/Everglades; introduced by John Tradescant junior

1640*c. Anthyllis barba-jovis* Jupiter's Beard; south-western Europe/Mediterranean region

Robinia pseudoacacia False Acacia/Black Locust; eastern and mid-western USA; introduced via France *c*.1635
Spiraea hypericifolia; south-eastern Europe, naturalized in parts of North America

1648 *Citrus aurantifolia* Lime; Tropical Asia
Citrus limonia Lemon; Asia
Citrus medica Citron; Asia
Prunus lusitanica Portugal Laurel; Spain/Portugal; v. hardy

1650*c. Jasminum humile* Afghanistan to Yunnan/Szechwan

1656 *Celtis occidentalis* Hackberry/Nettle Tree; eastern North America
Cornus stolonifera North America
Pistacia terebinthus Chian Turpentine Tree; Asia Minor/Mediterranean region

1656*c. Acer rubrum* Red/Scarlet/Virginian Maple; eastern North America; Philip Miller '…was rais'd from Seeds, which were brought from Virginia many Years since by Mr John Tradescant, in his Garden at South Lambeth'
Cotinus coggygria Venetian Sumach/Smoke Tree; central/southern Europe

1663*c. Platanus x hispanica* (syn: *acerifolia*) (hybrid: *P. occidentalis* and *P. orientalis*) London Plane; extensively planted as a street tree

1664*c. Juniperus virginiana* Pencil/Red Cedar; eastern/central USA and eastern Canada

1669 *Myrica cerifera* Wax Myrtle; eastern USA/Caribbean Isles

1676 *Hypericum calycinum* Rose of Sharon; South-East Europe/Asia Minor

1679 *Acer pseudoplatanus* 'Corstorphinense'; came to notice on 26 August when Lord Forrester is said to have been murdered by his sister-in-law by it near Edinburgh

1680 *Fagus sylvatica Atropurpurea* Purple Beech; first discovered at Buchs canton of Zurich. Legend relates that the tree was discovered on the spot where 5 brothers all fought & killed each other

Ononis fruticosa western Mediterranean region

1680c. *Cupressus lusitanica* Mexican cypress/Cedar of Goa; Mexico/Guatemala

Magnolia virginiana Sweet/Swamp Bay; eastern USA; probably the first magnolia to be introduced to Britain

1683 *Acer lobelii* Lobel's Maple; southern Italy; named for Mathias de l'Obel (1538-1616)

Baccharis halimifolia Bush Groundsel; eastern North America

Crataegus pedicellata Scarlet Hawthorn; eastern North America

Juniperus phoenicea Phoenicien Juniper; Mediterranean region

Lindera benzoin Spice Bush; eastern USA

Sorbus chamaemespilus; mountains of central & southern Europe

1683c. *Euonymus americanus*; eastern USA

Pinus halepensis Aleppo Pine; southern Europe/Asia Minor; resin used in oil of turpentine/Greek wine retsina

1686 *Juglans nigra* Black Walnut; eastern/central USA; nuts not used; one of the world's most valuable timber trees

1687 *Physocarpus opulifolius* Nine Bark; eastern North America

1688 *Acer negundo* Box Elder/Ash-leaved Maple; eastern/central North America; grown by Bishop Compton

Aralia spinosa Devil's Walking-stick/Hercules Club/Angelica Tree; south-eastern USA

Melianthus major; South Africa

Rhus copallina; eastern North America

1688c. *Quercus prinus* Chestnut Oak; eastern USA

1689c. *Populus balsamifera* Balsam Poplar/Tacamahac; balsamic odour when leaves are unfurling

1690 *Genista monosperma*; southern Europe/northern Africa

Grewia occidentalis; South Africa

Psoralea pinnata; South Africa

1690c. *Thuja orientalis* Chinese Cedar/Chinese Arbor-vitae; northern/western China

1691 *Crataegus crus-galli* Cockspur Thorn; central/eastern North America

Myrsine Africana; Himalayas/China/Azores/mountains of eastern and southern Africa

Quercus coccinea Scarlet Oak; north-eastern USA; introduced by Bishop Compton

1692 *Ostrya virginiana* Ironwood/Eastern Hop Hornbeam; eastern North America; introduced by Bishop Compton

1696 *Abies balsamea* Balm of Gilead; eastern North America; introduced by Bishop Compton; species from which Canada Balsam obtained

1699 *Castanea pumila* Chinquapin; North America

Quercus suber Cork Oak; southern Europe/northern Africa

1699c. *Salix babylonica* Weeping Willow; China

1700c. *Fraxinus ornus* Manna/Flowering Ash; southern Europe/Asia Minor; stem exudes a sweet sap; manna medical/laxative use

1700 *Gleditschia triacanthos* Honey Locust; central/eastern North America; planted southern Europe where fruit ripens

Picea glauca White Spruce; Labrador to Alaska/east side of Rockies, Montana, New York etc.; reaches higher latitudes than any other evergreen; shelter belt tree on heaths/dunes of Jutland

Prunus avium 'Plena' Double Gean; Europe

1700c. *Aronia arbutifolia* Red Chokeberry; eastern North America

Aronia melanocarpa Black Chokeberry; eastern North America

Broussonetia papyrifera Paper Mulberry; China/Japan; bark used in paper-making. Fine cloth woven which Captain Cook saw being worn at Otaheite on Tahiti; widely grown in the East/Polyanesia; used as street tree in some Dalmatian towns, e.g. Spalato

Picea mariana Black Spruce; north-western North America; spruce beer made from leaves; timber used in Canada

Pinus rigida Northern Pitch Pine; eastern North America

Prunus cerasifera Cherry Plum/Myrobalan; Balkans; cultivated central Europe for fruit; found in Britain hedgerows etc.

Ptelea trifoliata Hop Tree/Stinking Ash; southern Canada/eastern USA

Salix alba var. *caerulea* Cricket-bat Willow; original tree found in Norfolk; the best wood for making cricket bats

1704 *Ptelea trifoliata* Hop-tree; eastern North America/Mexico

1705 *Pinus strobus* Weymouth Pine; eastern North America; timber tree originally v. prolific in USA; first planted at Longleat, Wiltshire

Bibliography

Acetaria: A Discourse of Sallets, John Evelyn (1699), Devon edition 1996

Alston Moor: Its Pastoral People, Its Mines and Miners, William Wallace (1890), Newcastle, reprint 1986

An Ear to the Ground, Ken Thompson, London, 2003

British Botanical and Horticultural Literature, B. Henrey, London, 1975

British Gardeners: A Biographical Dictionary, London, 1980

Cheshire's Modern Real Property, tenth edition, London, 1967

Complete Book of Herbs, Kay Sanecki, London, 1974

Culpeper's Complete Herbal, Foulsham edition, London, 1653

Dictionary of British and Irish Botanists, Ray Desmond, London, 1977

Dictionary of Wines, Spirits and Liqueurs, André Simon, London, 1958

Diary of Samuel Pepys, 11 volumes, Latham/Latham, London, 1995

English Custom and Usage, Christina Hole, London, 1941

John Evelyn and his Family Circle, W. G. Hiscock, London, 1955

John Evelyn and his Times, Beatrice Saunders, Oxford, 1970

John Evelyn and his World, John Bowle, London, 1981

John Evelyn's Elysium Britannicum and European Gardening, editors: Therese O'Malley, Joachim Wolschke-Bulmahn, Washington DC 1998

English Law Suits from William I to Richard I, volumes 1 and 2, Selden Society, 1990/1991

The English Park, Denys Louis Lasdun, London, 1991

Evelyn's Diary, editor: William Bray, London, 1818

Five Hundred Points of Good Husbandry, Thomas Tusser (1580), London, 1984

Flora Britannica, Richard Mabey, London, 1996

Flora Europaea, 5 volumes, editors: T. G. Tutin et al, Cambridge, 1968

French Garden 1500–1800, William Howard Adams, London, 1982

The Garden Book of Sir Thomas Hanmer of 1659, Clwyd, 1991

The Garden in Ancient Egypt, Alix Wilkinson, London, 1998

The Garden Makers, George Plumptre, London, 1993

The Genius of the Place, John Dixon Hunt/Peter Willis, London, 1975

The Glass Industry of the Weald, G. Kenyon, Leicester, 1967

Holy Bible, Knox Version, London, 1963

History of Ships, Peter Kemp, London, 1978

Hommes & Plantes, CCVS journal, Paris, 2001–2005

I Planted Trees, Richard St Barbe Baker, London, 1944

In Search of Ancient Italy, Pierre Grimal, London, 1964

In Search of English Gardens, Priscilla Boniface, Wheathamstead, 1987

The Kitchen Garden, David C. Stuart, London, 1984

Landscape and Memory, Simon Schama, London, 1995

Landscape with Trees, Miles Hadfield, London, 1967

Old & New London, Edward Walford, London, 1893

Oxford Companion to the Decorative Arts, editor: Harold Osborne, Oxford 1975

Oxford Companion to Gardens, editors: Jellicoe/Goode/Lancaster, London, 1986

Oxford History of England, 16 volumes, reprint 1985

Pursuit of Paradise, Jane Brown, London, 2000

Recusant History, Journal Volume 27, No. 2, October, 2004

The RHS A–Z Encyclopedia of Garden Plants, Christopher Brickell, London, 1996

The RHS Dictionary of Gardening, Fred Chittenden, 5 volumes, Oxford, 1951

Selden Society Centenary Guide, 1987

Sylva: a Discourse of Forest Trees, John Evelyn, second edition, London, 1669

Tourists Travellers and Pilgrims, Geoffrey Hindley, London, 1983

Travels of Peter Mundy 1608–1667, volume 5, Hakluyt Society, London 1937

Trees of Great Britain & Ireland, Elwes & Henry, 7 volumes, Edinburgh, 1906–13

25 Legal Luminaries from 'Vanity Fair', Rupert Collens, London, 1990

Wealden Iron, Ernest Straker (1931), Newton Abbot, reprint 1969

Acknowledgements

Researching the horticultural and silvicultural life of John Evelyn, I have been delighted to accept help from so many people – all of whom have given me so generously of their time and expertise – and I thank them all. I would especially like to acknowledge the research grant I received from the Authors' Foundation, which made it all possible. Among the many friends and colleagues whom I wish to thank are: Mavis Batey, Vice-President, Garden History Society; Georgie Beanland, Bernwode Plants, Bicester; John Campbell-Smith, Sue Castle-Smith and the staff at Wotton House, Dorking; Brian Cooper (my computer guru); Gina Douglas, Librarian, the Linnean Society; Moira and Richard Doyle, Anne Durham, Elizabeth Gilbert and the RHS Lindley Library; Professor Grenville Lucas, the Linnean Society; Dr Francis Harris, the British Library; Corinne Julius; Roy Lancaster; Fiona Lidstone; Richard McGurk; Mikinori Ogisu; the Oxford Botanic Garden; Trish Swain; Geraldine Watts; Dr Jan Woudstra, Sheffield University.

Many thanks to Pat White, my literary agent, whose cheerful voice – usually over the phone – urged me ever onwards whenever things seemed to get too difficult.

The steadfast encouragement and loving support I received from Claire, Steph and Justin, went well beyond the bounds of ordinary family life. To my husband, Michael, most grateful thanks for his unstinting generosity in living with the 'other man' in my life for the past two years.

My hope is that this introduction to the writing of John Evelyn will make us all realize how right he was in his passion for the planting and good husbandry of trees – something fundamental to our well being. While researching, I became aware of a charity that seems particularly to exemplify all that Evelyn cared most deeply about. It is TREE AID (Charity no: 296708), whose mission is 'to see thriving, self-reliant communities in Africa's dry lands, through the sustainable use of trees and woodlands'. For those who may wish to find out more, their website address is: www.treeaid.org.uk.

Maggie Campbell-Culver FLS
Brittany

Picture Credits

All the botanical line drawings are from the 1776 edition of John Evelyn's *Silva*, with additional notes by Alexander Hunter, unless otherwise credited. Bark photos by Clive Loveless: 10 London plane, 44 larch, 62 sweet chestnut, 210 Atlas cedar, 236 horse chestnut, 252 Austrian pine and as captioned. '*The book I had saved up to buy ...*' from *Boxwood: Sixteen Engravings by Reynolds Stone illustrated in verse by Sylvia Townsend Warner*, 1958. Enlarged. © Estate of Reynolds Stone: 6; from Henri Louis Duhamel du Monceau, *De l'Exploitation des Bois*, 1764: 8, 142, 216, 225; Bridgeman Art Library: 9 (portrait of John Evelyn, by Robert Walker, 1648. Private Collection, © Philip Mould, Historical Portraits Ltd), 22 (*View of the Villa Aldobrandini* by Alessandro Spechi, (1668–1729). Private Collection/The Stapleton Collection), 102 (Bibliothèque Municipale, Poitiers/Giraudon), 105 (Norton Simon Collection, Pasadena, CA), 113 bottom (Hat Trick Side Chair. © Museum of Fine Arts, Houston, Texas, Gift of Dr and Mrs Peter Marzio), 124 (Victoria & Albert Museum, London), 129 (Österreichische Galerie, Belvedere, Vienna), 173 (Kunstmuseum, Basel/Peter Willi), 233 (Victoria & Albert Museum), 259 (Prior Park, Avon); The Royal Society of London: 13; Wellcome Library, London: 16; British Library, London: 25; Bodleian Library, Oxford: 26 (MS Rawl. A. 315), 31 (MS Aubrey4 f.95); from *Sylva* by John Evelyn, 1670: 35, 224, 235; Harry Ransom Humanities Research Center, University of Texas at Austin: 31; from Henri Louis Duhamel du Monceau, *Élémens de l'Architecture Navale*, 1758: 54, 244; National Maritime Museum, London: 56/7 (*Blackwall Yard from the Thames* by Francis Holman, 1784), 254; from Moses Cook, *The Manner of Raising ... Forest Trees*, 1717: 59; Edward Parker: 65, 133, 243, 270/71; woodcut by Thomas Bewick from Revd Dr John Truster, *The Progress of Man and Society ...*, 1791; illustrations by C. F. Newall from C. S. Cooper and W. Percival West, *Trees & Shrubs of the British Isles*, 1909: 5, 70, 93, 118 top, 135 bottom, 141, 149 top, 150, 168, 171, 188/9, 196 bottom, 199, 200, 230/31; CORBIS: 71 (© Francesc Muntada), 80 (© Roger Tidman), 85 (© Niall Benvie), 160, 164 (© Minnesota Historical Society), 181 (© Charles O'Rear), 207 (© Historical Picture Archive); from Henry J. Elwes and Augustine Henry, *Trees of Great Britain and Ireland*, 1906–13. Reproduced by permission of the Linnaean Society of London: 77, 111, 143, 158, 177, 183, 196 top, 265; Andrew Lawson: 82, 118 bottom; Alamy: 88 (© David Boag), 145 (© Apis|Abramis), 147 (© E J Images), 149 (© Nick Hanna), 170 (© Andrew Holt), 184 (© Holt Studios International Ltd), 186 (CuboIImages srl), 187 (© Nigel Cattlin), 213 (© Bryan and Cherry Alexander); © Crown Copyright 2006/Forestry Commission: 91 (Thelma Wood), 113 top (John White), 268; London Stereoscopic Company/Getty Images: 97; Nature Picture Library: 107 (© Brian Lightfoot), 116 (© Geoff Simpson), 151 (© Adrian Davis), 153 (© Niall Benvie); Edifice: 121; Heather Angel/Natural Visions: 135 top, 190, 203; Royal Horticultural Society Library: 201, 264 both; Evelyn Binns: 202; © from Jean de la Quintinie, *The Complete Gardener*, translated by John Evelyn, 1693. Collection of Rachel Lambert Mellon, Oak Spring Garden Library, Upperville, Virginia: 218; from *The Graphic*, 16 February 1878. Illustrated London News Picture Library: 225; from William Gilpin, *Remarks on Forest Scenery ...*, 1808: 251, 258.

Index

Page numbers in **bold** denote an illustration

A

Acacia 73, 78, 195–6
  Boswellia spp. 49
  False (*Robinia pseudoacacia*) 272
  Virginia (*R. pseudoacacia*) 195
Accademia del Cimento 15
Accademia degli Investignati 15
Accademia dei Lincei 15
Acetaria: A Discourse of Sallets (Evelyn) 39
Adam and Eve 2, **3**
Aelfric, Abbot (*c*.955–1020) 101, 106, 112, 139, 198
  Glossary to Grammatical Latino-Saxonica 66, 95, 131
Agapanthus 40
age of trees 220–1
Aiton, William (1766–1849) 259
  Hortus Kewensis 259
Albert, Prince 156
Albury Park (nr Guildford) 34–5, **35**
Alden, John (*c*.1598–1687) 75
Alder (*Alnus*) 61, 130, 132, 137–9, **138**, 216
  Black (*A. nigra baccifera*) 139
  Common (*A. glutinosa*) 137, **137**, 139
  Grey (*A. incana*) 139
  propagation 138
  uses of timber 138
Aldobrandini Palace (Italy) 22, **22**
Alexander the Great 175
Alexander, Norman (d.1657) 75
Allestry, James (d.1670) 60
Allspice 205
Alston Moor (Cumbria) 50
American War of Independence (1775–83) 260
Anglicus, Bartholomaeus
  De Proprietatibus Rerum 4
Anglo-Dutch Wars 55
Anne of Denmark, Queen (1574–1619) 103
ant hills 214
Aphrodite 188
Arabs 188
Arborvitae (*Thuja*) 175–7
  Chinese (*T. orientalis*) 177, 273
  Japanese (*T. standishii*) 177
  Korean (*T. koraiensis*) 177
  Western Red Cedar (*T. plicata*) 177, **177**
  White Cedar (*T. occidentalis*) 175–6, 176–7

Arbutus 61, 196–7
  A. x andrachnoides 196
  Common (Strawberry Tree) (*A. unedo*) 194, 196–7, **196**, **228**
Argentina 49
Arlington, Earl of (Henry Bennet) (1618–85) 35–6
Arnold Arboretum (Massachusetts) 267
Ash (*Fraxinus*) 48, 71, 84, 87–9, 113, 130, 216, 223, 242
  beliefs and superstitions connected with 87–8
  Common (*F. excelsior*) 87, **87**, 88, 89
  felling of 229
  Manna (*F. ornus*) 88–9, 273
  uses 73, 89
  White (*F. americana*) 89
Aspen (*Populus tremula*) 134–5, **135**, 241
Atholl, Dukes of 262–3, 272
Atkyns, Sir Robert (d.1711)
  Ancient and Present State of Gloucestershire 92
Aubrey, John (1626–97) 78
augers 224
Austen, Ralph (d.1676) 257

B

Bach, Johann Sebastian (1685–1750) 8
Bacon, Francis (1561–1626) 224–5
  Of Gardens 257
  Sylva Sylvarum 257, **257**
Baker, Henry (1698–1774) 261–2
Balm of Gilead (*Abies balsamea*) 159, 273
Banister, Reverend John (1650–92) 156
Banks, Sir Joseph (1743–1820) 206
Banyan Tree (*Ficus benjamina*) 221, **221**
Barberry (*Berberis*) 234
barrels 73–5
Barron, John (1844–1906) 200, 264–5
Barron, William (1800–91) 200, 264–5
  The British Winter Garden 265
Bartram, John (1699–1777) 115, 129, 200
Bay 198–9
  Sweet (*Laurus nobilis*) 198
Bean, W. J. (1863–1947) 67, 138, 167, 260
  Trees and Shrubs Hardy in the British Isles 266

Beech (*Fagus*) 48, 61, 71, 81–6, 113, 118, 130, 241–2, **270–1**
  Common (*F. sylvatica*) **81**, 83–4, 272
  Oriental (*F. orientalis*) 83
  origins 83
  understorey of wood 84
  uses 86
Beetham and Dowson 155
Benbow, Vice-Admiral (1653–1702) 30
Berkeley Square (London) 170, **170**
Bible 179, 188, 250
Bilberry (*Vaccinium myrtillus*) 189, **189**
billets 217, 230
Birch (*Betula*) 48, 61, 128–30, 132, 216
  Birch/River (*B. nigra*) 129
  Dowony (*B. pubescens*) 128, 129
  Dwarf/Arctic (*B. nana*) 128
  sap 130, 235
  Silver (*B. pendula*) 128–9, **128**, **130**
Birch Wood (Klimt) **129**
birdlime 202, 204
Bishop's Palace (Ely) 170
Bittersweet 192
  Climbing (*Celastrus scandens*) 192
Blackwell Yard **56–7**
Blenheim, Battle of (1704) 8
Bligh, Captain 206
Blissett, Matthew 26
Blount, Colonel Thomas 208
Bobart, Jacob (1599–1680) 66
  Catalogue of the Trees and Plants in the Physicke Garden of the University of Oxford 66–7, 91, 96, 112, 115, 132, 135, 156, 167, 184, 187, 192
Bocklin, Arnold (1827–1901) **173**
Bombyx mori (silkworm) 102
Bowyer, Sir Edmond 201
Box (*Buxus sempervirens*) 199–200, **199**, 223, 227, 229
Box Hill (Surrey) 200
Boyle, Sir Robert (1627–91) 15, 16, 17
Brazil wood 234
Breadfruit, Tahitian (*Artocarpus communis*) 206, **206**
Bresal (monk) 197
brewing industry 50, 53
Broad-leaved Alder (*Platylophus trifoliate*) 139
Brompton Park Nursery 38–9
Brooke House (Hackney) 207
Brouncker, Lord (1620–84) 15

Brown, Sir Ambrose 28
Brown, 'Capability' (1716–83) 86, 92, 101, 126, 179, 256, 258
Browne, Sir Richard 21, 27
Browne, Samuel (d.1698) 157
Browne, William (1591–c.1643) 129
Bruce, Lord 86
Bryanston School (Dorset) 170
Buckingham Palace 35, 103
Buckland Churchyard (Dover) 200, **201**
Buckthorn (*Rhamnus*) 182–3
    Alder (*R. frangula*) 139
    Italian (*R. alaternus*) 28, 182–3
Burghley, Lord William (1520–98) 103, 188
Burke, Edmund (1729–97) 247
Burnham Beeches 83
Burning Bush 250
Bush Groundsel (*Baccharis halimifolia*) 273
Buttonwood/American Sycamore (*Platanus occidentalis*) 272

C
Callinicus 160
Camden, William (1551–1623)
    Britannia 230
Camellia 189
Canaletto, Antonio (1697–1768) 8
candle wood 161
Canterbury Cathedral 124
Capitulare de Villis 91, 95, 131
Carlo, Colonel William 70
Carob tree (*Ceratonia siliqua*) 234
casks 73–5
Cassiobury (Hertfordshire) **36**, 37, 78, 123, 257
Castanea pumila 273
Castle Ashby (Northants.) 126
Catalogue of the Trees and Plants in the Physicke Garden of the University of Oxford
    see Bobart, Jacob
caterpillars 214
Catesby, Mark (1682–1749) 156
cattle 214
Cecil House (London) 188
Cecil, Robert *see* Salisbury, 1st Earl of
Cedar 61, 175–9
    Blue Atlas (*Cedrus atlantica*) 177
    Deodar/Indian (*Cedrus deodara*) 177–8
    Japanese Red (*Cryptomeria japonica*) 178
    of Lebanon (*Cedrus libani*) **172, 176**, 177, 178, 179, **179**, 272
    Pencil/Red (*Juniperus virginiana*) 178, 204, 272
    sited in the Bible 179
    Smooth Tasmanian (*Athrotaxis cupressiodes*) 178
    Summit (*Athrotaxis laxifolia*) 178
    see also Arborvitae

Cedrela toona 178
Chairs of Forestry 266
Chaldaeans 2
charcoal 48–9, 50, 161, 197
Chardin, Jean (1643–1713) 37
Charlemagne, Emperor (*c*.742–814) 91, 95, 101, 131
Charles I, King (1600–49) 7, 12, 15, 17, 88, 248
Charles II, King (1630–85) 8, 12, 23, 25, 29, 55, 60, 69–70, **70**, 124, 245
Chaucer, Geoffrey (*c*.1345–1400) 69, 113, 139
cheese moulds **72**
Chelsea Physic Garden 92, 98, 105, 155
Chermes illicis 69
Cherry 242
    Black/Rum (*Prunus serotina*) 272
    Cherry Plum (*Prunus cerasifera*) 273
Chestnut (*Castanea*) 73, 90–3, 216, 223, 262
    nuts of 92
    origins 90
    Sweet/Spanish (*C. sativa*) 61, 90, **90**, 91, 92, 93
    uses 91
    see also Horse Chestnut
China 131, 222, 223
    silk industry 102, **102**
    Tree of Immortality 2
Chiswick House (London) **207**
Chokeberry
    Black (*Aronia melanocarpa*) 273
    Red (*A. arbutifolia*) 273
Christmas tree 156
Cicero 169
Ciennich tree 222
Citron (*Citrus medica*) 272
Civil War 7, 12, 20
Clarendon, Lord (Edward Hyde) (1609–74) 41
classification, pre-Linnaeus 198
Clayton, Sir Robert (1629–1707) 98
Clumber Park (Nottinghamshire) 126
coal 46, 50, 51, 83
Collinson, Peter (1694–1768) 92, 129
Columella 149
Comber, Harold (1897–1969) 187
compass timber 54
Compleat Gard'ner 38
Compton, Hon. Henry (1632–1713) 115, 156, 272, 273
concentric rings 223–4
conifers 264–5
Constable, John (1776–1837) 136
Cook, Moses
    The Manner of Raising, Ordering and Improving Forest Trees 37, 257

Cooper, Samuel 58
cooperage 73–5, 225
copses 215–17, 244
Cordia latifolia 204
Cordia myxa 204
cork 61
Cork Oak *see* Oak, Cork
Cornbury (Charlbury) 34–35
Cornwall 50, 149
Council of Trade and Foreign Plantations 23–4
Covent Garden market 97
Cowley, Alexander 255
Cowper, William (1731–1800) 126
Coys, William 41
Crab Apple 148
Crawley 70
cricket bats 142
Crimean War 99
Cromwell, Oliver 7
Culpeper, Nicholas (1616–54) 97, 98
    Complete Herbal 95
Cypress 73, 172–5, 221
    and ancients 173–4, 221
    'false' 174
    Hinoki (*Chamaecyparis obtuse*) 174
    Italian/Mediterranean (*Cupressus sempervirens*) 172
    Leyland (*Cupressocyparis leylandii*) 173–4
    Mexican/Cedar of Goa (*Cupressus lusitanica*) 273
    Monterey (*Cupressus macrocarpa*) 174
    Swamp (*Taxodium distichum*) 174, 272
    virtues of timber 175

D
Dampier, William (1652–1715) 7
Danvers, Henry 34
Darell, Christopher 241
Date Palm 171
    Wild (*Phoenix sylvestris*) 130
David, Elizabeth 189
David, King of Israel (d.*c*.993 BC) 179
De Bonnefons, Nicolas 38
Deane, Sir Anthony (*c*.1638–1721) 56, 57–8
Defoe, Daniel 262
Deptford Church of St Nicholas 124
Dering, Sir Edward (1625–84) 57
Devil's Walking-stick (*Aralia spinosa*) 273
Devon 149, 150
Dioscorides, Pedanius
    De Materia Medica 144
Directions for the Gardiner at Says Court (Evelyn) 30
diseases, tree 212–15
Ditchley Park (Oxfordshire) 98
Dittany (*Dictamnus albus*) 250

Dogwood 171
    Cornelian Cherry (*Cornus mas*) 171, **171**
    Cornus sanguinea 151, 171, **171**
Dorking 70
Douglas, David (1799–1834) 259–60
Dryden, John (1631–1700) 7, 8
Dunkeld estate (Scotland) 262–3
Dutch East India Company 222, 232
Dutch Elm disease 80, **80**
Dutch reed *see* Horsetail
Dyers Company 69

E
earwigs 214
East India Companies 55
Eastland Company 54
ebony 229
Edward I, King 239
Egypt/Egyptians, ancient 4, 185, 188
'elbows' 54
Elder 130, 235
    Box (*Acer negundo*) 115, 273
    Sambucus nigra 107, 150, **151**
Elector IV, Prince 249
Elizabeth I, Queen 55
Elm (*Ulmus*) 48, 71, 76–80, 218, 223, 227, 229, 242, 262, 269
    Caucasian (*U. elliptica*) 79
    disappearance from countryside 80
    and Dutch elm disease 80, **80**
    Dutch (*U. x hollandica*) 78
    English (*U. procera*) 76–7, **76**, 77, 79
    Mountain (*U. montana* now *glabra*) 78–9
    origins 76–7
    requirements for growing 78
    sap of 235
    uses 79
    Weeping 79
    Wych (*U. glabra*) 79
Elvaston Castle (Derbyshire) 264–5
Elwes, Henry (1846–1922) 118, 265, **265**, 266
Ely Cathedral 153
Elysium Britannicum (Evelyn) 39, 40
English East India Company 55
English Vineyard Vindicated, The 39
Epic of Gilgamesh 4–5
Escorial Monastery 77
Essex, Earl of (1631–83) 37, 38, 123
eucalyptus 73
Euonymus americanus 273
Euston Hall (Suffolk) 35–6
Evelyn, Captain George (cousin) 21
Evelyn, George (brother) 20, 21, 31, 32

Evelyn, John
    attacked on journey 239–40
    birth 18
    designing and planting of Sayes
        Court's gardens 25–31
    diarist 19–20
    early interest in estate
        management 18–19
    education 18
    foreign travels and gardens
        visited 20–3, 26, 208
    garden adviser 33–7
    gardening style and taste 33
    interest in hedges 21
    living at Wotton 32–3
    marriage 21
    and music 228
    portraits 9, 13
    public service career 23, 24, 59
    relief sculpture of 254
    and Royal Society 15–16
    writings 38–43 see also Sylva
Evelyn, John (son) 254, 255
Evelyn, Mary (wife) 21, 25
Evelyn, Richard (brother) 31, 235
Evelyn, Richard (father) 18
Exeter, 1st Earl of (1542–1623)
    188
Ezekiel, Prophet 162, 178

F
faggots 230–1
felling 58–9, 224–8, 226, 229,
    268, 268
ferme ornée 258
Fig 221
Fir 152–3, 157, 223, 259, 264
    Douglas (Pseudotsuga menziesii)
        260
    European Silver (Abies alba)
        152, 153, 155, 155, 163, 261
    Grand (A. grandis) 260
    Noble (A. procera) 260
    see also Pine; Spruce
First World War 247, 267
Fisher, William (1846–1910) 267
Flamsteed, John (1646–1719) 16
Forest of Dean 50, 246, 247, 266,
    268
Forestry Act (1919) 247–8
Forestry Commission 247–8, 263,
    267–8
Fortune, Robert (1812–80) 177
fossilized wood 229
France 5, 55, 165, 198, 244
    barrel production 74
    royal forests 244
    silk industry 102–3
French East India Company 55
French Gardiner, The 38
fruit trees 220
fuel
    timber used for 46–50, 229–31
Fulham Palace 156
Fumifugium (Evelyn) 23, 38
furniture-making 79, 96

Fustic (Rhus cotinus) 234
Future Forests 269

G
Galilei (1564–1642) 17
Gascoyne, Joel (fl.1680–1705) 30
Gay, Jacques (1776–1864) 181
Gehry, Frank 113
Genista monosperma 273
George I, King 124
Gerard, John (1545–1612) 69, 171,
    183, 191, 196
    The Herball 69, 199
Germany 244, 249
    development of forestry
        planting 267
Gibbons, Grinling (1648–1721)
    123–5, 234
Gibbons, Orlando (1583–1625)
    7
Gilbert, William (1540–1603) 14
Gilpin, William (1762–1843) 251,
    258
Gingko Tree 222–3
Gladstone, William 226
glass manufacture 46, 50, 81, 83
Glastonbury 133
Glenbervie, Lord (Sylvester
    Douglas) 247
glue 234–5
Goddard, Dr Jonathan (1617–75)
    59
Goodwood estate 179
Goring (West Sussex) 68
Gorse (Ulex europaeus) 149–50, 149
Grape, Malvasia (Vitis vinifera) 208
Great Fire of London (1666) 8, 12,
    60, 123
Great Storm (1987) 68, 269
'Greek fire' 160
Greeks, ancient 172, 188, 198
green timber 227–8
Greenwich Park 29
Gresham College 14, 15
Gresham, Sir Thomas (1519–79)
    14
Grew, Nehemiah (1641–1712)
    The Anatomy of Plants 17
Grewia occidentalis 273
Grey Squirrel (Sciurus carolinensis)
    132
groves, sacred 250
Guaiacum officinale 189, 191
'gum naval stores' 161
gunpowder 19, 48, 75, 132
Gunter, Edmund (1581–1626)
    226
Gunter's line 226

H
Hackberry/Nettle Tree (Celtis
    occidentalis) 272
Haddington, 6th Earl of (Thomas
    Hamilton) (1680–1735) 262
Hampton Court Palace 110, 115,
    124, 125

Handel, George Frederick
    (1685–1759) 8, 169
Hanmer, Sir Thomas (1612–78)
    41, 184
    Garden Book 69
Hannay, Patrick (d.c.1629) 135
Hanseatic League 54
Hare's Ear (Bupleurum fruitcosum)
    191
Harvard, John (1607–38) 7
Hatfield House 103, 126, 176,
    184, 188–9, 208
Hawthorn (Crataegus) 147
    C. laevigata 147
    C. monogyna 146, 147
    Scarlet (C. pedicellata) 273
Hazel (Corylus) 48, 131–3, 213,
    216
    C. avellana 132
    C. maxima 132
    C. sylvestris 132
    folklore attached to 133
    uses of timber 132–3
hedgerows 249, 258
hedges 146–51
    gorse 149–50
    growing from seed 149
    and hawthorn 147
    planting and maintaining 148
    quickset 147
    trees suitable for 150–1
hemp (Cannabis sativa) 161, 182
Henri III, King of France 195
Henri IV, King of France
    (1553–1610) 103
Henry, Dr Augustine (1857–1930)
    Trees of Great Britain and Ireland
    265–6, 266
Henry VIII, King 58, 248
Henshaw, Thomas (1618–1700)
    38
Herodotus (c.485–425 BC) 73,
    168
hewn timber 228
Hicks, David (1929–98) 118
Hickory
    Shagbark (Carya ovata) 272
Hiram, King of Tyre 179
Historie of Plantes 116
Holly (Ilex) 113, 149, 205, 223,
    227, 234, 260, 266
    I. aquifolium 202, 202, 204
    Winterberry/Black Alder
        (I. verticillata) 139
Home, Captain Sir Everard 178
Honey Locust (Gleditschia
    triacanthos) 273
Honeywood v Honeywood 242
Hooke, Robert (1635–1703) 14,
    16, 229
Hop Tree (Ptelea trifoliata) 273
Hornbeam 48, 113, 117–19, 118,
    241, 243
    Carpinus betulus 61, 117
    Hop (Ostrya carpinfolia) 119
    uses 118

Horse Chestnut (Aesculus
    hippocastanum) 3, 92, 206
Horsetail
    Dutch Reed (Equisetum hyemale)
        234
Hortensus 169
horticulture
    split between botany and 17
Hospital for Seamen(Greenwich)
    23
Howard, Lord see Norfolk, Duke of
Huggens, Christiaan (1629–93) 17
Hunter, Dr Alexander
    (1729–1809) 256
    Georgical Essays in which Food of
    Plants is particularly Considered
    256
Hypercium hircinum 272
Hyte, Henry (c.1529–1607) 116

I
Ice Age 71, 113, 117, 128, 131
Iceman 119
Icica altissima 178
Imart, Father Eustachius 232
India 130
Indigofera tinctoria 231
Iran 2, 49
Iraq, ancient 4
Ireland 197, 240
iron manufacturing 19, 46, 48, 240
Isle of the Dead (Bocklin) 173
Italy 22
    silk industry 103

J
Jamaica 205
James I, King (1566–1625) 103,
    248
James II, King 8
japanning 232
Jardin Royal des Plantes
    Médicinales (later Jardin des
    Plantes) 195
Jasminum humile 272
Jessel, Sir George (1824–83) 242
Johnes, Thomas 263
Jones, Inigo (1573–1652) 103
Juniper (Juniperus) 260
    J. communis 204–5
    Phoenician (J. phoenicea) 273
    Savin (J. sabina) 204
    see also Cedar, Pencil
Jupiter's Beard (Anthyllis
    barba-jovis) 272

K
Kaempfer, Engelbert (1651–1715)
    Amoenitates Exoticae 222
Kalendarium Hortense (Evelyn)
    40–1, 42
Kalm, Peter (1715–79) 256
Keffler, Dr 230
Kensington Palace 124
Kepler, Johannes (1571–1630)
    16–17

King William Pine (*Athrotaxis selaginoides*) 178
Klimt, Gustav (1862–1918) **129**
Knatchbull, Sir Norton (1601–84) 36
Knebworth (Hertfordshire) **121**
'knees' 54
Kneller, Sir Godfrey (1646–1723) 7
Koehne, Emil 267

L

La Quintinie, Jean de (1626–88) 38
lacquer 232
Lambert, Aylmer (1761–1842)
    The Genus Pinus 263
Lambeth garden 115, 191, 192
Lancaster, Roy 222
landscape movement 5, 193, 255, 258–9
Larch (*Larix*) 166–8, 262–3
    European (*L. decidua*) 159, 166, **166**, 272
    Hybrid (*L. x marschlinsii*) 263
    Japanese (*L. kaempferi*) 263
    Siberian (*L. russica*) 167
Laurel (*Prunus*) 209
    Cherry (*P. laurocerasus*) 209
    Portugal (*P. lusitanica*) 209, 272
laws concerning trees 238–43
Lawson, Charles 263–4
    Pinetum Britannicum 264
Lawson, William (*fl.*1570s–1610s)
    The Country Housewife's Garden 219
    A New Orchard and Garden 219–20, **219**
Le Nôtre, André 33, 38, 93
lead mining/smelting 50
l'Ecuse, Charles de (1526–1609) 183
Leicester, Earl of (RobertDudley) (*c.*1532–88) 197
Lely, Sir Peter (1618–80) 8
Lemon (*Citrus limonia*) 272
Lichfield, 2nd Earl of (George Henry Lee) (1690–1742) 98
Lime (*Tilia*) 71, 120–7, **127**, 223
    aesthetic appeal 125
    avenues 125
    Common (*T. x Europaea*) **120**, 122, 125
    cost of 126
    and Gibbons 123–4, **124**
    Large-leaved (*T. platyphyllos*) 120
    name 122
    Small-leaved (*T. cordata*) 120, 122
    use of timber 126–7
Lime (*Citrus aurantifola*) 272
Lime Walk (Buxted) 125
Linnaeus (Carl Linné) (1707–78) 67, 69, 92, 95, 112, 119, 122, 136, 140, 156, 191, 255
linseed oil 215, 229, 231

Liverpool 155
Lobb, William (1809–64) 177, 187
L'Obel, Matthias de (1538–1616) 114, 273
London, George 31, 38 (*fl.*1681–1714)
Lotus 171
Loudon, John Claudius 39, 265
    Encyclopaedia of Gardening 39
Louis XVI, King 7, 165
Lucas, William (d.1679) 178, 183, 192
Lutyens, Sir Edwin **121**
Luxembourg Gardens (Paris) 21, 119
Lyon, David 68

M

Magnolia virginiana 273
Maidenhair Tree *see* Gingko Tree
Mansfield 70
Maple (*Acer*) 48, 112–16, 130, 169, 228, 241
    Ash-leaved (*A. negundo*) 115, 273
    Field (*A. campestre*) **112**
    Italian (*A. opulus*) 114
    leaves 112
    Lobel's (*A. lobelii*) 114, 273
    Norway (*A. platanoides*) 114, 115
    origins 113
    Red (*A. rubrum*) 114–15, 272
    Smooth Japanese (*A. palmatum*) **113**
    Sycamore (*A. pseudoplatanus*) **114**, 115–16, **116**, 130, 216, 272
    uses 114
    virtues of timber 113–14
Marden estate 98
Mariotte, Edmé (d.1684) 17
Markham, Gervase (*c.*1568–1637) 225
marquetry **233**, 234
Martin, John (*fl.*1649–80) 60
Mary II, Queen 8
Mascall, Leonard (d.1589) 53
Mason, Peter 98
Mastic Tree (*Pistacia lentiscus*) 185, **186**, 187
masts 58, 162–5
May, Hugh (1622–84) 34, 37
Mayflower 7, 75
Meader, James
    The Planters Guide **264**
Meadowsweet (*Filipendula ulmaria*) 144
Melianthus major 273
Menzies, Archibald (1745–1842) 259
Merret, Dr Christopher (1614–95) 59
mice 214
Michaux, André (1746–1803) 165
Middleton, Admiral Sir Charles (1726–1813) 261

Midgely, John 126
Miller, Philip (1691–1771) 92, 98, 105, 114, 155, 272
Milton, John (1608–74) 8
Mines Law Court 50
Mitchell, Alan 78
moles 214
Molière, Jean (1622–73) 7
Mollet, André (d.c.1665) 34, 195, 207
Mollet, Claude
    Théâtre des plans et Jardinages 33–4
Monceau, Duhamel du 267
Monck, General George (1608–70) 248
Montiverdi, Claudio (1567–1643) 7
Moray, Sir Robert (?1608–73) 59
Morin, Pierre 21, 26, 28
Moser, William Gottfried von 267
Moses 179, 250
Mouillefert, Pierre 267
Mount Edgcumbe House (Cornwall) 68
Mulberry (*Morus*) 61, 100–5
    Black/Common (*M. nigra*) 100, **100**, 101, 103, 104
    origins 101
    Paper (*M. papyrifera*) (later *Broussonetia papyrifera*) 105, 273
    propagation of 101
    Red (*M. rubra*) 104, 272
    and silk industry 102–3, **102**
    spread of 'mulberrymania' through America 104
    uses 100
    White (*M. alba*) 100, 101, 102, 103, 104
Mulberry Garden (London) 103
Mulberry Tree, The (van Gogh) 105
Mundy, Peter (*c.*1596–1667) **28**, 165
Muscovy Company 55
musical instruments 228–9
Myrsine Africana 273
Myrtle 187–9
    and ancients 188
    Common (*Myrtus communis*) 187–8, **187**
    M. lechleriana (now *Amomyrtus luma*) 187
    M. luma (now *Luma apiculata*) 187
    Wax (*Myrica cerifera*) 272
myrtle oil 189

N

Naples 34–5
Napoleonic Wars 98, 261
Naseby, Battle of (1645) 7
National Forest 269
National Memorial Arboretum 269
Navigation Act (1651) 55

Navy Board 153, 161, 163, 182
navy, British 55–6
Nelson, Lord 261
Netherlands 21, 55
    tulipmania 104
New England 163, 164–5
New Forest 247, 268
New Hall (Essex) 125, 167, 248
Newcomen, Thomas (1663–1724) 16
Newton, Sir Isaac (1642–1727) 8, 16, 231
Nine Bark (*Physocarpus opulifolius*) 273
Nisbet, Professor John (1853–1914) 267
nitric acid 215
Norfolk, Duke of (Henry Howard) (d.1684) 34–5, 223
Normans 69, 150
North American Indians 2
Northumberland, 10th Earl of (Algernon Percy) (1602–68) 36
Nusmismata, A Discourse of Medals Ancient and Modern (Evelyn) 38

O

Oak (*Quercus*) 5, 48, 54, 61, 64–71, **65**, 84, 130, 220–1, 235, 242, 249
    affection held for 69
    Chestnut (*Q. prinus*) 273
    Cork (*Q. suber*) **180**, 181–2, **181**, **183**, **193**, 273
    felling of 229
    Holm/Ilex (*Q. ilex*) 48, 67–8, **68**, 206
    Kermes (*Q. coccifera*) 69
    origins of word 71
    Pedunculate (*Q. robur*) **64**, 66, **66**
    planting of 262
    Scarlet (*Q. coccinea*) 273
    Sessile/Durmast (*Q. petraea*) 66, **66**
    significance of 70
    stature 223
    Turkey (*Q. cerris*) 67
    used for making barrels 73–4
    used for shipbuilding 56–7, 71
    used as symbols in town/county crests 70
Oak Apple Day 70
oars 89
Oatlands Palace (Surrey) 103, 208
Oeggl, Dr Klaus 119
off-square 58
Ogisu, Mikinori 222
Olive Tree (*Olea europaea*) 89
Orange 206–7
    Seville (*Citrus aurantium*) 207
    Sweet (*C. sinensis*) 206
Orange, Prince of 21
Order of the British Empire for Gallantry 70
'ornamental farm' 258

Osier (*Salix viminalis*) **140**, 141, 144

Oxford Botanic Garden 36, 66, 96, 112, 118, 144, 149, 167, 170, 191
  see also Bobart, Jacob:*Catalogue*

Oxford Philosophical Society 14

P

Padua (Italy) 22

Pakenham, Thomas
  Remarkable Trees 92

paradise 250

Paris 21

Parkinson, John (1567–1650) 17, 104, 185, 196
  Paradisi in Sole Paradisus Terrestris **3**, 17, 167

Patrick, St 133

peanut 222

pear wood 227, 228

Pembroke, 5th Earl of (Philip Herbert) (1619–69) 36

Pendar, William 126

Pentaceras australis 178

Pepys, Samuel (1633–1703) 5, 7, 19, 24, 29, 38, 48, 50, 51, 56–8, 59, 97, 109, 153, 161, 165, 191, 206–208, 226, 246

Persimmon (*Diospyros virginiana*) 171, 272

Peter the Great (1672–1725) 30–1

Petty, William (1623–87) 15

Philip II, King of Spain (1527–98) 76–7

Phillyrea 183–4

Phillyrea angustifolia 149, 183

Phoenicians 162

pianos 118

Pine (*Pinus*) 61, 71, 157, 157–9, 259, 260, 264
  Aleppo (*P. halepensis*) 273
  extracting tar from 160–1
  Longleaf (*P. palustris*) 158
  Maritime (*P. pinaster*) 157, 158
  Monteray (*P. radiate*) 260
  Northern Pitch (*P. rigida*) 273
  and resin 158–9
  Scots (*P. sylvestris*) 58, 152, **152**, 158, **158**, **161**, 162, 260, 262
  Slash (*P. caribaea*) 158
  and turpentine oil 159
  used for masts 162, 163
  White (*P. strobus*) 163, **164**, 273
  see also Fir; Spruce

Plague 8, 12, 23, 212

Plane (*Platanus*) 168–70
  London (*P. x hispanica*) **168**, 169–70, 272
  Oriental (*P. orientalis*) 168–9, **168**

'plantation' 24

Plat, Sir Hugh (1552–1608) 130, 230
  Jewell House of Art and Nature 227

'Plena' Double Gean (*Prunus avium*) 273

Pliny the Elder (AD 23–79) 22, 64, 94–5, 113, 141, 169, 181, 198–9, 220, 221, 257
  Historia Naturalis 66

Plukenet, Leonard (1642–1706) 115

polishing of wood 229, 234

Pomegranate (*Punica granatum*) 184–5, **184**

Pomona 43

Poplar (*Populus*) 48, 61, 73, 84, 130, 134–6, 216
  Aspen (*P. tremula*) 134–5, **135**, 241
  Balsam (*P. balsamifera*) 273
  Black (*P. nigra*) 134, **135**, 136, **136**
  Grey (*P. canescens*) 134–5
  use of timber 136
  White (*P. alba*) 134, **134**, 135

Poussin, Nicholas (1594–1665) 8

Powderham Castle (nr Exeter) 77

preservation laws and statutes 238–44

Privet (*Ligustrum vulgare*) 192

pruning 217–20

Prunus x amygdalo-persica 272

Psoralea pinnata 273

Purcell, Henry (1659–95) 7, 8

Pyracantha coccinea 272

Q

Quarterly Journal of Forestry 266

Quebracho Tree, White 49

Quercus agrifolia 67

Quicksets 147

R

Rackham, Dr Oliver 147

rainforests 270

Rapinus, Renatus 255

Ravenscroft, Edward (1816–90) 264

Ray, John (1627–1705)
  Historia Plantarum Generalis 17, 167

Rea, John (*fl.*1620s–81)
  Flora, Ceres and Pomona 257

recorders 228–9

Red Alder (*Cunonia capensis*) 139

Reformation 12

Rembrant van Rijn (1606–69) 8

Rennie, John 79

Repton, Humphrey (1752–1818) 37, 256

resin 158–9, **160**

Restoration 55

RHS *see* Royal Horticultural Society

RHS A–Z Encyclopaedia of Garden Plants 195

Rhus copallina 273

Rialto Bridge (Venice) 138

Richelieu, Cardinal (1585–1642) 55

Richmond, Duke of 179

Rickets, George (*fl.*1680s–1710s) 126

Robin, Jean (1550–1629) 195

Romans 49, 70, 76, 90, 95, 114, 132, 167, 169, 188, 198, 238–9

Rooke, Hayman
  Remarkable Oaks in the Park at Welbeck 92

rope 161

Rose, John (*c.*1621–77) 38–9
  Rose, the Royal Gardener (painting) 39

Rose of Sharon (*Hypericum calycinum*) 272

Rosewood 234

Rowan (Mountain Ash) (*Sorbus aucuparia*) 106–7, **106**, **107**, 109

Royal African (Guinea) Company 55

Royal Botanic Gardens (Kew) 67, 138

Royal Dockyard 57

Royal English Arboricultural Society 266

Royal Forests 53, 57, 245–9, 260–1

Royal Horticultural Society (RHS) 171, 199, 259–60

Royal Hospital (Chelsea, London) 70

Royal Indian Engineering College 266

Royal Scottish Arboricultural Society 266

Royal Society 8, 13–16, 43, 59, 60, 104, 160, 229, 255, 256

Royal Society of Arts 261–2

Royal Sovereign (ship) 165

S

sacred groves 250

saffron 49

St George's Chapel (Windsor) 127

St James's Park 78, 125, 195, 218

St Mary Magdalene church (Worcestershire) 124

St Paul's Cathedral 124

St Peter's Church (Rome) 175

Salisbury, 1st Earl of (Robert Cecil) (1563–1612) 126, 176, 184, 188

Sandwich, 1st Earl of (Edward Montagu) (1625–72) 77–8

sap 130, 235

Sargent, Charles Sprague (1841–1927) 267

Sassafras albidum 272

Savery, Thomas (1650–1715) 16

Sayes Court (Deptford) 25–31, 60, 174
  designing and planting of the Grove 28–9, 30, 96, 98, 198
  letting of 30–1
  Oval Garden 26, 30
  plan of gardens (1652) 26, **27**

planting of trees in Great Orchard 26

Sayes Court Workhouse 31

Schlich, Sir William (1840–1925) 266–7

scientific discovery 12–13, 16–17

Scopoli, Giovanni (1723–88) 119

Scotland
  tree planting developments 262

Scudamore Crab 43

seasoning of timber 227–8

seaweed 230

Second World War 268

Seed and Nursery Company 264

Seven Years War (1756–63) 260

Shakespeare, William (1564–1616) 69

Shenstone, William (1714–63)
  Unconnected Thoughts on Gardening 86

Sherwood Forest 71

shipbuilding 53–4, **54**, 55–7, **56**–7, 161
  and masts 58, 162–5
  timber used 53–4, **54**, 55, 56–7, 58, 71, 79, 153–5, 229, 260
  use of tar and pitch 160

Shoreham-by-Sea 155

sideration 212

silk industry 101–4, 208

Sion House 36

Slingsby, Henry (*c.*1621–*c.*90) 207

Smythson, John (d.1634) 125

snails 214

'snapwood' 53

Society of Arts 263

Society for the Encouragement of Arts, Manufactures and Commerce 261

Somalia 49

Sorbus chamaespilus 273

Sorbus genus 106–11

Spain 67, 244

Spencer, Lady Ann 256

Spice Bush (*Lindera benzoin*) 273

Spindle Tree (*Euonymus europaeus*) 150, **151**

Spiraea hypericifolia 272

split timber 228

Spruce (*Picea*) 152, 156, 157
  Black (*P. mariana*) 156, 273
  Norway (*P. abies*) 153, **153**, 156, **157**, 228
  Sitka (*P. sitchensis*) 260
  used for masts 163
  White (*P. glauca*) 156, 273
  see also Fir; Pine

Stalker, John and Parker, George
  A Treatise of Japanning and Varnishing 232

Stallenge, William 104
  Instructions for the Increasing and Planting of Mulberry Trees 103, 104

Steuart, Sir Henry (1759–1836)
  Planter's Guide 265

Stone, Reynolds (1909–79) **6**
Storax (*Styrax officinalis*) 206
storm (1703) 195
Stourhead (Wiltshire) 86
Stowe 78
Strafford, Earl of (Thomas
    Wentworth) (1593–1641) 7, 20
Strawberry Tree *see* Arbutus,
    Common
Sumach
    Stag's Horn (*Rhus typhina*) 272
    Venetian (*Cotius coggygria*) 272
Sutton Hoo (Suffolk) 114
Sweden 133
Switzer, Stephan (1682–1745) 257,
    258
Sycamore (*Acer pseudoplatanus*) **114**,
    115–16, **116**, 130, 216, 272
Sydenham, Thomas (1624–89) 16
Sylva: A Discourse of Forest Trees
    (Evelyn) 6, 41, 43, 46, **47**, 59,
    60–1
    contents 60–1
    dedication to Charles II 60,
        245
    editions 254–6, 265
    publishing of 60
    success 254–5

T

Tagg, Thomas 98
tar and pitch 158, 160–1
Tatton Park (Cheshire) 126
taxation 241
Temple of Apollo (Utique) 178
Tetraclinis articulate 234
Thailand 49
Theophilus 83
Theophrastus (*c.*372–286 BC)
    91–2
    Enquiry into Plants 122
thickets 148
Thirty Years War 16, 267
Thorn, Cockspur
    (*Crataegus crusgalli*) 273
Thucydides (*c.*460–*c.*400 BC) 175
timber
    acquiring of different properties
        according to seasons 227
    commercial/industrial uses of
        46, 50, 54
    corruption in supply of 57–8
    cutting methods **115**
    domestic use of 53
    formula for keeping healthy 215
    imports of 155
    legal definition of 242
    measuring 226
    naturally coloured 234
    painting and staining 231–2
    polishing 229, 234
    production brought under state
        control 267–8

purchase of foreign 58
seasoning and preserving of
    227–8
and shipbuilding 53–4, **54**, 55,
    56–7, 58, 71, 79, 153–5, 229,
    260
shortages of 46, 57, 59
use of in brewing industry 50,
    53
used for fuel 46–50, 229–31
varnishing 232–3
tin smelting 50
tithes 241–2, 244
toddy 130
Tottenham Park (Wiltshire)
    86
Tournefort, Joseph Pitton de
    (1656–1708) 143–4
trade 54–5
Tradescant the elder, John
    (*c.*1570–1638) 66, 67, 103, 112,
    126, 132, 135–6, 167, 176,
    184, 185, 188–9, 191, 195,
    208, 248
Tradescant the younger, John
    (1608–62) 67, 74, 91, 110,
    114–15, 122, 148
Trajan, Emperor 175
Treasure Upon Fruit Trees, A 39
Tree Purslane (*Atriplex halimus*)
    191
tree-planting schemes 269
trees
    definition and origins of word
        2, 4
    differences between British and
        European 5
    introductions (1620–1706) 17,
        272–3
    particulars and peculiarities of
        220–35
    planting for commemoration
        249
    planting of 245–9, 262
    practical use 4
    size and stature 221–2
    spiritual influence 2, 250
    use of in ancient times 4–5
Trophonius 173
True Service Tree (*Sorbus domestica*)
    110, **111**
tubs 73–5
Tulip Tree (*Liriodendron tulipifera*)
    136, 272
Turner, Reverend William
    (*c.*1508–68) 84, 91, 196
    Names of Herbes 167
turpentine oil 159, 161
Turpentine Tree
    Chian (*Pistacia terebinthus*)
        272
    P. lentiscus 220–221
Tusser, Thomas (*c.*1520–80) 146

Tynningham House (Scotland)
    262

U

United States
    barrel production 74
    'mulberrymania' 104
Uzbekistan 102

V

van Gogh, Vincent **105**
Vanbrugh, Sir John (1644–1726) 7
Vancouver, Captain George
    (*c.*1758–98) 259
varnishing 232–3
Varro, Marcus 214
Vaux-le-Vicomte 93
Veitch, John Gould (1839–70)
    263
Venice 167
Verrio, Antonio (*c.*1640–1707) 207
Viburnum tinus **190**, 191–2
vine 208, **208**, 235
violins 228
Vivaldi, Antonio (1678–1741) 8
Vranen, Christian van 125

W

Wade, Edward 262
Wallace, William 50
Wallis, John (1616–1703) 14
Walnut (*Juglans*) 8, 61, 94–9, 229
    Black (*J. nigra*) **95**, 96, 273
    Butternut/White (*J. cinerea*) 96,
        272
    Common (*J. regia*) **16**, 94–5, **94**,
        96, 97
    and furniture-making 96
    nuts 97–8
    origins 94–5
Walpole, Horace **124**
Walpole, Sir Robert (1676–1745) 8
Walsingham, Sir Francis
    (*c.*1530–90) 197
Waltham Forest 58
Walton, Izaak (1593–1683) 8
Warren, Sir William 154, 163, 164
warships
    classification and rating of 154
Waterloo Bridge (London) 79
Wayfaring Tree (*Viburnum opulus*)
    151
Weeping Willow (*Salix babylonica*)
    143–4, **145**, 273
Wellingtonia/Big Tree
    (*Sequoiadendron giganteum*) 2
Wentworth, Thomas *see* Strafford,
    Earl of
Weston Park (Staffordshire) 126
White Alder (*Clethra acuminate*) 139
White, Thomas 263
Whitebeam (*Sorbus aria*) **108**,
    109–10

Wild Service Tree
    (*Sorbus torminalis*) 109
Wilkins, Dr John (1614–72) 15, 29
William III, King 8, 30, 124
Willis, Thomas (1621–75) 16
Willow (*Salix*) 61, 134, 140–4, 216,
    223
    Almond-leaved (*S. triandra*) 144
    Crack (*S. fragilis*) 141
    Creeping (*S. repens*) 141, **141**
    Cricket Bat (*S. alba* var. *carulea*)
        142, **143**, 273
    Dwarf (*S. herbacea*) 141
    and pain relief 144
    Purple (*S. purpurea*) 144
    Pussy (*S. caprea*) 142
    Silver (*S. alba* var. *sericea*) 141
    uses 142, **142**
    Weeping (*S. babylonica*) 143–4,
        145, 273
    White (*S. alba*) 141–2
    see also Osier
Willow-bay (*Salix pentandra*) 141
Wilson, Ernest Henry
    (1876–1930) 136, 177, 254
Wimbledon House 125
Windsor, Baron (d.1687) 205
Windsor Castle 124, 138
Windsor Great Park **52**
Winthrop, John (1606–76) 59,
    160–1
Wise, Henry 30
witches 107, 133
wood *see* timber
Wood Mote Court 53
'wood naval stores' 161
Wood, William 164–5
Woodland Trust 269
Worcester, Battle of (1651) 7,
    69–70
World Tree of Buddha 2
Worlidge, John (*c.*1630–93) 84, 86
    Systema Agriculturae 184
Worshipful Society of Apothecaries
    17
Wotton estate (Surrey) 18–19, **19**,
    21, 31–3, **31**, 241
Wren, Sir Christopher
    (1632–1723) 14, 16, 31, 123
Wyche, Mary 32–3
Wyche, Sir Cyril (*c.*1632–1707)
    32–3

X

Xerxes, King 168–9

Y

Yew (*Taxus baccata*) 200–1, **200**,
    223, 228, 229, 260
Yucca
    filamentosa 148–9
    gloriosa 41